THE
ERNST & YOUNG
GUIDE TO
FINANCING
FOR GROWTH

Also from Ernst & Young

The Ernst & Young Almanac and Guide to U.S. Business Cities
The Ernst & Young Business Plan Guide, Second Edition
The Ernst & Young Guide to Total Cost Management
The Complete Guide to Special Events Management
Development Effectiveness: Strategies for IS Organizational Transition
Managing Information Strategically
Mergers and Acquisitions, Second Edition
The Name of the Game: The Business of Sports
Understanding and Using Financial Data: An Ernst & Young Guide For Attorneys

Forthcoming from Ernst & Young

Privatization: Investing in Infrastructures Around the World

The
Ernst & Young Guide To Financing For Growth

Daniel R. Garner
Robert R. Owen
Robert P. Conway

John Wiley & Sons
New York • Chichester • Brisbane • Toronto • Singapore

Copyright © 1994 by Ernst & Young
Published by John Wiley & Sons, Inc.

Library of Congress Cataloging-in-Publication Data:
Garner, Daniel R.
    The Ernst & Young guide to financing for growth /
Daniel R. Garner, Robert R. Owen, Robert P. Conway.
      p. cm.--(Ernst & Young entrepreneur series)
    Includes index.
    ISBN 0-471-59904-2 (alk. paper).
    ISBN 0-471-59903-4 (pbk. : alk. paper)
    1. Corporations—United States—Finance.   2. Capital.
3. Venture capital.   I. Owen, Robert R.
(Robert Randolph)   II. Conway, Robert P.
III. Title.   IV. Series.
HG4061.G368   1994
658.15—dc20   93-34164

Printed in the United States of America

91 92 10 9 8 7 6 5 4 3 2 1

PREFACE

As an entrepreneur at the helm of a small or mid-sized company, or a manager who is considering acquiring your operation, one of the most interesting and potentially rewarding experiences you will have is raising capital to take advantage of growth opportunities. Yet nothing in your business life is likely to prepare you for the limitless variety of methods available to fill your capital needs.

At some point, your company will require more research and development, new products, product improvements, modern factories, or wider markets or will exhibit some other manifestation of growth. Financing this growth will bring you into the world of financiers—investment bankers—who will sell your stock to the public, banks, venture capitalists, and to government agencies with outright loans and loan guarantees. It also will bring you in close contact with business advisors such as the accountants and consultants who comprise the Entrepreneurial Services group of Ernst & Young, whose contributions to this book are based on their knowledge and experience in helping businesses mesh their capital-raising strategies with their overall business strategies.

Through our work with hundreds of growing companies, we have seen that suppliers of capital have been nothing if not imaginative in devising techniques to match your requirements and that they have been equally creative in their expectations of how you will pay them for risking their money.

As methods differ, so do suppliers. They have different goals. Some have conservative operating styles, while others relish risk in the hope of greater reward. Some will take no hand in runnning your company, while others will move in aggressively as an active participant in management. If government is the lender, the scenario changes further, since the principal motivation is often to achieve a social goal and save jobs.

Keeping current with this changing picture is literally impossible for anyone whose focus is running the day-to-day affairs of a company and plotting its future. Historically, change has been a major factor behind the raising of money. Periodically, great events have occurred that launched significant bursts of growth and demands for capital. For example, during the Civil War, the need for great quantities of supplies gave sudden impetus to mass production, which had more or less languished until then. Similarly, when the economies of many European and Asian nations were in ruins at the close of World War II, global operations became feasible for American companies. Now, entering the global market may be necessary for the survival of many organizations.

In recent years, we have also seen how high-technology companies have created a computer-driven revolution in information handling that is transforming even the smallest business. New products and technological processes have created a feverish growth environment and a huge need to raise capital.

Another element fueling the need for growth capital has recently entered the picture in almost every corner of the world. That is the distinct turn toward less government regulation in the belief that this will spur competition and encourage more aggressive, imaginative, and better-managed companies to search for new opportunities in the best tradition of an old fashion entrepreneurship.

By any measurement, growth financing has become a growth industry of its own. There is more money available from more sources, and in a truly amazing variety of instruments and strategies, than we could have imagined only a few years ago.

The purpose of this book is to help entrepreneurs and those professionals who advise them get a clear, current picture of this ever-expanding array of financing methods. In drawing upon our own experience as well as those of our colleagues in Ernst & Young's Entrepreneurial Services, Corporate Finance, and other service areas of our firm, we have sought to provide an array of professional insight. You will read how the different methods work and learn about the advantages and disadvantages of the various financing techniques and the kind of outside help from which you might benefit.

Our hope is that you find this book both interesting and useful. We also hope that you find it a reliable reference for your bookshelf, readily at hand the next time a growth opportunity begins to take shape on your company's horizon.

DAN GARNER
BOB OWEN
BOB CONWAY

New York, New York
January 1994

≡ ABOUT THE AUTHORS ≡

Daniel R. Garner is Partner and National Director of the Ernst & Young Entrepreneurial Services Group. He is also a member of the Small Business Council of the U.S. Chamber of Commerce. Garner is a Certified Public Accountant and earned his BA in accounting from the University of Texas at Austin.

Robert R. Owen is Partner and National Director of Industry Services at Ernst & Young. A Certified Public Accountant, Owen earned his BA in accounting at Southern Methodist University and graduated from the Advanced Management Program at the Harvard University Graduate School of Business.

Robert P. Conway is Partner and National Director of Special Services at Ernst & Young, with overall responsibility for Corporate Finance, Restructuring and Reorganization, and Valuation Services. He has been advising clients on all aspects of corporate finance for more than 18 years as both a banker and consultant.

≡ ACKNOWLEDGMENTS ≡

The scope of experience reflected in this book is the result of contributions from many professionals at Ernst & Young. As accountants and consultants, we advise and help emerging and medium-sized companies select and gain the means of financing that appear right for them. We have learned from our vast experience that few business activities are more critical than raising capital, and all of us thought we could make an especially meaningful contribution by sharing our knowledge in this area with growing businesses.

The Ernst & Young contributors are:

Stephen C. Blowers, Washington, D.C.
Herbert S. Braun, Cleveland
Jim Collet, Dallas
Henry Evans, Palo Alto
Michael Evans, San Francisco
Janet Green, New York
Andy Hajducky, Boston
Mark Hauser, Cleveland
David Jessen, Raleigh
Mindy J. Kaplan, Los Angeles
Bernard Leone, Metro Park
Alan Levine, Boston
Curt Noel, Atlanta
J. Wayne Norsworthy, Atlanta
Rick Post, Dallas
Ralph Sabin, Orange County
David L. Shafer, Kansas City
Warren Williams, Houston

Other important contributions were made by a number of Ernst & Young professionals, including A. J. Matsuura, Century City; Robert Snyder, Philadelphia; Michael Moneymaker, Joan Sweeney, Bill Washecka, Dimitri Plionis, Marianna Bertucci, and Tatiana Iliczewa, Washington, D.C.; Alan Kline and Tony Walters, Chicago; Michael Elliott, Atlanta; Nancy Clark and Edward Beanland, Dallas; Ronald H. Silver, Woodland Hills; Eric R. Pelander, Chicago; Ronald C. Diegelman, Baltimore; Lanny Latham, Kansas City; Kenneth Lee, Michael Hildreth, and Hank Settle, Palo Alto; Gregory Ericksen, Indianapolis; and John Romney, Cleveland.

Special thanks also go to Gerald Rama of CoreStates Philadelphia National Bank who lent his expertise in export financing, to Barbara Amen of Ballantrae International in Seattle for her expertise on international expansion, and to Jon Zonderman who provided especially valuable help as an editor of the manuscript.

Finally, we thank Mort Meyerson, Ernst & Young's director of public communications, who first suggested this book, and then helped to plan and develop it.

CONTENTS

1. Trends in Financing   1
2. The Going Public Decision   14
3. Private Placements (Exempt Offerings of Securities)   40
4. Venture Capital   55
5. Traditional Financing: Debt   71
6. Obtaining a Loan   88
7. Joint Ventures and Other Strategic Alliances   111
8. Leasing   121
9. Government Financing   133
10. Business Combinations and Divestitures   158
11. Research and Development   166
12. Cash Management   205
13. Management Buyouts   226
14. Employee Stock Ownership Plans   236
15. Franchising   251
16. Tax Planning   257
17. International Expansion   298
Appendix A: Summary of Financing Alternatives   327
Appendix B: Glossary of Commonly Used Terms   336
Appendix C: Sample Timetable for Going Public   341

**Appendix D: Comparison of Registration Forms S-1 and
              SB-2 and Annual Report 10-K Information
              Requirements**   344

Appendix E: Strategic Alliance Checklist   348

Appendix F: Outline of a Joint Venture Agreement   350

Index   355

1

TRENDS IN FINANCING

Capital markets can and do change quickly. Chief executives and owner-managers alike are, by necessity, becoming more innovative in their approach to securing financing. Maturing companies are finding that they have to use a variety of techniques to obtain the money they need to continue their growth.

In the early 1980s, venture capital was hot. But in the early part of the 1990s, new-venture financing was in a lull, partially because venture capital investors did not realize such heady gains as they had earlier from initial public offerings of companies they had earlier backed in the second half of the last decade. However, the rapid positive change in the market for initial public offerings (IPOs) that occurred in 1992 and the early part of 1993, coupled with the significant reduction in debt yields, has created new interest in venture capital investments and financing for entrepreneurs. This volatility in the capital markets has again rewritten the rules for financing and created a more complex and exciting financing environment.

In this new environment, companies have to deal with the continued tough underwriting requirements of traditional credit sources and the incredible valuations bestowed upon successful entrepreneurial companies that go public. Leasing, debt financing, joint ventures, research and development partnerships, mergers and acquisitions, and financing from positive cash flow are still some of the most promising techniques for raising capital.

One rule of thumb for growth companies is to avoid strategies that use excessive amounts of cash. Start by contracting out production,

1

renting instead of buying, and using sales representatives with variable commissions instead of hiring your own sales force.

The following is a brief insight into many of the trends in financing for growth.

JOINT VENTURES AND OTHER STRATEGIC ALLIANCES

Joint ventures are formed when a new company is created from the contribution of assets or a business by two or more separate companies. The entity operates as a separate business, apart from the corporate owner's operation, for the benefit of the owner. Strategic alliances involve two or more companies combining to share risks, rewards, and resources to achieve specific but perhaps different strategic goals. Strategic alliances range from full ownership control to contractual control only.

The past decade has brought an explosion in the number of joint ventures and other strategic alliances, even among the largest corporations. Industry sources estimate that the number of strategic alliances has grown from only 345 in the 1950s to more than 3,500 in 1991.

The rapid growth in strategic alliances is most noticeable by the wave of joint ventures in the automotive and computer industries, where the fiercest competitors have teamed up to build automobiles or computers. Such alliances are not only evidence of the feverish pace of strategic alliance activity, but they also present an opportunity for smaller companies seeking financing for growth. Small companies focused on niche applications can often command a high premium to joint venture with their larger brethren who may have difficulties reacting quickly to emerging markets and products.

MANAGEMENT BUYOUTS

Leverage buyouts (LBOs) captivated Wall Street during the 1980s, while management buyouts (MBOs) flourished in obscurity. MBOs are LBOs in which pre-buyout managers acquire and hold a substantial ownership and equity position after the buyout. The motivation for MBOs is usually tied to management's desire to avoid sale of their division or company to unknown and perhaps unfriendly new owners, as well as the opportunity to control their destinies and fortunes.

The problems common to the great majority of management groups who desire to own their company encompass the whole range of transaction issues as well as issues specific to an MBO, such as independence and fiduciary responsibility. The acquisition process becomes complicated due to the position of the management group. They know more about the company than anyone else. They could control the outcome of the price negotiations for the company by managing profits down for a period of time. Similarly, management could themselves profit by buying the company just prior to a turn upwards in company operations. Management must remain sensitive to these and other issues when structuring a management buyout.

The opportunities for LBOs and MBOs were abruptly reduced during the 1991–1992 recession. Lending practices and additional equity requirements reduced private company valuations and investor yields. These trends seem to be reversing at present due to easing credit requirements and the decreasing yield expectations of investors. Management's ability to invest significant personal equity in MBOs remains a key ingredient for success.

LEASING

Equipment/asset leasing, including the sale and subsequent leaseback of an asset, is a major source of capital. Leasing ranks behind only public offerings as a source of funds for small to mid-sized companies. Smaller businesses reluctant to tie up cash in purchasing equipment can expand their capital with asset-lease arrangements, which generally have lower repayment terms than equipment purchases. By 1990, leasing had grown to a $100 million annual source of growth funding.

Leasing arrangements can take various forms, and flexibility in negotiated terms can positively affect a company's balance sheet. For instance, certain leases can be deemed purchases, while others can afford off-balance-sheet financing to a growing company.

Whether leasing assets or selling presently owned assets and then leasing them back, the cash-flow benefits can be greater than purchasing an item with borrowed funds. Considerations when leasing are significant. Tax, accounting, and cash-flow factors need to be analyzed. Sometimes this requires the help of outside professionals.

RESEARCH AND DEVELOPMENT ARRANGEMENTS

Research and development (R&D) funding arrangements can take one of a number of configurations—limited partnerships, corporate joint ventures, partnerships, foreign R&D arrangements, government participation—and have numerous applications for financing growing companies. Among the fastest growing small public companies, an average of nearly 10 percent of sales is committed to research and development. Therefore, a substantial portion of such businesses can be financed through an R&D arrangement.

VENTURE CAPITAL

In addition to experienced management, a good forecast, and a solid business plan, what are venture capitalists looking for today?

Size. A venture capital firm will rarely look at a financial deal below $250,000.

Risk. Business risks that are identifiable and understandable.

Growth. Businesses with large upside possibility—the ability to grow very large in a short period of time.

Product. A product that is through the development stage and thus ready for distribution, or a product in development for which the need and market is obvious. For example, an attractive company is one that will grow by producing more assembly-line type products versus one that will grow by adding more people; in other words, venture capitalists typically don't look for labor-intensive services or products such as contract software.

Uniqueness. A "niche" business—one with a product or service that has some sort of competitive edge. An idea that is unique, proprietary, or special, and that is in demand now or is likely to be in the near future.

Market. A company with potential sales and profits that are significant for its industry and likely to provide the required return on investment. Generally ten times their investment in five years.

Exit. The venture firm or private investor will require some mechanism or strategy to facilitate sale of its interest in the business or acquisition of control. Large-company investors want a situation that will allow them to purchase a minority interest (5 percent or greater) with the thought of buying the company outright at some point. Written into the first equity deal may be an option to acquire within four or five years.

Overseas Potential. Foreign investors, intent on marketing U.S. products overseas, are investing in U.S. companies that have foreign-market product potential.

CASH MANAGEMENT

Through creative cash management, combined with full use of tax deductions, exemptions, credits, expensing, and so forth, smaller companies can increase their working capital by 10 to 50 percent.

Banks now offer sophisticated cash-management products to borrowers of all sizes. Companies are educated to minimize excess cash in noninterest-bearing checking accounts. Cash is collected quicker through the use of lockboxes and through checking accounts that consolidate balances both from different institutions and within the same bank. Payment of company bills from a bank account located out of state is encouraged: a "remote disbursement service" allows a company to maximize the "float time." During this one- to three-day float period, the funds remain available within the company's account for working capital. Banks offer systems to report this collection and disbursement information throughout the day via a telephone linked to a company's computer. Cash management systems can be established to automatically advance daily cash needs into a master account from a line of credit and, conversely, to reduce bank debt or make overnight investments with excess funds.

TAX STRATEGIES

Currently, some of the most popular methods for creating cash internally include the following:

Expensing. The company takes a tax deduction of up to $17,500 in the first year of useful life on the cost of purchased property. There are complicated rules about what kind of property qualifies but, in general, it must normally be subject to depreciation and does not include real estate. Usually, you will want to choose first-year expensing for the property with the longest recovery period under the modified accelerated cost recovery (MACRS) depreciation system.

Credits. Deductions reduce taxable income but tax credits generally cut taxes dollar for dollar. Many smaller companies are unaware of all the credits available to them. For instance: (1) There are rehabilitation credits for substantial renovation of existing properties. Credits range from 10 to 20 percent depending on the age of the building. (2) Research and development credits can help companies recover up to 20 percent of the costs of developing new technology, including wages. (3) A "targeted" jobs credit is available for a portion of the wages paid to employees who are members of certain economically disadvantaged groups. Most of these credits are currently being reviewed and may be changed or repealed.

Income Deferral. Many companies realize revenues for products or services provided over one to two years. Income recognition over the life of the agreement or the period in which the production service is provided will defer the cash tax requirement.

Capital Structure. The magic of LBOs and real estate was and is debt leverage. Interest costs are deductible while dividends are not. Many companies decrease their cost of capital and increase cash flow through prudent but aggressive capital structures.

PRIVATE PLACEMENTS

The private sale or placement of exempt (unregistered* but not un-regulated) securities (debt or equity) to one or more investors is an excellent prelude or alternative to going public. For smaller companies, private placement is the third largest source of capital after going public and equipment leasing. Private placements are an especially

---

* Transactions exempt from federal registration requirements may not be exempt from registration under laws of the state(s) in which the securities are to be offered.

effective tool for raising second- and third-round capital. Successful companies can usually raise between $4 million and $5 million. In times when venture capitalists are concentrating on current portfolio companies, and looking very cautiously at new investments, it may be possible to secure second- and third-round capital exclusively through the sale of exempt securities to current investors. Securities and Exchange Commission (SEC) regulations allow for an unlimited range of offering sizes when combined with time and/or buyer stipulations.

GOVERNMENT FINANCING

Both federal and state governments provide a wide range of financing assistance to smaller businesses. The Small Business Administration (SBA) remains the primary agency for assisting small companies. There are also non-SBA initiatives that have much to offer. Two of these are decided bright spots.

The Small Business Enhancement Act of 1992 provides SBA-funded capital to Small Business Investment Companies (SBICs) of up to 300 percent of its committed capital. This new law (unlike its 1958 predecessor) allows SBICs to make equity investments.

Export Assistance. The Export-Import Bank (Eximbank) assists smaller U.S. exporters through a small-business credit program, working capital loan guarantee program, and export credit insurance.

State and Local Aid. Increasingly, state and local governments are furnishing assistance funds for small business development. Capital is being made available for both expansion and start-up.

More than half the states are now participating in venture capital financing, principally through state employee pension funds and public business development corporations. As it offers the states an opportunity to support job creation and retention, state financial assistance can only be expected to grow. A section that views sample state programs is included in Chapter 9.

TRADITIONAL FINANCING

Traditional financing includes the standard sources of debt financing—commercial banks, finance companies, savings and loan companies, investment banks, insurance companies, and pension funds—and the standard instruments—credit lines, asset-based loans, term loans, mortgage financing, and factoring of accounts receivable. Yet there is much that is new.

Asset-Based Bank Loans. Although asset-based loans—loans secured by accounts receivable and/or inventories—were once available only from commercial finance companies, most commercial banks are now aggressively offering them. These loans are typically short-term; intended for working capital, generally available in amounts up to 55 to 80 percent of receivables, and up to 25 to 60 percent of inventory; and may cost up to seven percentage points above the prime rate.

Subordinated and Mezzanine Debt. This is a layer of debt between senior term debt and equity. Loans to finance this type of debt are typically unsecured, and generally allow for payment of interest only for the first two or three years while senior debt is being repaid. Interest rates tend to be fixed rates at prime plus 3 to 6 percent. Repayment is likely to be due within five to eight years. Equity rights in the form of warrants or options may be required.

Hybrid Lenders. In the late 1980s, some institutions set up groups called "hybrid lenders." These lenders financed primarily mergers, acquisitions, and leveraged buyouts with senior, term, and mezzanine debt, as well as equity. Hybrid lenders functioned as a "one-stop shop" to facilitate obtaining a commitment and financing. Very few financial institutions in today's market offer these services.

Equity Funds. Numerous funds have been established to invest directly as principal in leveraged buyout transactions and recapitalizations, and to support major growth.

Syndications and Underwriting Loans. Historically, banks made a loan and held it until the loan was repaid. More stringent regulatory requirements, including a greater capital base against loans, have resulted in banks selling off loans rather than holding them. Distribution networks have been established where banks have existing relationships with other lenders willing to purchase loans in order to increase their interest income.

These networks allow banks to quickly commit to large borrowing requests with the knowledge that they can sell these loans. This substantially quickens a borrower's response time from a bank over the bank-by-bank approval process previously necessary in a multibank transaction. The networks also allow a bank to offer creative products with the knowledge that the risk will be sold off or diversified among many. Banks receive income up front for the initial commitment, as well as a fee or interest rate spread over the syndicated loan.

Pricing Options. Historically, the interest rates associated with bank debt have been based on the prime rate of interest. Interest rates in today's environment still include the prime rate or "bank-reference rate," which may stem from a bank's depository base. Banks also may go to the domestic or international marketplace and purchase a particular block of funds against which they will make specific loans. This is known as "matched funding," and generally allows banks to charge rates below prime. Some of these "subprime" financing rates include London Inter-Bank Offering Rate (LIBOR), Certificate of Deposit rate, Treasury Bill rate, and Bankers' Acceptance rate. A bank's pricing structure may be influenced by a combination of interest rates, noninterest-bearing checking account balances, up-front loan fees, annual commitment fees, and fees based on company performance such as profits or excess cash flow.

Lender Liability Issues. The lending environment has recently experienced a number of legal changes. Changes in bankruptcy law have extended the preference period and may have an impact on a bank's ability to retain cash it has collected or offset against company balances. The bank, acting in the role of an owner, may be seen by the law as exerting undue influences over management, and may therefore be considered as assuming the risk of an investor rather than a lender. In a liquidation, this may also alter a bank's priority claim on assets from that of a senior lender to that of an equity investor. Fraudulent conveyances laws have been enforced to protect existing vendors against excessive lending by a bank that may have directly contributed to a company becoming insolvent.

Consumer and retail laws have been enacted to protect unsophisticated borrowers from "sophisticated lending institutions," potentially affecting a bank's ability to force a company in bankruptcy to make a loan repayment. These laws could also affect the bank's priority on assets in a liquidation. One may expect lenders to assume a more conservative position in credit decisions where these and other issues are concerned.

Environmental Issues. Court rulings specifically related to toxic-waste cleanup may hold a bank, in part, responsible for contaminated property owned by a borrower.

Real Estate Lending Terms. The Savings and Loan (S&L) industry has experienced much upheaval in recent years, in part due to funding fixed-rate, long-term real estate loans with variable-rate (certificate of deposit), short-term dollars. During inflationary times, S&Ls would be required to pay higher rates of interest to attract depositors (their source of lendable funds) than they received from interest paid on real estate loans. As a result, loans now typically have shorter maturities. A loan may be structured with a 20- to 40-year amortization, but the loan may be due for payment or review in a shorter period, such as 5 to 10 years.

Accounts Receivable as Security. Selling receivables as a way to finance seasonal growth was traditionally used by many industries such as the garment trade. This service has recently been adopted by large banks and their subsidiaries to further generate fee income. Consumer and corporate receivables resulting from the sale of assets, such as automobiles or real estate, can now be bundled together. These receivables are backed by a credit-enhancement feature such as a standby letter of credit, or by significantly more collateral than the amount of the investment. These investments are sold publicly or privately to investors. The investor receives a secured investment, backed by a tangible asset, as well as current income.

Interest-Rate Protection Products. The high rate of interest during the 1980s created concern about burdensome interest-rate expense. As a result, insurance-type products were created to limit the upside risk of rising rates. These products may be an attractive alternative to fixed-rate financing, which may have a prepayment penalty. An interest-rate cap is an insurance policy to limit a borrower's upside interest expense. In general, the lower the amount of the interest-rate spread—for example, 1 percent—the more costly the interest-rate cap protection. This would be true because there would be a greater likelihood that interest rates would increase 1 percent. Conversely, it is less likely that interest rates would increase as much as 5 percent, so the cost for such an interest-rate cap would be lower.

Collars. Collars represent the complement to caps. They are both a maximum and minimum interest exposure to a borrower. The upside risk is limited with the cap product. The downside floor works similarly. Because of the somewhat limited insurance exposure, the fees are typically less than those associated with caps.

GOING PUBLIC

Now or Later. If the capital required is available from other sources, at reasonable rates, consider a delay. This alternative source capital, if used to increase the company's growth potential, could increase the value of stock brought out at a later date.

Momentum. Investors and underwriters look for a company with years of strong, steady growth and rising profits. Both indicate management's ability to compete over the long haul.

Market. Even if the economic climate is bad, a company may still go public successfully if it has an experienced management team, a good financial record, and an important product or service.

Pricing. Underwriters will sell the shares at a price based on how similar offerings have fared and on the current state of the market. Post-IPO price and market support by the underwriter is crucial for a truly successful stock offering.

FRANCHISING

If your company has developed a sound product or business format and needs or wants to grow rapidly, franchising or licensing your business format to others may provide the workforce and other resources to achieve this goal. There are over 2,000 different franchisors, and this is one of the most rapidly growing forms of doing business. Consumer-product and service companies have found this to be an excellent way to promote their products and name recognition on a national and international scale.

EMPLOYEE STOCK OWNERSHIP PLANS

Over the last ten years, Employee Stock Ownership Plans (ESOPs) have been transformed from employee benefit plans to powerful tools of corporate finance. This transformation is due in large part to the increased merger and acquisition activity the 1980s generated. Employee Stock Ownership Plans have become an important financing alternative in corporate acquisitions, particularly in leveraged buyouts, where a substantial amount of debt must be financed.

Although some companies still participate in unleveraged ESOP plans, the most popular type of plan in use by companies at present is the leveraged ESOP, which provides tax incentives for both the borrower and the lender. Both types of ESOP have one fundamental advantage as a vehicle to raise capital: they reduce a company's after-tax cost for debt servicing. Ancillary advantages to an ESOP are that the plan can act as a buyer of shares and as a defense against hostile takeovers.

HOW MUCH DEBT IS TOO MUCH?

Some people believe that the healthy smaller company has a total liability-to-equity ratio of 3.0 to 1.0, while others believe 1.5 to 1.0 is sufficient. Some believe that smaller companies should borrow as much as they can, thinking of money as an investment. However, on one thing almost everyone can agree:

> A highly leveraged business allows little room to maneuver against the unexpected, such as falling markets, widely fluctuating interest rates, increases in costs, or seasonal or cyclical changes.

And there is no doubt that

> a disproportionately large number of businesses entering Chapter 11 bankruptcy (protection from creditors for the purpose of reorganization) are highly leveraged. Many companies borrowed so heavily that the tremendous interest payments overwhelmed them.

With no determining rule of thumb and only credit grantors' verdicts for temperance, each CEO must make the final decision on how much debt is too much for the company.

What Follows

Each of the financing categories below is the subject of a separate, in-depth discussion in the chapters that follow:

Going public

Private placements

Venture capital

Traditional financing

Debt

Obtaining a loan

Joint ventures

Strategic alliances

Leasing

Government financing

Business combinations

Research and development

Cash management

Management buyouts

Employee stock ownership plans

Franchising

Tax planning

International expansion

2

THE GOING PUBLIC DECISION

Going public is one of the most challenging experiences a top executive can have—selling stock in the company for the first time, satisfying all the requirements of federal and state regulatory agencies, and, in the process, giving up some of the control and privacy of the business.

As professional accountants and advisors, we have helped hundreds of companies go public, and we know that every company has its own special needs. This chapter will give you a better understanding of what lies ahead and help you reach sound decisions at one of the crucial moments in your company's history.

MAKING THE DECISION

Going public is one of the most important events in a company's life. As a method of raising capital, it has served American business remarkably well. Virtually all large U.S. companies and many smaller, vigorous companies with strong growth momentum have chosen to sell shares to the public.

Once a company makes this decision and sets the process in motion, nothing will ever be quite the same. Every facet of the company's character and operations will feel the effects.

If all goes well, the new capital can dramatically improve the company's potential to increase its financial leverage and, therefore, the rate of return to shareholders—by supplying funds to finance research, new-product development, plant construction and modernization, expansion into new markets, and, perhaps, a promising acquisition. On a personal level, going public can provide a vehicle for liquidity and possibly bring gratifying financial rewards.

However, going public goes far beyond just raising capital, and even when it is the best thing to do it is always a mixed blessing. For a start, you will give up the privacy and autonomy you previously enjoyed. Freedom of action will be curtailed as outside investors hold management accountable, and the company will be required to disclose important information to the public, including competitors.

In addition, many public offerings have fallen below expectations, or even failed, for a variety of reasons. Perhaps the offering was made just as the stock market slumped and prices dropped. Or the company's profits fell just before the offering. Or it was discovered, too late in the process, that the company didn't have the right lineup of advisors.

You need to clearly visualize the company's future direction and ask the right questions *before* you make a decision as important as this one. Some of the questions you should ask are as follows:

What kind of company do you want to become?

How much capital do you need?

How will the proceeds be used?

How much will it cost to raise the money?

Is going public the best financing method?

Is the timing right?

Do you have adequate internal systems and discipline to be a public company?

What are the advantages and disadvantages of going public?

At the very beginning of your deliberations, you will need the best advice you can get because this once-in-a-lifetime experience will set the company's course for the foreseeable future.

The discussions that follow will help bring into perspective the principal considerations for going public.

Advantages to the Company

- *Improved Financial Condition.* The sale by the company of shares to the public brings money that does not have to be repaid, immediately improving the company's financial condition. This improvement may enable the company to borrow funds at more attractive interest rates. Moreover, if the initial stock offering is successful and a strong "aftermarket" develops, the company may be able to raise more capital by selling additional shares of stock at terms even more favorable than those of the initial offering.

- *Using Stock for Acquisitions.* Public companies often issue stock (instead of paying cash) to acquire other businesses. Owners of a company you seek to acquire may be more willing to accept your company's stock if it is publicly traded. The liquidity provided by the public market affords them greater flexibility—they can more easily sell their shares when it suits their needs, or use the shares as collateral for loans.

  The public market also assists in valuing the company's shares. If your shares are privately held, you have to estimate their value and hope the owners of the other company will agree; if they don't, you will have to negotiate a "fair price." On the other hand, if the shares are publicly traded, the price per share generally is set every day in the stock market where the shares are traded.

- *Using Stock as an Employee Incentive.* Companies frequently offer incentives such as stock options, stock appreciation rights, or stock bonuses to attract and retain key personnel. These arrangements tend to instill a healthy sense of ownership in employees, who also benefit from certain tax breaks and the chance to gain if the value of the stock appreciates. Stock incentives are generally more attractive to employees of public companies, since the public market independently values the shares and enhances their marketability.

- *Enhancing Company Prestige.* One of the intangible, but widely recognized, potential benefits of going public is that the company becomes more visible and attains increased prestige. Through press releases and other public disclosures and daily listing in stock market tables, the company becomes known to the business and financial community, investors, the press, and even the general public.

While both good and bad news must be disseminated to enable investors to make well-informed decisions, a public company that is well run and compiles a record of success can gain a first-class reputation that can prove an immeasurable benefit in many ways. As a company's name and products or services become better known, not only do investors take notice, but so do customers and suppliers, who often prefer to do business with well-known companies.

Disadvantages to the Company

- *Loss of Privacy.* Of all the changes that result when a company goes public, perhaps none is more troublesome than its loss of privacy. When a company becomes publicly held, it is required by the Securities and Exchange Commission (SEC) to reveal highly sensitive information, such as compensation paid to key executives, special incentives for management, and many of the plans and strategies that underlie the company's operations. While these disclosures need not include every detail of the company's operations, information that could significantly affect investors' decisions must be disclosed.

   Such information is required at the time of the initial public offering, and it normally will have to be updated on a continuing and timely basis thereafter.

   As a result of this loss of privacy, some companies feel that special arrangements with key personnel or other related parties that are normal for a private company but that might be misconstrued by outsiders should be discontinued.

- *Limiting Management's Freedom to Act.* By going public, management surrenders its right to act with the degree of freedom that it enjoyed when the company was private. While the management of a privately held company generally is free to act by itself, the management of a public company must obtain the approval of the board of directors on certain major matters, and on special matters must even seek the consent of the shareholders. (Obtaining directors' approval or consent need not be a significant problem. The board of directors, if kept informed on a timely basis, can usually be counted on to understand management's needs, offer support, and grant much of the desired flexibility.)

Shareholders generally judge management's performance in terms of profits, dividends, and stock price, and apply pressure to increase earnings and pay dividends each quarter. This pressure may cause management to emphasize near-term strategies instead of longer-term goals.

- *The High Cost of Going Public.* The cost of an initial public offering is substantial. The largest single cost will be the underwriters' commission, which can be as much as 10 percent of the offering price. In addition, legal and accounting fees, printing costs, registration fees, and the underwriters' expenses can easily total more than 10 percent of the offering price for small offerings. Costs depend upon such factors as the complexity of the registration statement, the extent to which legal counsel must be involved, and the availability of audited financial statements for recent years.

  Beyond the initial offering, there are the continuing costs of the periodic reports and proxy statements filed with regulatory agencies and distributed to shareholders, and the increased professional fees paid to attorneys, accountants, registrars, and transfer agents for additional services. The time management will spend preparing the ongoing reports and statements must also be considered, since this responsibility will divert its attention from managing operations.

  The company may also need to upgrade its management and accounting information systems to enable it to maintain adequate financial records and systems of internal accounting controls to meet the accounting provisions of the Foreign Corrupt Practices Act, which are included in the Securities Exchange Act of 1934. Upgraded systems may also be necessary to report timely financial information.

Advantages to the Owners

- *Obtaining Marketability.* Once a company goes public, the owners will often find themselves in a new and more favorable position. Instead of holding shares with limited marketability, they will hold shares that can easily be sold in the market (subject to certain restrictions if their shares are unregistered) or used as collateral for loans.

- *Getting a Better Price.* One of the principal benefits of going public is that the value of the stock may increase remarkably, starting with the initial offering.

  Shares that are publicly traded generally command higher prices than those that are not. There are at least three reasons why investors are usually willing to pay more for public companies: (1) the marketability of the shares, (2) the maturity/sophistication attributed to public companies, and (3) the availability of more information.

- *Diversification of Personal Portfolios and Estate Planning.* Spreading investment risk through a diversified investment portfolio may be as relevant an objective for the shareholders of a private company as it is for an institutional investor. Many private companies, however, earn returns well in excess of normal investment returns. You need to consider your company's prospects, the degree of inherent risk in your industry, and the return now earned by your company's shareholders compared with what you believe could be earned in alternative investments. Diversification may be, but need not always be, an appropriate objective.

  Should owners of a private company wish to diversify their investment portfolios, going public can achieve that objective. Initial public offerings frequently include a secondary offering of shares owned by existing shareholders in addition to a primary offering of previously unissued shares. Of course, a secondary offering should not be perceived as a "bailout" from a faltering business.

  Estate planning may also be facilitated by going public. The liquidity of a shareholder's estate will be increased by the sale of shares. An existing public market for the shares retained will also facilitate future secondary offerings. Should that future secondary offering be precipitated by the death of a major shareholder who plays a significant management role, however, the offering may not be well received by investors, who are generally sensitive to management changes.

  The taxable value of a decedent's estate will be more readily determinable if the shares owned are publicly traded. The value of those shares, however, will often be increased by a public market. Whereas executors may be forced to sell a private company in order to pay estate taxes, shares in a public company can more readily be redeemed to pay estate taxes. (A specific relief provision, though, may allow the estate of the owner of a privately held business to pay estate taxes over a 14-year period.) And many of the estate tax benefits available to a privately held company will also be available once your company is public.

Disadvantages to the Owners

- *Constraints on Activities.* Privately held companies frequently engage in transactions with their owners, management, and directors. Such transactions might involve sales, leases, or joint ventures. Since such transactions might not be advantageous to public investors, or there may be the perception that they are not appropriate, it might be appropriate to forgo them once a company decides to go public.

  A second constraint relates to your investment in the company after it goes public. As part of management, you have access to important information before it is released to the public. Since this "insider information" could give you an edge over outside investors, the Securities and Exchange Commission prohibits your using it to buy or sell the company's securities. In addition, officers, directors, and persons holding 10 percent or more of the company's stock must give the company any profits they make on sales of the company's stock held less than six months.

  A third constraint results because securities owned are "restricted securities" unless they have been registered in a public offering. Restricted securities must be held at least two years before they can be sold, and the number of shares that can be sold in any three-month period thereafter is limited.

  Underwriters usually limit the number of shares the owners can register in an initial offering to avoid the appearance of a bailout by existing shareholders and to maximize the proceeds to the company.

- *Potential Loss of Control.* If a company goes public and enough shares are issued, an investor or a group of investors could take control away from the present owners. If a large block of shares finds its way into the hands of dissidents, they may vote to bring in new management. This can and does happen.

  However, if the stock is widely distributed, management usually can retain control even if it holds less than 50 percent of the shares. Retention of voting control can be accomplished by is-suing a new class of common stock with limited voting rights. However, such stock may have limited appeal to investors, and accordingly may sell for less than ordinary common stock.

- *Estate Valuation for Tax Purposes.* Any increased value that results from going public could result in higher estate and in-heritance taxes.

Is This the Time?

Suppose you have weighed all the pros and cons, and have decided that the best thing for the company is to go public. But when? Timing is crucial and raises several questions.

- *Is Now the Best Time to Go Public?* If needed capital is available from nonpublic sources at reasonable cost, you may want to delay going public. If funds raised from other sources can be used to increase the company's growth potential, the value of the com-pany's stock may increase. At a later date, the increased stock value may result in raising more capital or selling fewer shares.
- *Are Your Plans in Order?* After the offering, the stock's price may decline unless the company continues to show good progress and profits. A well-developed strategic business plan (including a multiyear financial plan) can help minimize adverse surprises by identifying the critical elements for continued success and providing benchmarks against which to monitor the company's progress.
- *Is Management Ready?* Now is the time, before the decision is irreversible, for management to analyze itself. Can it comfortably adjust to the loss of the relative freedom to act as it sees fit and to the loss of privacy? Are senior executives ready to cope with the public's scrutiny of the company's actions? Are they ready to admit outsiders to the decision-making process? Do they have the leadership capability to grow as the company grows? Does management command credibility in the financial community?
- *Are the Company's Information Systems Adequate?* As a public company, it will be required to provide timely and reliable fi-nancial information to investors. If the company's management and accounting information systems are inadequate, now is the

time to get them in first-class working order. There are legal liabilities for reporting false or misleading information, not to mention the loss of investors' confidence if information is not timely and accurate.

- *Does the Company Have Impressive Momentum?* Investors buy stock with the expectation that its value will go up if the company prospers. That's why investors (and underwriters) tend to look for companies with several years of strong, steady growth and rising profits, indicating management's ability to compete over the long haul. If the momentum is not there when the company goes public, investors will likely turn to more promising opportunities and the offering may fizzle.

There are no hard-and-fast rules, but some underwriters will not consider taking a company public unless it can point to revenues of at least $10 million and annual net income of $1 million, with anticipated growth of 25 to 50 percent a year for the next few years. There are exceptions, of course, such as new companies in the relatively new glamour industries. Each company must consider its own circumstances, bearing in mind that few elements in the overall picture will impress the investor as much as momentum.

- *Is the Market Right?* The market for initial offerings has varied dramatically from the depressed levels of the mid-1970s, when fewer than 50 companies a year went public, to the record highs of the early 1990s. In deciding whether this is the right time to go public, one of the critical questions is whether the mood of the market is right. Is the market strong or slumping? Are prices rising or falling? Is trading volume up or down?

One of the ironies is that even though your company might more than satisfy every criterion for going public, market conditions might sour just at the time you are ready to make your offering. Or, you may catch the market when prices and volume are strong and investors are eager for new opportunities.

Many things influence the market—political developments, interest rates, inflation, economic forecasts, and sundry matters that seem unrelated to the quality of your stock. The market is admittedly emotional, and investors' moods change from bullish to bearish and back again to the consternation of everyone, even the experts.

Underwriters track these changes to anticipate when investors are likely to be receptive to new offerings. When the market is favorable, many companies go to the market to obtain funds that they will not need until some time in the future, thereby eliminating the need to speculate on future market conditions.

- *What Are the Risks of Going Public at the Wrong Time?* The most obvious risk is that the offering will not be completed and the costs that have been incurred will have gone for nothing. This may occur because changes in the market or disappointing financial results cause the underwriter to back out. Another risk is that the stock may have to be offered at a lower price per share to attract investors.

Even offerings that sell enthusiastically can fail in the aftermarket, particularly if subsequent operating results are less than anticipated. A company that loses credibility in the financial community faces a long, difficult process in regaining investors' confidence, and a stock that loses value can also be vulnerable to shareholders' lawsuits.

The price you pay for bad timing can be almost beyond calculation.

ASSEMBLING THE REGISTRATION TEAM

Team Members

After making the decision to go public, you must assemble the group of specialists needed to guide you through the complex registration process. The team should include members of the company's management, legal counsel, the managing underwriter, the underwriter's counsel, and the independent accountants.

The lawyers and independent accountants you choose should have the expertise to work effectively with the SEC during the registration process, and to help the company meet SEC reporting requirements after the public offering is completed. It is not uncommon for companies to hire new counsel and independent accountants when they go public.

Choosing an Underwriter

In seeking an underwriter, you can turn to certain trusted sources for guidance—your legal counsel, independent accountants, or acquaintances in your local investment community—or you can ask companies that have recently gone public, especially those in your own industry. Here are six suggestions for choosing an underwriter:

1. Review the underwriter's performance in other offerings and its general reputation earned over the years. A helpful source of this kind of information is *Going Public: The IPO Reporter*, which tracks initial pubic offerings and their performance in the aftermarket.

2. Look for an underwriter that understands the important characteristics of your industry.

3. Check whether the underwriter has experience with offerings of the size you contemplate.

4. Determine the extent of the underwriter's distribution capabilities. If you want the company's stock to be widely distributed, you will want a firm with nationwide facilities. On the other hand, if the company's operations are regional, a regional underwriting firm might be a better choice.

5. Find out whether the underwriter will provide support in the aftermarket once the initial offering is sold. This support can take the form of bringing your stock to investors' attention, providing market research, or offering financial advice to your company.

6. Don't be unduly swayed by the highest offering price mentioned when you are interviewing potential underwriters. Reputable underwriters usually will sell the shares at approximately the same price, based on the results of similar offerings and the current state of the market.

Once the registration team has been chosen, the process of going public can begin.

THE GOING PUBLIC PROCESS*

The sale of securities to the public is governed by the Securities Act of 1933 (1933 Act), which requires a registration statement containing

---

* As you would expect, the process of going public is highly technical and complicated. While we will keep the discussion of this complex process relatively simple, from time to time we will use technical terms. They are described in Appendix 2–1.

specified financial and other information about the company and the proposed offering to be filed with the SEC. The 1933 Act provides certain exemptions from the requirement that a registration statement be filed; these exempt offerings are not considered public offerings and are covered separately in Chapter 3, "Private Placements." The process of going public generally takes from 60 to 180 days, depending upon the complexity of the registration statement and the SEC's backlog of filings in process (registration periods of less than 90 days are unusual). The more significant steps in the registration process include the following:

- Planning
- The initial meeting of the registration team
- Preparing the initial registration statement
- Filing the initial registration statement and the initial regulatory review
- Amending the registration statement
- Selling the securities
- The closing

A sample timetable for the steps involved in going public is contained in Appendix C.

Planning: Questions to Be Considered

After you have decided to take your company public, consider the steps needed to ensure a smooth transition from private to public company. You may need to do some corporate housekeeping. You will have to determine whether the necessary information for the registration statement is available and, if not, make plans to assemble it.

Corporate Housekeeping. Corporate housekeeping generally begins during the planning stage and may not be completed until the registration statement is filed with the SEC. You should consider whether the existing corporate, capital, and management structures are appropriate for a public company and whether transactions with owners and management have been properly documented and recorded. The following are typical questions to be considered during this phase:

- Should the company's capital structure be changed? You may want to simplify it by issuing common shares in exchange for preferred stock or special classes of common stock.
- Should additional shares of stock be authorized? Additional shares might be needed for the public offering or for future acquisitions or sales.
- Should the stock be split before you go public? Reducing the per share price, possibly to $10–$20 per share, can increase marketability.
- Should affiliated companies be combined? Affiliated companies might provide services to each other, compete with each other, or sell related products and services. The combined entity may well be more attractive to investors and thus command a higher price in the market.
- Should the company's articles of incorporation or bylaws be amended? A private company may have special voting provisions that are inappropriate for a public company, or it might be desirable to establish certain committees of the board of directors, such as audit and compensation committees.
- Are the company's stock records accurate and up to date? Accurate shareholder information is a must for a public company. (While reviewing the stock records, be alert for problems with previous issuances of unregistered securities.)
- Are the company's transactions or arrangements with the owners and members of management appropriate for a public company, and are they adequately documented? Since related-party transactions can be a problem, they should be identified and discussed with the company's legal counsel early in the process.
- Have important contracts and employment agreements been put in writing? Do they need to be amended? Should a stock-option plan be implemented? Should additional options be granted under existing plans?
- Does management possess sufficient depth and experience for a public company? The company may need to supplement or upgrade its financial and/or operating management before it goes public. Changes in the board of directors are often appropriate— for example, adding outside directors.

Information Requirements. The registration statement will require substantial amounts of financial information and disclosures about the company's history and business. Obtaining the required information about predecessor companies and acquired companies, both as defined, can be especially difficult.

The registration statement must include audited financial statements, usually for the preceding two or three years. If the company's financial statements have not been audited previously, you should determine whether financial records are adequate and auditable.

The Initial Meeting of the Registration Team

During the registration team's initial meeting, responsibilities for the various portions of the registration statement are assigned and the proposed terms of the offering are discussed. The registration form to be used should also be decided upon.

Form S-1 is the registration statement form most commonly used in initial public offerings for larger companies. Form S-1 imposes no limitation on the amount of funds that can be raised.

In August 1992, the SEC adopted Regulation S-B, which includes rules making it easier for small businesses to raise money in the capital markets. The rules somewhat simplify the initial and ongoing disclosure and filing requirements for qualifying small businesses and broaden the limits of existing rules relating to small offerings. To file a registration statement under Regulation S-B, your company must be a United States or Canadian company with annual revenue of less than $25 million in the last fiscal year and voting stock that does not have a public float of $25 million or more. In adopting Regulation S-B and amendments issued to date, the SEC has introduced two new registration statements for eligible small business issuers, Forms SB-1 and SB-2. Form SB-2 imposes no limit on the amount of funds that can be raised; however, Form SB-1 establishes a limit of $10 million in any 12-month period.

Following the initial meeting, the offering timetable and a letter of intent between the company and the lead underwriter should be formalized. The timetable should detail the tasks to be performed, the identity of those responsible for each, and the completion date of each task. (See Appendix C for a sample timetable.) The nonbinding letter of intent confirms the intended nature of the underwriting (i.e., "best efforts" or "firm commitment"), the underwriters' compensation, the number of shares expected to be issued, and the anticipated price. A binding underwriting agreement is not signed until the registration statement is about to become effective.

Preparing the Initial Registration Statement

A registration statement usually requires a considerable period of time to prepare. The statement must contain all disclosures, both favorable and unfavorable, necessary to enable investors to make well-informed decisions, and the document must not include any materially misleading statements. The SEC's disclosure requirements are contained in Regulations S-K and S-X. Regulation S-K specifies the requirements for the nonfinancial statement portion of the document, while Regulation S-X specifies the financial statements to be included and their form and content. Regulation S-B, on the other hand, sets forth the financial and nonfinancial disclosure requirements for small business issuers.

Information Requirements. The registration statement consists of two parts. Part I is also printed in booklet form and initially constitutes the preliminary prospectus, or "red herring," which is distributed to prospective investors prior to the effective date of the registration statement. Part II contains information that is not required to be included in the prospectus.

Exhibit 2–1 summarizes the information required in a Form S-1 registration statement. (Appendix D contains a more detailed discussion of the information required in Forms S-1 and SB-2.) Item 11, "Information with respect to registrant," is the most time-consuming and difficult item to prepare. Item 11 contains the requirements for information about the company's business, properties, and management; for financial statements and other financial information; and for management's discussion and analysis of financial condition and results of operations.

The entire registration team ordinarily participates in the initial drafting of the registration statement. The company and its legal counsel generally prepare the nonfinancial sections (if the company's legal counsel is inexperienced in preparing registration statements, the underwriters' counsel assists). The managing underwriter and underwriters' counsel prepare the description of the underwriting arrangements and, in some cases, the description of the offering. The company prepares the required financial statements and schedules,

EXHIBIT 2-1. Form S-1 Information Requirements

PART 1: INFORMATION REQUIRED IN PROSPECTUS

Item

1. Forepart of registration statement and outside front cover page of prospectus
2. Inside front and outside back cover pages of prospectus
3. Summary information, risk factors, and ratio of earnings to fixed charges
4. Use of proceeds
5. Determination of offering price
6. Dilution
7. Selling security holders
8. Plan of distribution
9. Description of securities to be registered
10. Interests of named experts and counsel
11. Information with respect to registrant
12. Disclosure of Commission position on indemnification for Securities Act liabilities

PART II: INFORMATION NOT REQUIRED IN PROSPECTUS

Item

13. Other expenses of issuance and distribution
14. Indemnification of directors and officers
15. Recent sales of unregistered securities
16. Exhibits and financial statement schedules
17. Undertakings

---

as well as other financial disclosures. The independent accountant usually advises the company about the financial statements and disclosures.

Financial Statement Requirements. Form S-1 registration statements require audited balance sheets as of the end of the last two years and audited income statements, statements of changes in shareholders' equity, and statements of cash flows for each of the three fiscal years preceding the latest audited balance sheet. The SEC recognizes the difficulty of providing audited financial statements immediately after year-end. Thus, for registration statements that become effective within 45 days after year-end, the most recent audited balance sheet may be as of the end of the second preceding year.

Condensed interim financial statements, which may be unaudited, are required unless the date of the latest year-end financial statements presented is within 134 days of the effective date of the registration statement. Exhibit 2–2 shows the latest financial statements required under various circumstances in an initial public offering for a company with a December 31 year-end.

Separate financial statements may also be required for entities for which the company's investment is accounted under the equity method, and for entities that the company has acquired or plans to acquire. (The need for separate financial statements depends on the relative significance of such entities to the registrant.)

Preparation Procedures. After the registration statement has been drafted and circulated to the registration team, the company's management, and possibly the directors, the registration team meets to review it. The draft is modified as appropriate (several redrafts may be necessary), and the amended copy is sent to the printer for the first proof. The printer's proof goes through the same circulation, comment and revision process. When the registration team is satisfied with the document, it is distributed to the board of directors for review and approval prior to filing with the SEC and the appropriate state agencies.

Preparing a registration statement that is acceptable to all the parties is extremely difficult and often involves a series of compromises. For example, underwriters' counsel may insist on disclosures about the company that management is initially reluctant to make. These discussions, when coupled with severe time pressures and changing market conditions, can result in frazzled nerves and frayed tempers, particularly as the proposed offering date approaches.

Filing the Initial Registration Statement and the Initial Regulatory Review

The SEC and the states have concurrent jurisdiction over securities offerings. The registration statement must be filed with the SEC, with any state in which the securities will be offered, and with the National Association of Securities Dealers (NASD). The SEC review is designed only to assess compliance with its requirements, including the adequacy of disclosures about the company, without addressing the merits of the offering. In addition to reviewing the adequacy of the dis-

EXHIBIT 2-2. Form S-1 Financial Statement Requirements

Expected effective date	January 1, 19X2 to February 14, 19X2	February 15, 19X2 to May 14, 19X2	May 15, 19X2	July 15, 19X2
The most recent audited financial statements must be as of a date no earlier than[a]	December 31, 19X0[b]	December 31, 19X1	December 31, 19X1	
The most recent condensed unaudited interim financial information must be as of a date no earlier than[c]	September 30, 19X1	None	January 31, 19X2[d]	

[a] If the annual audited financial statements included in the registration statement are "not recent" (e.g., nine months old at the effective date), underwriters often require audited interim financial statements as of a more recent date.

[b] Unless later audited financial statements are available.

[c] In addition to the condensed unaudited interim financial information describing the results of subsequent months may be necessary to prevent the registration statement from being misleading (e.g., if the company incurs operating losses or develops severe liquidity problems).

[d] Filings made 134 days after the company's fiscal year-end must include a balance sheet as of an interim date within 135 days of the date of filing.

closures, some states also consider the merits of the offering under their "blue sky" laws (i.e., whether the offering is "fair, just and equitable"). Some states perform in-depth reviews, while others perform cursory reviews. The primary purpose of the NASD's review is to determine whether the underwriters' compensation is excessive.

Based on the reviews, the SEC (and sometimes one or more of the states) may issue a formal comment letter, generally 30 to 60 days after the initial filing. The SEC's letter describes the ways in which it believes the filing does not comply with its requirements. The comment letters often focus on the specific uses of the proceeds (including the adequacy of the proceeds for the designated purposes), management's discussion and analysis of financial condition and results of operations, and disclosures about risk. Comments on the financial statements may question such matters as accounting policies and practices, related-party transactions, unusual compensation arrangements, off-balance-sheet financing methods, or the relationship among certain components of the financial statements.

Amending the Registration Statement

The registration team should address *all* of the comments in the regulatory review response letters, either by amending the registration statement or by discussing with the SEC and state regulators the reasons why revisions are unnecessary and obtaining concurrence with that conclusion.

A draft of the amended registration statement is distributed to the registration team for review, any necessary changes are made (including updating the financial statements), and the amended registration statement is filed. After all the parties involved are satisfied with the technical and disclosure aspects of the registration statement, the pricing amendment is filed. The pricing amendment discloses the offering price, the underwriters' commission, and the net proceeds to the company.

Although technically there is a 20-day waiting period after the final registration statement is filed before it becomes effective, an "acceleration request" is usually filed concurrently with the pricing amendment. The request asks the SEC to waive the 20-day waiting period and declare the registration statement effective immediately.* The SEC usually approves acceleration requests.

After the registration statement becomes effective, the final prospectus is printed and distributed to everyone who received a copy of the preliminary prospectus and to others who expressed an interest in purchasing the stock.

The Closing

The registration process culminates with the company issuing the securities to the underwriters and receiving the proceeds (net of the underwriters' compensation) from the offering. The closing for firm-commitment underwritings generally occurs five to seven business days after the registration statement becomes effective. The closing for best-efforts underwritings generally is 60 to 120 days after the effective date, provided the underwriters have sold at least the minimum number of shares specified in the registration statement.

Publicity During the Offering Process—Restrictions

The SEC has established guidelines limiting the information that may be released during the "quiet period," which begins when you reach a preliminary understanding with the managing underwriter and ends 90 days after the effective date of the registration statement.

You are prohibited from offering a security prior to the initial filing of the registration statement. The term "offer" has been broadly interpreted by the SEC to include any publicity that "has the effect of conditioning the public mind or arousing public interest in the issuer or in its securities." However, the SEC encourages you to continue publishing the company's normal advertisements and financial information.

If you issue new types of publicity, the SEC may delay the effective date of your registration statement, so you should consult your attorneys and underwriters before issuing any publicity releases during the quiet period.

---

* Acceleration is particularly critical in firm-commitment underwritings, since underwriters are generally unwilling to risk deterioration in the market after the offering price has been set.

After the initial filing, the SEC prohibits the company from distributing any written sales literature about the securities except the preliminary prospectus, which may be distributed to prospective investors. Oral presentations are permitted, such as the "road show," in which you and your underwriters discuss the offering with prospective members of the underwriting syndicate, financial analysts, and institutional investors. However, sales of the securities may not be made until after the registration statement has become effective.

In Regulation A offerings, the SEC will permit companies to "test the waters" for potential public interest in the company prior to the preparation or filing of the registration statement with the SEC. In these circumstances, companies are allowed to test the market through oral presentations as well as newspaper and other media advertisements. These communications have specific requirements and are not allowed in all states as a result of more restrictive state laws.

Liability Claims and Due Diligence

Material misstatements in, or omissions from, the registration statement can result in liabilities under the federal securities laws. Purchasers of the securities can assert claims against the company, the underwriters, the company's directors, the officers who signed the registration statement, and any experts (such as accountants or attorneys) who "expertized" certain portions of the registration statement.

The company cannot avoid liability as a result of material misstatements or omissions. On the other hand, the other parties (e.g., accountants and attorneys) may be able to assert the "due diligence" defense. That is, they may be able to avoid liability by demonstrating that, with respect to the applicable portions of the registration statement, they had conducted a reasonable investigation and thus had a reasonable basis for belief and did believe that the statements in the registration statement were true and not misleading at the time the document became effective, and that no material facts were omitted from the document.

The members of the registration team begin performing their due diligence procedures at the initial meeting, and continue them throughout the registration process. As part of these procedures, underwriters usually require the independent accountants to provide them with letters ("comfort letters") that contain assurances about the unaudited financial data in the registration statement. In addition, the members hold a due diligence meeting shortly before the registration statement becomes effective. Representatives of all the firms in the underwriting syndicate usually attend this meeting.

Suggestions for Facilitating the Process of Going Public

Based on our broad experience with many initial public offerings, we have a number of suggestions for facilitating the process of going public. Some suggestions are designed to prevent delays in the registration process, while others address steps to take before or during the registration process. (See also the section "Planning: Questions to Be Considered" earlier in this chapter.)

- Begin planning and considering the implications of going public long before you finalize the decision. For example, develop a well-thought-out strategic business plan, including a multiyear financial plan, that considers alternative means of financing and the effects the decision to go public will have on future operations.
- Establish relationships with an investment banker, a law firm, and an independent accounting firm experienced with federal securities laws.
- Before the offering process begins, establish a program of providing information about your company to the financial community and potential investors. Unless your company has established a practice of releasing information through the media or through advertising, the company may be prohibited from doing so during the registration process. Public visibility can enhance the initial sales effort and maintain the public's interest in your company's stock in the aftermarket.
- Consider engaging an independent accounting firm to observe the taking of the year-end inventories—even though it may be several years before you go public and your company's financial statements currently are not being audited. Observation of significant physical inventories by the independent accounting firm is usually essential if you are to receive an acceptable audit opinion on prior years' financial statements as required by the SEC.

- Consider whether the company's accounting principles are appropriate or should be changed to conform with prevalent industry practice.

- Anticipate potential accounting and disclosure problems, such as accounting for noncash and other unusual transactions, and disclosures about legal proceedings and transactions with owners and officers. Be prepared to explain to the SEC why the disclosures or methods of accounting reported in the registration statements are appropriate. In some cases, a prefiling conference with the SEC may be helpful. The early resolution of accounting and disclosure problems can prevent subsequent delays in the registration process.

- Establish a timetable for the registration process and stick to it. An isolated delay may not be significant, but the cumulative effects of several delays can be. Significant delays may force your company to provide more recent interim financial statements or cause the underwriters to question whether your company is really ready to go public.

- Avoid entering into significant business combinations or disposing of significant amounts of assets during the registration process. Pro forma financial statements and audited financial statements of acquired companies may be required in such cases and for combinations or dispositions that are probable but have not yet occurred. The preparation of these financial statements requires gathering additional information and can significantly delay the registration process.

- Limit the number of revisions that the printer must process, since typesetting, printing, and circulating drafts is costly. One member of the registration team should be designated to gather comments from the parties, make the appropriate changes, and then submit all the approved changes to the printer at one time.

- Make arrangements for the SEC's comments to be delivered by express mail, telephone, or fax. This can save one or two days in the registration process.

- Respond promptly and completely to all SEC comments. One easy way to provide a complete response and to facilitate the SEC's review of the amended registration statement is to number the comments on a copy of the comment letter, which should accompany the amended statement. The statement should be marked to indicate where each comment has been addressed.

Certain of the SEC's comments may not be appropriate, because the SEC staff misinterpreted the information in the statement. You should arrange to discuss these comments with the SEC. If the SEC suggests insignificant changes, it is usually better to make them than to delay the registration process while discussing them with the SEC.

REPORTING REQUIREMENTS FOR PUBLIC COMPANIES

Under the Securities Act of 1933, after the initial public offering, a company has to file with the SEC certain nonrecurring reports, including Form S-R, which describes the securities sold, the proceeds to the company, and the use of the proceeds. Further, under the Securities Exchange Act of 1934, a company has to file an annual report on Form 10-K or Form 10-KSB in its initial year as a public company. Only those companies registered under the 1934 Act must file a Form 10-K or Form 10-KSB in subsequent years.

Companies that elect to be listed on a national stock exchange* and companies with 500 or more shareholders of a class of equity securities and total assets of more than $3 million must register under the 1934 Act on Form 10 or Form 8-A. (Form 10 is the basic 1934 Act registration statement and requires disclosures similar to those required by Form S-1. Form 8-A is a simplified 1934 Act registration statement that can be used to register securities issued in an initial public offering, provided that the statement becomes effective within one year after the end of the last fiscal year for which audited financial statements were included in a 1933 Act filing.)

Companies registered under the 1934 Act must file the following periodic reports:

- *Form 10-K†.* This annual report must be filed within 90 days after the end of the fiscal year. The financial statement requirements

---

* Companies that elect to list their securities on a national or regional stock exchange must file a listing application with the exchange. Certain exchanges may require additional disclosures that were not included in the registration statement.
†Regulation S-B created Form 10-KSB as an annual report form and Form 10-QSB as a quarterly report form. Pursuant to Regulation S-B, Form 10-KSB provides for financial and nonfinancial statement disclosures that are more limited than those required in Form 10-K. Form 10-QSB requires essentially the same disclosure and financial information as Form 10-Q; however, one difference is that Form 10-QSB does not require a balance sheet as of the preceding fiscal year-end.

and the required nonfinancial disclosures about the registrant are similar to those in Form S-1, except that interim financial statements are not required. (Appendix D compares Form 10-K with Forms S-1 and SB-2.)

- *Form 10-Q.* This quarterly report must be filed within 45 days after the end of each of the first three quarters of the fiscal year. Comparative financial statements and notes are required, but they may be condensed and need not be audited. In addition, other disclosures relating to the occurrence of certain events during the period are required.

- *Form 8-K.* This form is used to report changes in control, acquisitions, or dispositions of significant assets; bankruptcy; changes in independent accountants; and resignations of directors. A Form 8-K reporting changes in control, acquisition, or disposition of assets; bankruptcy; or change in fiscal year must be filed within 15 calendar days after the occurrence of the reportable event. A Form 8-K reporting a change in independent accountants or a resignation of a director must be filed within five business days after the occurrence of the event. Financial statements of significant acquired businesses must be filed, and certain pro forma information must be provided. An extension of time is available for filing the required financial information about acquired businesses. Form 8-K can also be used to disclose other events the company believes are important to security holders; when used for this purpose, the 15-day filing requirement does not apply.

A public company is required to disclose all information that is material to investors. Such information cannot be disclosed selectively; it must be disclosed regardless of whether it is favorable or unfavorable, and it must be released simultaneously to all shareholders.

The SEC's integrated disclosure system has standardized the required financial statements and other disclosures in 1933 Act registration statements and 1934 Act annual and quarterly reports. This facilitates the filing of future registration statements. In fact, after a company has been subject to the reporting requirements of the 1934 Act for three years, it is eligible to file "short-form" 1933 Act registration statements, which can incorporate by reference information previously included in annual, quarterly, and current reports. This can expedite significantly the registration process and result in lower accounting, legal, and printing costs.

Registration under the 1934 Act also subjects the company (and certain shareholders and members of management) to a multitude of SEC rules, including those on soliciting proxies, insider trading, and tender offers.

- **Proxy Rules.** These rules require a company that solicits proxies from its shareholders to distribute a proxy statement containing a description of the matters to be voted on and detailed disclosures of the compensation earned by the company's highest-paid executives. In addition, the rules require that the annual report to shareholders be distributed with, or prior to, the proxy materials for the company's annual meeting. Even if proxies are not solicited, the rules prescribe certain disclosures for the company's annual report (e.g., the financial statements must comply with Regulation S-X, management must discuss and analyze the company's financial condition and results of operations, and the company's business during the past year must be discussed).
- **Insider Trading.** Officers, directors, and persons holding 10 percent or more of a company's stock must file reports on their holdings and changes in their holdings of the company's stock. Changes in security holdings in one month must be reported by the tenth day of the next month. Those reporting are required to turn over to the company any profits they realize on sales of the company's stock held less than six months, and are prohibited from selling the company's securities short.
- **Tender Offers.** Persons who tender to become owners of more than 5 percent of a company's stock must make certain disclosures to the company and the SEC. The tender offer rules also describe the mechanics for making a tender offer and limit a company's activities in resisting a tender offer.

This chapter has merely introduced the going-public process; it does not include all the possible considerations that will affect a particular company. Nothing can take the place of the firsthand advice of experienced professionals—attorneys, independent accountants, and investment bankers. They can consider your special circumstances and tailor their advice to your needs to help you make the important decisions that will set the future course of your company.

3

PRIVATE PLACEMENTS (EXEMPT OFFERINGS OF SECURITIES)

Many entrepreneurs at the head of small and growing companies dream of taking their companies public not only as a means of raising capital for growth, but for two other enticing advantages: the prestige of being a public company and the considerable financial gain earlier investors can often realize. But what if this is not the time? Three factors typically prevent initial public offerings: (1) your company does not yet have the financial strength or reputation to attract enough investors for a public offering; (2) you cannot afford the expense of going through the public-offering process; and (3) you need the money now and cannot wait for the lengthy process to run its course.

Going public will be feasible eventually, but how can your company obtain needed financing now? The answer may be an exempt offering, commonly called a private placement.

A private placement is "exempt" because you do not have to file a registration statement with the Securities and Exchange Commission (SEC), a significant advantage because it cuts down paperwork and saves precious time. A private placement is so called because you can offer the stock or debt to a few private investors instead of the public at large.

Saving time and money for small companies in need of growth capital was exactly what Congress had in mind when it spelled out these exemptions in the Securities Act of 1933. The aim was to simplify compliance with securities laws and make it easier for companies to raise capital. The Small Business Investment Incentive Act of 1980 expanded exempt-offering opportunities, and the resulting changes in SEC regulations have made private placements an increasingly popular method of raising capital. The SEC's 1992 Small Business Initiatives further simplified and expanded the exempt-offering process.

While "exemptions" is the key word, you do not have a completely free hand—far from it. For one thing, while your private placement may be exempt from federal registration, it may not be exempt from registration under state laws. Some states require registration, some do not. Also, private placements are not exempt from antifraud provisions of the securities laws. This means that you must give potential investors the necessary information about your company to make a well-informed decision. You must exercise meticulous care not to omit or misstate the facts or give them a rosier hue than they deserve.

WHEN TO CONSIDER A PRIVATE PLACEMENT

There are other considerations in a private placement, as your attorney or independent accountant will tell you.

Broadly defined, the private placement market includes a wide variety of larger corporate finance transactions, including senior and subordinated debt, asset-backed securities, and equity issues. This sophisticated, highly developed market is dominated by institutional investors (including insurance companies, pension funds, and money management funds), larger corporate issuers, and investment bankers or other corporate finance intermediaries. In recent years, debt financing in the institutional market totalled over $50 billion in the United States Equity financing, though smaller in dollar volume, is also substantial. If your company is contemplating a debt financing of $10 million to $15 million or an equity financing of $5 million to $10 million, your financial advisor can help you determine whether the institutional market is a viable alternative.

As privately negotiated transactions, private placements can be designed to meet the specific situation your company faces. Debt securities can have amortization schedules tailored to match anticipated cash flow. By attaching warrants or other equity "kickers," you can improve returns on debt securities for investors while not causing any immediate dilution or control implications for current ownership. Equity financing has the advantage of requiring no current servicing, thus conserving the company's cash flow for investment in the business. Creative securities can be structured to minimize the transfer of control to outside investors.

While private placements can involve debt, equity, or both, this chapter focuses on the registration exemptions for small issuers emphasizing equity transactions. This chapter discusses why you might undertake a private placement, who the potential investors might be, and the types of exempt offerings that you should understand before you decide to proceed.

PRIVATE PLACEMENT CAPITAL SOURCES

Compared with a public offering, your private placement will probably involve only a few investors. They might be relatives, friends, neighbors, or business acquaintances. If you know enough of such people and feel comfortable laying your proposition before them, fine. More likely, you will place the job of finding investors in the hands of a broker or financial advisor who makes a business of keeping track of investors who are willing to take risks with small companies.

In all, there are at least three different groups of investors that might have a special interest in your situation:

1. Suppose you manufacture a product and sell it to dealers, franchisors, or wholesalers. These are the people who know and respect your company. Moreover, they depend on you to supply the product they sell. They might consider it to be in their own self-interest to buy your stock if they believe it will help assure continuation of product supply and perhaps give them favored treatment if you bring out a new product or product improvement.

   One problem with this type of arrangement is when one dealer invests and another does not; can you treat both fairly in the future? Another problem is that a customer who invests might ask for exclusive rights to market your product in a particular geographical area, and you might find it hard to refuse.

   These professional investors are often focused on a particular industry, a specific geographic area, or companies at a defined development stage. Examples are prominent in fields such as high technology or biotechnology. Many professional investors or funds invest in companies that have developed products but need to build manufacturing capacity. If your situation matches the investors' criteria, and your management team is strong enough to stand up to the intensive scrutiny that is typical of professional investors, this may be a good source of private capital for your company.

2. There are other investors searching for opportunities to buy shares of small growth companies in the expectation that the company will soon go public and they will benefit as new investors bid the price up, as often happens. For such investors, news of a private placement is a tip-off that a company is on the move and worth investigating, always with their eye on the possibility of its going public. These investors usually have no interest in taking a hand in running the company, so you have no fear of losing control or suffering their interference.

3. Private placements also often attract venture capitalists who hope to benefit when the company goes public or when the company is sold. To help assure that happy development, these investors get intimately involved at the board of directors level, where their skill and experience can help the company reach its potential.

Whatever the source of private capital, it is critical for the future growth and development of the company that the current owner and the new investors share a common outlook on the eventual "exit strategy" for the investors. Shared expectations with respect to the timing and structure of a public offering, a recapitalization financing, or the sale of the company to a larger corporation are as important to both the entrepreneur and the investors as the terms and conditions of the private placement.

TYPES OF EXEMPT OFFERINGS

There are several types of exempt offerings. They are usually described by reference to the securities regulation that applies to them.

Regulation D

Regulation D is the result of the first cooperative effort by the SEC and the state securities associations to develop a uniform exemption from registration for small issuers. A significant number of states allow for qualification under state law in coordination with the qualification under Regulation D. Heavily regulated states, such as California, are notable exceptions. However, even in California, the applicable exemption is fairly consistent with the Regulation D concept.

Although Regulation D outlines procedures for exempt offerings, there is a requirement to file certain information (Form D) with the Securities and Exchange Commission, usually within 15 days following sale of the security. Form D is a relatively short form that asks for certain general information about the issuer and the securities being issued, as well as some specific data about the expenses of the offering and the intended use of the proceeds.

Regulation D provides exemptions from registration when securities are being sold in certain circumstances. The various circumstances are commonly referred to by the applicable Regulation D rule number. The rules and their application are as follows:

- *Rule 504.* Issuers that are not subject to the reporting obligations of the Securities Exchange Act of 1934 (nonpublic companies) and that are not investment or "blank check" companies may sell up to $1 million of securities over a 12-month period to an unlimited number of investors.

- *Rule 505.* Issuers that are not investment companies, and issuers disqualified because of specific acts of misconduct with respect to the securities laws, may sell up to $5 million of securities over a 12-month period to no more than 35 nonaccredited purchasers, and to an unlimited number of "accredited" investors (defined in Exhibit 3–1). Such issuers may be eligible for this exemption even though they are public companies (subject to the reporting requirements of the 1934 Act).

- *Rule 506.* Issuers may sell an unlimited amount of securities to no more that 35 nonaccredited but sophisticated purchasers (described under "Requirements and Restrictions" following) and to an unlimited number of accredited purchasers. Public companies may be eligible for this exemption.

EXHIBIT 3–1. Accredited Investor Definition as Defined by Regulation D

To determine whether the exemptions in Rules 505 and 506 apply, one must understand the term "accredited" purchaser or investor. Regulation D enumerates eight categories of accredited investors:

1. Institutional investors (e.g., banks, brokers or dealers, and insurance companies), including ERISA (Employee Retirement Income Security Act) plans, with total assets in excess of $5 million
2. Private business development companies (defined in the Investment Advisors Act of 1940)
3. Tax exempt organizations that are defined in Section 501(c)(3) of the Internal Revenue Code, with total assets in excess of $5 million
4. Certain insiders of the issuer, such as directors, executive officers, and general partners (these persons need not meet the financial criteria set forth in items 5 and 6 below)
5. Any person whose individual net worth or joint net worth with that person's spouse at the time of purchase exceeds $1 million
6. A person who has an individual income in excess of $200,000 in each of the two most recent years or joint income with that person's spouse in excess of $300,000 in each of those years, and has a reasonable expectation of reaching the same income level in the current year
7. Any trust, with total assets in excess of $5 million, not formed for the specific purpose of acquiring the securities offered, whose purchase is directed by a sophisticated person (as defined)
8. An entity in which all the equity owners are accredited investors

Requirements and Restrictions

The Small Business Exemption (Rule 504). Rule 504 is an attempt to establish a clear and workable exemption for small offerings (up to $1 million) that are not regulated at the federal level but are left to the states to oversee. Although the federal antifraud and civil liability provisions are still applicable, the company is not required to register at the federal level. The exemption is not available to issuers who are subject to the reporting obligations of the Securities Exchange Act of 1934 (public companies). The 1992 SEC Small Business Initiatives lifted the previous ban on general solicitation of investors and eliminated the restriction on resales. However, state security regulations must be followed.

The $5 Million Exemption (Rule 505). Only 35 investors who are not accredited may participate in an exempt offering under Rule 505, while an unlimited number of accredited investors may participate

EXHIBIT 3–2. Comparative Chart of Regulation D Exempt Offerings

Restrictions and Requirements	Small Business Exemption (Rule 504)	$5 Million Exemption (Rule 505)	Unlimited Exemption (Rule 506)
Maximum dollar amount	$1 million (12 months)	$5 million (12 months)	Unlimited
Number of investors	Unlimited	Unlimited	Unlimited
Types of investors	Anyone	Accredited (35 may be nonaccredited)	Accredited (35 may be nonaccredited, but must be sophisticated)
Offering solicitation restrictions	General solicitation, including advertising, meetings, and seminars, is allowed (subject to state regulation)	General solicitation is not allowed	General solicitation is not allowed
Security resale restrictions	Resale not restricted (subject to state regulation)	Restricted (see Exhibit 3–3)	Restricted (see Exhibit 3–3)
Who can issue	Any company other than investment companies or public companies	Any company other than investment companies	Any company
SEC notification	Required as a condition of exemption. Five copies of a notice on Form D must be filed with the SEC no later than 15 days after the first sale.		

Disclosure requirements	None specified, but enough should be disclosed to ensure compliance with antifraud provisions	None specified if investors are all accredited purchasers, but enough should be disclosed to ensure compliance with antifraud provisions

If investors include nonaccredited purchasers:

Nonpublic companies (those not registered under the Securities Act of 1934) must furnish:

- Offerings up to $2 million—the same kind of information as would be required in Part II of SEC Form 1-A
- Offerings up to $7.5 million—the same kind of information as would be required in Part I of SEC Form SB-2
- Offerings over $7.5 million—the same kind of information as would be required in Part I of a registration statement filed under the Act on the form that the issuer would be entitled to use

Public companies must furnish:

Annual report to shareholders, definitive proxy statement, and Form 10-K, if requested, plus subsequent reports and other updating information *or* information in most recent Form S-1, Form SB-2, or Form 10 or Form 10-K plus subsequent reports and other updating information

Issuers must make available prior to sale:

- Written information given to accredited investors
- Opportunity to ask questions and receive answers

under this rule, which allows up to $5 million in securities to be sold. (See Exhibit 3–1 for a definition of "accredited.")

Even though a company is exempt from registration under Rule 505, proof that all investors are indeed accredited involves a substantial legal and paperwork process.

Furthermore, if any nonaccredited investors (limited to 35) purchase the securities, Regulation D specifies that minimum disclosures about your company and the offering must be made to them. When an issuer provides required information to nonaccredited investors, it should consider providing such information to accredited investors as well, in view of the antifraud provisions of the federal securities laws.

The information that needs to be provided depends on the size of the offering. Offerings up to $2 million require the disclosures called for in Part II of SEC Form 1-A, except that an audited balance sheet, dated within 120 days of the start of the offering, must be provided. For offerings between $2 million and $5 million, the issuer must provide the same kind of information required in Part I of Form SB-2. This includes, among other things, compliance with the requirements of the Industry Guides whenever applicable. The issuer must give proposed purchasers the opportunity to ask questions in any transaction depending upon Rule 505 or Rule 506. The process of undertaking an exempt offering under Rule 505, as well as meeting any state regulatory requirements, can involve substantial legal and financial costs. Offerings under Rule 505 are limited to $5 million.

The Unlimited Exemption (Rule 506). Disclosure requirements for sales to nonaccredited investors under Rule 506 are similar to those of Rule 505 (see Exhibit 3–2). Rule 506 adds one further stipulation for the maximum of 35 nonaccredited investors who may purchase securities in this unlimited offering—all nonaccredited investors in a Rule 506 offering must meet the following description:

> Each purchaser who is not an accredited investor either alone or with his purchaser representative must have such knowledge and experience in financial and business matters that he is capable of evaluating the merits and risks of the prospective investment, or the issuer reasonably believes immediately prior to making any sale that such purchaser comes within the description.

As in Rule 505, an unlimited number of accredited investors may participate under Rule 506.

To determine whether potential investors qualify as either accredited or sophisticated, you should, with the aid of counsel, draw up a questionnaire to be completed by the prospective investor. These completed questionnaires should be retained by the seller as evidence of compliance with Regulation D.

For offerings between $5 million and $7.5 million, the company must provide the same kind of information as required in Part I of Form SB-2. This includes, among other things, compliance with the requirements of the Industry Guides whenever applicable. If the company is not qualified to use SB-2, it would be required to present the same kind of information as prescribed in the registration form that would be appropriate under the circumstances.

The requirement that the financial statements be audited is different than in the registration statements on which the disclosures are based. If Form SB-2 can be used in determining the disclosures needed, only the financial statements for the latest fiscal year need be audited. The prior year's financial statements may be unaudited. If the issuer must base its disclosures on a registration statement that requires three years of audited financial statements, only the latest two fiscal years' financial statements are required to be presented and only the latest year need be audited.

In all cases, the financial statements need only comply with generally accepted accounting principles; Regulation S-X does not apply.

If obtaining an audit of the most recent fiscal year would result in "unreasonable effort and expense," only a balance sheet, dated within 120 days of the offering, needs to be audited, for any issuer other than a limited partnership. Limited partnerships that cannot, without unreasonable effort and expense, obtain the required financial statements may present audited financial statements prepared on the basis of federal income tax requirements. The SEC has interpreted that this provision may apply to all financial statements in a limited partnership offering.

The provisions that allow for the financial statements to be audited for only the latest fiscal year and that provide alternatives where the audits are not available without unreasonable effort and expense apply also to any financial statements that may be required for the acquisition of a business or real estate operation.

Form SB-2 provides that the issuer should present the audited balance sheet as of the end of the most recent fiscal years of any corporation or partnership that is a general partner of the issuer. For any general partner that is a natural person, the issuer must disclose that individual's net worth in the disclosure document, based on the estimated fair market value of the person's assets and liabilities with provisions for estimated income taxes on unrealized gains. The SEC has administratively required these disclosures in registration statements by limited partnerships on forms other than Form SB-2 (or its predecessor, Form S-18).

For offerings over $7.5 million, the issuer must provide the same kind of information as specified in Part I of the registration form that the issuer could use (Form SB-2 or Form S-1 in most cases). However, if the requirements cannot be met without unreasonable effort and expense, the following are permitted:

- Audit requirements for issuers that are not limited partnerships may be limited to a balance sheet dated within 120 days of the offering; the other statements (generally two years of balance sheets and three years and interim periods of current-year and prior-year statements of income and cash flows) may be presented as unaudited.
- Limited partnerships may furnish audited financial statements prepared on the basis of income tax requirements rather than generally accepted accounting principles (GAAP).

Regulation D does not require that any particular information be furnished to accredited investors; however, as stated previously, consideration should be given to providing them all information given to nonaccredited investors.

For an overall comparison of the requirements and restrictions for Regulation D exempt offerings, see Exhibit 3–2.

Intrastate Offerings

To qualify for this exemption, all the securities must be offered and sold to persons living within the state in which the company is incorporated and does a significant portion of its business, and the securities must remain in the state. Difficulties in monitoring and controlling trading limit the use of this exemption.

Regulation A

The Regulation A exemption is available for sales of less than $5 million of securities. Although sales under Regulation A are labeled as "exempt offerings," Regulation A requires the filing of an offering circular that includes the types of disclosures required in registration statements. However, the required financial statements need not be audited, although state securities laws or the underwriters may require them to be audited. The 1992 SEC Small Business Initiatives lifted a number of restrictions on Regulation A offerings. The changes include allowing issuers to "test the waters" through distribution of factual material to determine investor interest prior to filing the mandated disclosure statement. Most state securities regulators, however, did not immediately follow the SEC in revising limitations. Regulation A is used infrequently because of the small amounts of capital that can be raised, the extensive disclosure requirements, and the reluctance of underwriters to permit issuers to use it.

STATE SECURITIES REGULATION

Each of the states has rules for private placements, and while there are some similarities there are many and wide differences as well. While three-quarters of the states have adopted the Uniform Securities Act to reduce such differences, subsequent amendments and other changes to the laws mean that whatever uniformity was achieved initially has not been maintained. Therefore, whenever securities are sold in a state, the state's regulations, as well as Regulation D, must be complied with. The extensive differences among the states may make it necessary to retain local counsel in each state in which the securities are offered, sold, or purchased.

State securities laws are known as "blue sky laws." The term originated from legislative and judicial actions to prevent the sale of securities for endeavors that had as much substance "as the blue sky." State securities laws are often different from and more confining than federal securities regulations. The purpose of the federal securities acts is the "full disclosure" of relevant data. This allows the sales of very poor quality, or high-risk, securities as long as full disclosure is made to the investing public. Many state securities laws go much further to protect potential investors. In many states, the administrators of securities laws are also responsible for the protection of citizens in that state against bad or risky investments. Thus, securities cannot be traded in certain states if they are not "fair, just and equitable. " The interpretation of this term is generally the responsibility of the administrator of the state's securities laws.

While it may appear easy to determine whether a state's blue sky laws apply to a particular situation, two potentially troublesome questions must be answered. First, it must be determined that a security is involved. There is no uniform opinion as to the meaning of the term "security"; it has been broadly interpreted to include such disparate items as stock, bonds, commitment letters, profit-sharing certificates, condominiums, orange groves, and other contracts in which it is anticipated that the purchaser will profit by the efforts of the issuer and its agents (an "investment contract"). Second, there must be an offer, purchase, or sale of the security "in this state" for state laws to apply. Yet there is a conflict among state laws as to how "in this state" should be applied to the many different and complicated transactions that can be involved. As indicated previously, one should use legal counsel to determine whether a state's blue sky laws must be observed.

PROCEED WITH CARE—COMMON PITFALLS

Although complying with exempt-offering regulations is generally less onerous than federal registration of securities, it still requires care and usually some professional assistance. Violations of the exempt-offering regulations can cause you to lose your exemption from registration and make you vulnerable to litigation brought by disgruntled investors.

Always follow the regulations and document your compliance with each. Be aware of these common pitfalls:

1. Do not advertise or solicit potential investors in a manner that could be construed to be the making of a general solicitation unless general solicitation is permitted under both the exemption from federal registration and applicable state securities laws. The offering could be determined to be "public" rather than "private."

2. Do not exaggerate or present information only in the most favorable light. You *must* point out the risks attendant to the investment. Emphasize positives and explain negatives.
3. Furnish all information required by the regulations, and if specific disclosures are not required, furnish enough information so the potential investor can make an informed decision.
4. Where qualification of investors is required, be sure you have documentation that proves your investors meet the qualifications.
5. Be sure investors understand the restrictions on resales of the securities. Failure to comply with this negates the exemption. The securities themselves should bear a legend disclosing the resale restriction (see Exhibit 3–3).
6. If you are thinking of a second exempt offering, or are planning an exempt offering before or after registering securities, make sure there is sufficient time delay so that the two offerings will

EXHIBIT 3–3. Restricted Resale of Exempt Stock

Restricted Stock: Securities whose resale or transfer is restricted because, among other reasons, it was issued in an exempt transaction (see Rule 144).

Rule 144: Rule 144 is not a part of Regulation D; however, a security issued pursuant to Regulation D can be sold in a broker's transaction (if other requirements are met) after a period of two years. After a period of three years, it can be sold basically without restriction.

Rule 144 Exception: The resale and transfer restrictions under Rule 144 do not apply to offerings made under Regulation D Rule 504, "The Small Business Exemption," if such offerings are registered at the state level and the state requires delivery of a disclosure document to all investors. In this case, all resale restrictions are lifted.

Resale Disclaimer: Regulation D provides that reasonable care in connection with limitations on resale may be demonstrated by

> written disclosure to each purchaser prior to sale that the securities have not been registered under the Act and, therefore, cannot be resold unless they are registered under the Act or unless an exemption from registration is available; and requires placement of a legend on the certificate or other document that evidences the securities stating that the securities have not been registered under the Act and setting forth or referring to the restrictions on transferability and sale of the securities.

Examples include the following:
> The securities in this offering must be held for two or more years before resale or transfer can take place under the regulations of the Securities Act of 1933, as amended.

Resale of the securities discussed in this disclosure may not be made unless the securities are registered under the Securities Act of 1933, as amended, or unless the resale is exempt from the registration requirements of the Securities Act of 1933, as amended.

---

not be considered as one. There must be at least six months between offerings. Likewise, beware of having sold some shares to a few investors prior to or immediately following an exempt offering. These sales might be construed as part of the exempt offering, subject to these requirements, or could cause you to lose your exemption.

PRIVATE PLACEMENT MEMORANDUM

To best present your company information to potential investors, you will want to prepare a private placement memorandum. At a minimum, it should include enough disclosure information to ensure compliance with antifraud provisions—enough information for investors to make a well-informed decision, with no omissions, misstatements, or enhancements of the facts. The contents of a private placement memorandum parallel the contents of a full business plan, and should be tailored to meet the circumstances of your company and the purposes of your offering. For example, a new venture or the launching of a new product would probably require the most detailed memorandum. The raising of second- and third-round capital may require only such information as funds required and their uses, historical and projected financial data, and a description of your company and its history.

Most private placement memorandums should also include certain disclaimers regarding the type of securities being offered, the confidentiality of information, the accuracy of projections, and so forth. As discussed previously, other than under Rule 504 and those private placement memoranda circulated solely to accredited investors, Regulation D specifies certain information required to be contained in an offering circular. Your financial advisor and legal counsel can assist you in developing an effective and thorough private placement memorandum.

4

VENTURE CAPITAL

One of the most promising ways to raise capital for growth is also one of the oldest. Venture capital—its modern name—dates as far back as business itself. The first time a person with a promising business idea asked an uncle, a friend, or a neighbor to help get a business going by putting in some money, and offered to share future profits, venture capital was born as a basic business concept.

To understand venture capital, start with the term itself: "venture" means risk. If your company has a promising but unproven idea (the risk factor), and needs money to take the next big step, yours is the kind of situation that attracts venture capitalists. They have the money you need and will supply it—by buying stock in your company, by lending it to you, or by some other method.

With an ownership stake, a venture capitalist will share your risk. If you fail, he or she fails. If you succeed, he or she shares your profits. Because it is a touch-and-go situation and the risks are high, venture capitalists will usually be interested only if they see a chance for a high return on their investment—30 percent or more a year is not uncommon. By comparison, common stock investors, with greatly reduced risks, will receive an average yearly return of only 10 to 15 percent. And while banks may lend you money, they will participate only if the risk is minimal and thus their return will be far less than venture capitalists expect.

The logic is simple: The more the risk, the higher the expected return. Nothing could be more aptly named than venture capital.

During the 1970s and for most of the 1980s, venture capital was itself something of a growth industry. There have always been wealthy individuals ready to invest in young, developing companies—at best, a minor factor in the world of business financing. But by the mid-1980s, the scale and orientation of venture capital had changed dramatically. Attracted by the creation of whole new high-technology industries, newly institutionalized venture capital began to multiply both in numbers of practitioners and in the amount of money available for investments.

By 1991, there were more than 600 venture capital firms in the United States. Many state governments, seeing a chance to help local firms and create new jobs, marched into the ranks of venture capitalists as well. In 1986, the aggregate investment of all these sources of risk capital peaked at $3.2 billion—hardly a minor factor any more. While investments decreased from 1986 through 1991, venture capital will remain a multibillion dollar industry with an important part to play in financing growing companies in the years ahead.

As you might imagine, large-scale venture capitalists have become far more than mere suppliers of money. To protect their investments and realize the high return they expect, venture capitalists tend to concentrate on industries with which they are thoroughly familiar. Therefore, they expect to have a voice in the management of your company. What they have to offer—valuable contacts, market expertise, sound strategic thinking, and a practical understanding of what you are trying to accomplish with your company—may turn out to be more important than their money.

Because the relationship between entrepreneur and venture capitalist is so intimate, before embarking on this arrangement it is important for both the entrepreneur and the venture capitalist to understand and be comfortable with the business objectives and financial goals of the other party, as well as each other. Venture capitalists have often said they invest in people as much as or more than companies.

The venture capitalist will examine your company in detail, particularly the quality of your management and your track record (possibly more important than your skills as an originator). And you will examine the venture capatalist to satisfy yourself that he or she understands your kind of business, that your objectives are compatible, and that he or she might bring expertise that can significantly add to your chances of making the venture successful.

To evaluate each other, both parties might bring in outsiders such as lawyers, accountants, or other experts who can train an objective eye on the facts that matter. It is important to approach the evaluation process with a constructive, nonadversarial attitude, recognizing that the resulting "partnership" must be mutually beneficial if it is to be truly profitable. This mutual evaluation is essential since the "marriage" is an important one and any subsequent divorce might be fatal to your company.

Venture capital, with its unique risk-sharing nature, may or may not be the best way for you to raise growth capital. But it is well worth your time to see what it is, how it works, what the advantages and disadvantages are, how to prepare for negotiations, and what factors enter into a well-reasoned decision.

SOURCES OF VENTURE CAPITAL

The demand for venture capital in recent years has caused a proliferation of financing sources that can be classified into seven distinct types. They are as follows:

1. Private venture capital partnerships (family money, pension funds, large individual investors, etc.)
2. Public venture capital funds
3. Corporate venture capital
4. Investment banking firms' venture capital funds
5. Small Business Investment Companies (SBICs) and Specialized Small Business Investment Companies (SSBICs)
6. Individual investors
7. State governments

Private Venture Capital Partnerships

This group has the largest number of venture capitalists and is the largest source of funds.

Originally, individuals who had been eminently successful in building enterprises of their own invested some of their profits in young companies still struggling for success. They saw opportunities that might be realized with an infusion of capital and perhaps the use of their own expertise and experience. They could afford the risk and expected a handsome return. Later, these adventurous entrepreneurs combined their money and formed partnerships. They invested in special situations where they believed they could apply their experience, contacts, and managerial skills to enhance a growing company's ability to profit and thus bring a high return.

Historically, low-risk investments such as money market instruments and bonds returned 5 to 10 percent a year, and riskier but still relatively secure equities brought 8 to 12 percent. Early venture capitalists showed that by carefully investing in companies whose business they understood and by getting personally involved in the management, they were able to achieve much higher returns commensurate with the risk. As a result, the venture capital industry as a whole now expects to generate a return on investment of approximately 30 percent a year. Since this 30 percent average includes successful and unsuccessful investments, many ventures will need to yield much more than 30 percent per year to meet the industry average. As you might expect, such results have brought many people and businesses into the venture capital field.

Among the family groups that became major factors in venture capital were Rockefeller, Phipps, and Whitney. In addition, firms were created by pooling funds.

These private pools of funds are usually partnerships in which limited partners have invested various sums of capital. These investments may range from as little as $25,000 each to tens of millions of dollars or more each. As a result, some funds are operating with relatively limited capitalization and concentrate on smaller deals. Other funds with very large capital bases—ranging in excess of $1 billion under management—will usually have a large number of investments in companies at various stages of their growth, and can concentrate on doing several very large deals concurrently. As private venture capital firms have succeeded, they have been able to attract funds from banks, insurance companies, pension funds, and other sources. By any measurement, they are a powerful force in the world of risk capital.

Public Venture Capital Funds

As the business of venture capital matures and the venture capitalists themselves need more capital, a few have raised funds by selling their stock in the public equity markets. The operation of these public firms is generally the same as private firms with one exception: they must disclose much more detail about their activities because they must conform to disclosure regulations imposed by the Securities and Exchange Commission. As a result, it is usually easier to get more information about the operation and investments of these public firms than about private venture funds.

Corporate Venture Capital

At one time, more than 50 major corporations had venture investment pools. More recently, the number of active corporate funds has fluctuated with changing corporate strategies and the varying circumstances of corporate mergers and restructurings.

These corporate venture funds typically operate in a very similar fashion to private funds. However, there may be a significant difference in the goals of a corporate fund and a private fund. Some corporate funds invest in developing businesses in the hope that the small company will succeed and become a choice acquisition target for the firm that supplied the capital. Others offer venture funds as a diversification move, hoping the investment will prove profitable. Many industrial companies view their venture capital investments as a type of research and development—a window on technology—a way of supporting and gaining access to new technology that could prove profitable to their company's future operations.

There are advantages and disadvantages to having a corporate venture fund as an investor, and these should be considered before entering a relationship with such a firm. On the plus side, profitable venturing corporations represent a stable, deep-pocket source of funding for subsequent phases of development and growth. Association with an established corporation may also bring broader resources for manufacturing, research, and marketing, as well as an in-place infrastructure and support system. On the other hand, corporations typically do not have the same type of culture as entrepreneurial companies, which may cause difficulties.

Investment Banking Firms' Venture Capital Funds

The investment banking business has long been a major factor in helping companies raise growth capital, and now it has entered the venture capital field. Traditionally, investment banks have provided expansion capital and later-stage financing by selling the stock of growing companies in the public and private equity markets. To provide more service to clients, some have formed their own venture capital firms. In this way, they can provide not only later-stage but also early-stage financing. While they can serve their clients better, these firms are also realizing the same high returns as other types of venture capital firms.

The SBICs and SSBICs

The Small Business Investment Companies (SBICs) and Specialized Small Business Investment Companies (SSBICs) are privately capitalized venture capital firms, licensed and regulated by the federal Small Business Administration (SBA). These firms receive loans from the SBA to augment capital they raise privately. Because of this special status, they are regulated to some degree, which means there are some restrictions. Restrictions include the level of private equity capital required for each funding (SBICs a maximum of $2.5 million and SSBICs a minimum of $1.5 million) and the type of enterprise funded (real estate transactions are usually excluded; see also Exhibit 4–1).

Individual Investors

While venture capital firms play a major role in raising funds for growth, there is still room for the individual investor, and individuals are a considerable force. They were the first venture capitalists when everything was on a much smaller scale. Many entrepreneurs prob-

EXHIBIT 4–1. SBIC Investment Restrictions

The following restrictions apply to SBIC investments:

1. To qualify for SBIC financing, a small business must meet the following two financial tests: (a) it does not have net worth in excess of $18 million, and (b) it does not have average net income after federal income taxes for the two preceding fiscal years in excess of $6 million.
2. An SBIC cannot take control of a small business in which it invests, through stock ownership, board control, or otherwise.
3. SBIC financings must have a term of at least five years.
4. SBIC financings of small concerns engaged in real estate activities are narrowly restricted.
5. SBICs cannot finance banks or other financial institutions engaged in relending or reinvestment.

---

ably overlook them when thinking about venture capitalism, but their contribution, if it could be measured, would undoubtedly surprise everybody. Their role in providing seed capital is important in that often the individual investor is willing to invest capital in a business opportunity that a private venture capitalist might consider too risky because it does not meet his or her firm's investment criteria or because the size of the investment is too small for a formal venture capital firm to justify. While these "early-stage deals" are definitely risky, if the business is successful it also has the potential to produce significant rewards. Individual investors are usually the source of funds for the true start-up company—the person with an idea or product but no track record.

State Governments

More than half of state governments have recognized the important contribution that support of fledgling companies can make to the economy. While the states hope to make a profit, their primary goal in providing early-stage or seed capital to companies that might have difficulty raising capital elsewhere is job creation. These seed-capital funds are also used as a vehicle to attract entrepreneurs and scientists to locate their businesses in that state. Some states have accumulated very large pools of capital, ranging from $5 million or $10 million to several hundred million dollars. However, compared with the larger private venture capital firms, they operate on a much smaller scale, generally making modest investments ranging from less than $100,000 to $500,000.

TYPES OF VENTURE CAPITAL FIRMS

Just like your own company, venture capital firms pick out a certain niche in their industry where they concentrate their activities. Some confine themselves to a certain geographic region. They study the investment opportunities in this region carefully and believe that being a home-grown operation gives them an edge. Others operate nationwide. And some consider the entire world to be their arena. Venture capital firms may also choose to differentiate themselves based on certain industries or types of products.

In the early days of venture investing, high-technology companies and products were traditionally viewed as the primary targets for venture firms. However, in recent years, the high-technology marketplace has matured. Attractive investment opportunities have arisen in other areas, and venture investors have expanded their portfolios to include nontechnology or "low technology" companies such as in the consumer products or retail industries. Recently, the venture capital industry has edged its way into the European market. With the current economic changes taking place in Europe, the venture capital industry has become more international, considering investments in the unexploited European venture market.

Many venture capital firms have refined their strategies for investment to reflect these overall changes in the marketplace, as well as to differentiate their niches within the industry. It can be of significant benefit to choose to work with a venture capitalist who understands your business, your competitive environment, and the critical factors for success in that environment.

Venture capital firms also differ in another way. Some specialize in early-stage financing; others favor expansion financing for more mature companies; still others supply funds for acquisitions and buyouts. The following table displays the compounded annual return a venture capitalist expects at the different stages of financing a company:

Stage of Financing	Expected Return
Seed or start—up	50% or greater
Second stage	30%—40%
Latter stage	25%—30%

We will examine these differences in some detail so you can see clearly how important it is to match your circumstances to those of the venture capitalist.

Early-Stage Financing

Some venture capitalists specialize in putting money into a company in its earliest stages. That is the point at which the risk is highest and, therefore, so is the chance for high rewards if the enterprise succeeds.

Suppose you have started a company. Right now it consists mainly of an idea—for a new product, a product improvement, or something else for which you are convinced there is a waiting market. Now the first steps must be taken, and that requires capital.

After considering other sources, you turn to the venture capital field and find a firm that specializes in your kind of situation. (See the section "How to Find a Venture Capitalist.") You state your case: You need funds to finance preliminary research and development, to prepare a business plan, and to provide a modest amount of working capital. The firm, impressed by your idea, your knowledge of the market, your objectives, and not least by your own level-headed intelligence, decides that your goals are compatible with its own, and the deal is made. They supply the necessary seed money. When the seed phase of your operation is completed, you take the next tentative step. This is the start-up phase. It takes additional capital, of course, to carry the research and development far enough to develop a prototype product and whatever else is necessary to show that your business has a solid chance to succeed. Again, this is an early-stage opportunity that some venture capital firms relish. They examine your product, your business, plan, and your objectives. They satisfy themselves that you have good people in key managerial positions and agree to supply the capital.

Early-stage financing might also include a third phase in which more funds are raised by the venture capital method to carry your business to the stage of manufacturing and marketing your product. These three early-stage phases may appear to be separate and distinct, and in some cases they are. But in other cases they blend and the capital is supplied by a single venture capital firm. Obviously, the needs differ from one industry to another and from one company to another.

Second-Stage Financing

Just as the term suggests, additional capital may be needed to assist your company through its second stage—the initial scale-up for manufacturing and marketing, building the necessary facilities, or establishing a working-capital base to support inventory, receivables, and other costs in moving the company into the commercial stage. The risk is still high and therefore appealing to venture capitalists who specialize in your kind of business, especially in these formative years of your development (see Exhibit 4–2).

EXHIBIT 4–2. The Venture Capital Funding Process

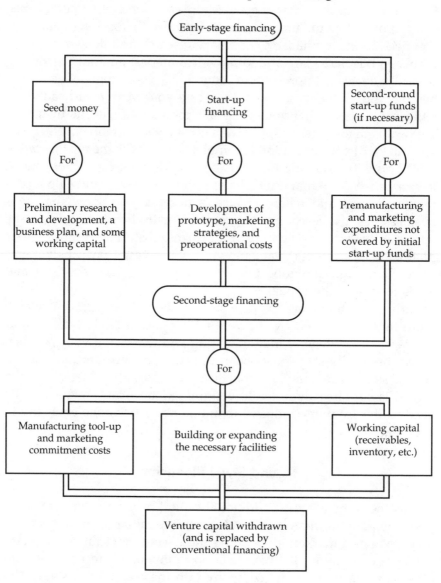

Acquisition and Buyout Financing

Venture capitalists use their money in many ways. As specialists in particular industries, they keep up to date on the affairs of individual companies and even divisions within those companies. In recent years, some venture firms have begun to use their expertise in an industry to identify opportunities for acquisition or buyout. If they identify an unusual opportunity, they may form a pool of investors, perhaps including the present management team, to buy out a division of a public company or to acquire a small private company. The new company can then be established as a new entity in the venture capital portfolio with its own management and capital base.

Venture firms invest in acquisitions and buyouts because they believe the new company can be made profitable and will produce the high returns they expect. Although buyouts and acquisitions are a new area of investment for many venture firms, as these firms react to changing market conditions, they will continue to expand their portfolios through acquisition and buyout financings.

WHEN VENTURE CAPITAL IS WITHDRAWN

When you arrange to bring venture capital into your company, one of the most important things to take into account is the basic nature of this relationship. At some point in the future, the firm that supplied the funds will want to cash in on its investment. As your company matures and the risk-reward quotient moderates, the venture capital firm moves on to invest in another high-risk opportunity.

You must prepare your company for this eventuality so that the investors can "cash in" without hindering your momentum or placing an unbearable stress on the operation.

At the very outset, it is wise for you to reach an understanding with the venture capitalist. Exactly what are the investment objectives? What are the liquidity needs? Making certain that your needs are compatible with the venture capitalist's instead of conflicting is probably the most critical step in the entire process of arriving at your decision.

HOW TO FIND A VENTURE CAPITALIST

With well over 1,000 individuals and firms in the business of supplying venture capital—many of them specializing in certain industries, some operating nationwide and others concentrating on smaller geographic areas, some interested in early-stage financing and others in growth and expansion—finding a few that fit your needs may sound like a formidable task. But it need not be; there is good help available.

A good way to begin is to consult a directory. Like venture capitalists themselves, some directories are national while others are regional. Many are published by industry groups such as the National Venture Capitalists Association, 1655 North Fort Meyer Drive, Suite 700, Arlington, Virginia 22201. A well-regarded directory is *Pratt's Guide to Venture Capital Sources,* produced by Venture Economics, Inc., 75 Second Avenue, Suite 700, Needham, Massachusetts 02194.

Directories usually give the names, addresses, and phone numbers of firms, list their officers, and specify the types of investments they are generally interested in—for example, the size and state of financing, the industries they specialize in, and whether they prefer to deal with national or regional companies.

Even when the directories have helped narrow the field, it is advisable to get further guidance from your attorney, accountant, or other consultant who can shed light on the current mood of the venture capital community, who understands the specific investment criteria of certain firms, who can identify firms that might be more compatible with your objectives, and who can help you assess which firms to approach. Based on their prior knowledge and experience, your advisors might also assist you with introductions to those firms.

The picture is not always what it seems in the cold facts of the directories. Take a venture capital firm that strikes you as likely to fill your needs. You check with your accountant. This advisor happens to know that because the firm is in the process of raising money for its own investment pool and has no money to invest at this moment, it would be a waste of time for you to meet with the firm. On the other hand, the accountant may know other firms that are well prepared to invest and are searching for opportunities.

It all comes down to a matter of avoiding pointless contacts and concentrating your time, your effort, and the expense of preparing a presentation on firms that you know are ready to talk seriously. If your state government is active in the venture capital field, a telephone call to your state office of economic development or state office of commerce should tell you how to set up a meeting. If you have problems making contact, are unsure whether your state has a venture capital program, or just feel you need counsel before or during state negotiations, your accountants, bankers, or business advisors may be able to provide some important assistance.

Once you have identified venture capital firms that might meet your professional goals, establishing contact with and getting the attention of those firms can be a challenge. A venture firm may receive many unsolicited phone calls, executive summaries, and business plans, in addition to having significant responsibilities for ongoing monitoring and assessment of their portfolio investments. As a result, an introduction from someone who is known to the venture firm may assist in getting attention to your business opportunity. In any case, whether your initial contact with the venture firm is through a cold call, an unsolicited business plan, or an introduction, the key to gaining the attention of the venture capitalist is a carefully prepared and well-presented business plan.

THE BUSINESS PLAN

The business plan—and in particular the executive summary—is a key document in initiating contact with a venture firm. As such, it should be a realistic reflection of how you as an entrepreneur and your management team expect to operate your business. The plan should reflect that you have carefully considered the many aspects of establishing and operating your business and have made the realistic decisions necessary to ensure its success. A cohesive, thorough plan of this nature will go a long way toward meeting the expectations of the venture capitalists.

What Do Venture Capitalists Expect?

Venture capitalists expect you to present a detailed and meticulously accurate account—in writing. This is usually done by preparing a business plan. The business plan will spell out such basics as these:

1. A succinct history of your company
2. The opportunity

3. Your estimate of how much capital is needed
4. The state of the market, as you see it, today and in the near future
5. Your assessment of present and potential competitors
6. New technologies and products that might affect the competitive environment
7. Your management team
8. Financial calculations, including cash flow for a number of years, expected profits, expected capital requirements, how this money would be used, and any other relevant facts
9. Your short- and long-term goals

Obviously, this list would change somewhat from one company to another, but it illustrates the kind of information needed. Committing all this to writing serves two good purposes: it helps you think things through in a careful, orderly manner, and it helps the venture capitalist evaluate your competence and weigh the risks that underlie his or her decision.

As you would expect, your business plan, no matter how thorough, is bound to raise questions and you will probably have to go back to supply further facts, address new problems that came to light in your meeting, and maybe even recast the plan. There is a good chance the venture capitalist will use the help of outsiders more expert than he or she in judging certain aspects of the plan. Thus, the process of getting to know each other goes on, often stretching into weeks and even months before an investment is structured that meets the objectives of both parties. These negotiations frequently involve attorneys and accountants for both sides to supply objective expertise in this delicate effort to create a relationship that will be fair and effective.

Major Concentration Points

A few features of the business plan deserve emphasis.

Many venture capitalists believe the most important ingredient is your management team. Accordingly, they carefully scrutinize the backgrounds of your key managers for assurance that these people have the intelligence, experience, and temperament to carry the business through the crucial years ahead when their money is on the line. They look for entrepreneurial skills, technical training; sophistication in research and development, production, distribution, marketing, finance, and administration; and any other qualifications that pertain to your type of business. And they expect to find enthusiasm and competitive spirit. All too often the basic business plan tends to dwell overwhelmingly on technical matters and neglects the human factor. This is always a mistake.

In creating the plan, another point of emphasis should be the size and attractiveness of the market. How big is the market? Is it completely saturated or can it be expanded? How do you rate your competitors? Have many new competitors entered the market recently and successfully gained a foothold? No matter how good your product may be, success will depend largely on how well you understand the dynamics of your market, so the venture capitalist looks for signs that you are thoroughly and realistically up to date on the state of the market.

Your plan must address a third significant issue: Exactly how is this venture unique? Do you have a unique product advantage? A unique packaging advantage? A unique method of distribution? A unique marketing edge? The venture capitalist expects you to define that element of uniqueness that sets you apart from your competitors and gives you the jump on the field. Winners usually have it and it deserves to be a major feature of your business plan.

There is much to consider when preparing a business plan. Some types of information will be applicable to your situation and some will not.

WHO GETS CONTROL OF YOUR COMPANY?

Nothing could be more natural than for you, as manager of the business, and maybe as founder and principal owner, to feel uneasy that control of the company might well pass to the venture capitalist. Pangs of worry may come and go as negotiations drag on, but it is important for the good of the company and your own peace of mind that you do not let these feelings become stumbling blocks.

One of the realities of running an expanding business is that, bit by bit, larger and larger portions of ownership pass from the original owners to investors as growth opportunities demand that you bring in outside capital.

It is not uncommon that first- and second-round capital might take 40 to 60 percent of the equity shares, and succeeding rounds of financing, including public offerings, may leave the original owners with as little as 5 to 20 percent of the stock.

The point to keep clearly in mind is that growth *depends* on this outside capital—without it, the company might fall behind the competition, lose its place in the market, and even go out of business. Another reassuring reality is that, though outside investors may own a majority of your stock and demand a voice in managing the company, they are not likely to wrest control away from you if your record proves that you are doing a good job and bringing them the returns they expect. Another consideration in getting comfortable with the role of a venture investor is to consider that most venture capitalists prefer a role as an advisor to your company and not a voice in the day-to-day operational management. Frequently, a venture investor is involved in multiple ventures at once and does not have the time to be deeply involved in any one company. Although there are a few venture capitalists who choose to become involved at a day-to-day operational level, most prefer a board-of-directors type of role, suggesting changes in the business to make it more profitable, assisting in finding new managers, and meeting with the entrepreneur to identify new opportunities for growth and success.

In considering the concepts of control, it is important not to lose sight of the fact that venture investment represents a "partnership" for growth. As such, owning a smaller percentage of a company that has grown successfully is far more attractive than owning 100 percent of a company that has not grown at all.

5

TRADITIONAL FINANCING: DEBT

As manager of a business, it is easy to picture yourself in this position: Your company is enjoying a good run of success. The problem now is to sustain that success, build on the momentum, and grow through plant modernization or expansion, new products, new markets, maybe an acquisition, or whatever opportunities beckon you into a promising future. At some point early in your planning, you will turn your mind to financing this growth and a bank loan may be the first possibility that occurs to you.

A good starting point is to list the reasons you might want to borrow. Some of these reasons are as follows:

- To limit the amount of equity investment required of company owners and investors
- To provide working capital
- To raise the funds to finance the acquisition of another business
- To refinance existing debt with a new lender
- To restructure the company's balance sheet
- To raise funds for product expansion
- To accommodate a lender's request for loan repayment

This chapter discusses how banks and finance companies operate, the advantages and disadvantages of debt versus equity, the best uses for borrowed funds, and the many kinds of loans. Chapter 6 tells how you and a bank should evaluate each other and how to carry out the negotiations for a loan.

SOURCES OF DEBT CAPITAL FOR GROWING BUSINESSES

The traditional sources of debt capital for growing businesses have been banks and finance companies. Finance companies offer forms of financing similar to banks, but are typically willing to assume more risk.

But more recently, the definition of "lender" has become more complex, especially in high-growth markets where lenders seek to establish their market niche. In an active financial market there are cash-flow lenders, secured lenders, asset-based lenders, and hybrid lenders. These terms refer as much to the lender's market niche as they do to their primary repayment sources and credit criteria. Within each of these categories, lending can be further defined by specific lending criteria such as the following:

- Minimum and maximum loan size
- Credit agreements (cash-flow lender) versus demand contract agreements (secured and asset-based lender)
- Pricing considerations
- Industry preferences
- Geographic preferences
- Purpose of loans: To finance receivables, inventory, equipment, fixtures, real estate, expansions, acquisitions, buyouts, or growth
- Types of loans: Lines of credit, term loans, mezzanine loans, or subordinated debt
- Equity interests

A "cash-flow lender" of today is your traditional handshake lender of yesterday. This lender is generally part of a commercial bank and is likely to be the most conservative of the lenders discussed here. The cash-flow lender may or may not require security, but does look primarily to the continuation of historical profits to repay the loan. The reliance on past profitability limits the attractiveness of cash-flow debt to early-stage companies. Credit criteria focus heavily on the use of the proceeds, leverage considerations (total liabilities to total net worth), and cash-flow coverage available to repay the principal and interest when due. The loan is generally monitored by a credit agreement with negotiated covenants and specified definitions and remedies for default of a loan. For the most part, the company remains in control of its cash.

A "secured lender" tends to be either the asset-based lending department within a commercial bank or a regional bank. This department is a cross between the cash-flow lender and the hard-asset lender because loan repayment from cash flow and profits remains an aspect of the credit decision, as does asset coverage for the loan. Less consideration is generally given to leverage issues because greater reliance is placed on the value of the assets and their collateral coverage. Pricing for secured loans tends to be higher than for cash-flow loans, as secured loans are perceived to have more risk and require more administrative attention to monitor the collateral. The increased risk is generally defined by a lack of strong operating trends, higher leverage, perceived industry difficulties, and so on.

Secured loans tend to be structured using a borrowing-base formula. This allows outstanding loans to be monitored against assets, with a typical borrowing base of 75 to 85 percent of eligible accounts receivable and 25 to 50 percent of raw material and/or finished-goods inventory. Secured-lender loans tend to be governed by demand agreements that generally allow the lender to control the receipt and disbursement of company cash.

The lender receives checks and cash daily from either a lockbox or a blocked account with a depository bank, or directly from the company. These proceeds are used to reduce the debt, and simultaneously re-advances are made available at the company's request according to availability under the borrowing-base formula. The loan contract typically specifies that the loan is outstanding for a one- to three-year time period, with prepayment penalties. While these secured-lending departments exist within commercial banks and tend to assume more risk in their lending activities, it is important to remember that these departments, like the bank itself, are subject to high levels of government regulatory scrutiny. Therefore, the "regulated" secured lender will typically have less flexibility in its lending practices than will unregulated commercial financing companies, often known as "asset-based lenders."

Asset-based debt represents funding from the typical commercial finance company. Similar to the secured loan from a commercial bank, an asset-based loan is secured with collateral provided by the borrower, such as accounts receivable, inventory, or plant and equipment, to support general working-capital needs, inventory build-up, loan refinancings, asset acquisitions, or a leveraged buyout.

The major differences between the secured-lending department at a bank and at a commercial finance company are the criteria by which borrowers are evaluated and the level of risk the institutions are willing to assume. Unlike asset-based departments of commercial banks, finance companies are not heavily regulated by the government and consequently have the ability to assume more risk in their loan portfolios and are paid accordingly. In granting secured loans, finance companies rely more on the strength of the company's collateral than on its operating track record or profit potential. Finance companies focus primarily on the liquidation value of the assets with little consideration for leverage.

Many small- and medium-sized businesses have found that finance companies provide an important source of funds that are not widely available through commercial banking channels. The typical finance company borrower is a company with erratic performance or one whose growth has outstripped its net worth and available working capital, and is unable to increase its bank borrowings. These tend to be highly leveraged companies. In many cases, asset-based lending is the sole source of working capital for these companies.

Finance companies charge higher interest rates than commercial banks and somewhat higher interest rates than secured lenders. This results from three factors: (1) the increased level of risk associated with highly leveraged and undercapitalized borrowers; (2) the greater amount of administrative time and costs required to monitor collateral; and (3) a higher cost of funds to the finance company, since a substantial part of its lendable dollars is often borrowed rather than in the form of depository balances.

The "hybrid lender" represents a cross between a cash-flow lender, a secured lender, and an equity investor. This type of lender typically represents a "one-stop shop" from whom a borrower may obtain both secured and unsecured debt, as well as revolving term debt and equity financing. These lenders are trained to assess cash flow and equity risks and receive the appropriate compensation for debt or equity funding.

This category of lender seems to have developed as the result of high-priced leveraged buyout transactions of the 1980s. The high purchase prices exceeded the comfortable credit limits of cash-flow lenders. Similarly, the purchase prices exceeded the lendable asset base. Many of the companies being acquired, such as those within the service industry, had little or no assets. This resulted in a layer of financing beneath senior and term debt and above equity, which is typically called mezzanine debt, subordinated (convertible) debt, and/or preferred stock.

Generally, mezzanine debt is repaid within two to four years, whereas subordinated debt is long-term by definition, with repayment beginning after other debt has been retired. Mezzanine or subordinated debt may be structured with features similar to equity and, over time, may be able to command an equity interest in the company, typically in the form of warrants or options. The hybrid lender considers cash flow and asset values, but focuses most heavily on the inherent value of the business enterprise and the ultimate rate of return on its investment. The repayment source in this case may be the sale of the company in order to receive a value for the stock.

This hybrid lender represents a blurring of lender categories, since various types of financing institutions operate within this area. Hybrid lenders can be found among large commercial finance companies, commercial banks, insurance companies, pension funds, public and private investment funds, and venture capital firms.

LONG-TERM DEBT

Fixed-Asset Acquisition

Capital assets are generally high-cost items of long-term utility that are difficult to finance internally through regular cash flow. They include assets that enable your business to expand its productive capacity and to serve additional customers more efficiently. In short, they are necessary for a young, growing business to continue expanding.

Banks often make capital loans—a specialized form of term loan— to finance the purchase of capital assets. The loan is usually secured by a lien on the asset being purchased, although more established bank customers are sometimes able to rely on their general earnings power and strong credit history with respect to prior loans and, hence, are able to obtain unsecured loans. The repayment period for a capital loan is generally five to seven years. If the loan is secured by a specific asset, the bank has the right to repossess the asset if the borrower does not meet its obligations.

Insurance companies, leasing companies, equipment and fixed-asset lenders, and pension funds also provide long-term financing for capital assets. Generally speaking, the longer the term the less likely a bank will be interested in the loan and the more likely other financing institutions will be the primary source of funds.

Expansion generally means an investment in additional plant and equipment and an increase in the overall amount of working capital required in the business. Companies borrowing to finance expansion have capital needs that differ greatly from those borrowing to supply basic working capital. When borrowing to finance an expansion, a company will find that it needs

- A large amount of long-term financing.
- Longer repayment terms.

Term Loans

The principal form of medium-term financing is the term loan. Term loans are distinguished from capital loans in that they are generally used for long- or intermediate-term credit needs, usually three to seven years. They are commonly used to increase working capital, to finance a major expansion of capital facilities, or to acquire another business. Principal payments may be structured to increase over time as cash is provided.

Banks are more cautious and have stringent credit policies regarding this type of credit because of the higher credit risk associated with the uncertainty about the future. Thus, term loans are often subject to higher interest rates, periodic fees, compensating bank account balance requirements, restrictive covenants, and annual anniversary reviews.

The interest rate on term loans is generally tied to the prime or bank reference rate and fluctuates with it. Thus, if the interest rate is "prime plus three," the borrower would pay 13 percent when the prime is 10 percent, 14 percent when it is 11 percent, and so on.

Larger than normal working-capital requirements can also be financed through the use of term loans. For this type of financing, the bank looks to the ability of the borrower to generate sufficient cash flow to repay the loan within the stipulated period.

Leases

As an alternative to buying equipment, businesses sometimes lease. Almost any capital asset can be leased, its acquisition effectively financed in a way similar to using a capital loan. Banks and leasing companies are the major sources of lease financing after equipment manufacturers.*

Leasing may be a preferred method of financing in some situations for the following reasons:

- Cancellation options are available. These are especially desirable when the asset being financed is associated with a technology that is advancing rapidly and unpredictably. A cancelable lease passes the risk of premature obsolescence to the lessor.
- Maintenance and other services are provided.
- One hundred percent of the asset cost, often including installation, may be financed.
- The terms may be longer and more flexible than under other types of financing.
- The tax deduction for the lease payment may be greater than the depreciation deduction that would apply if the asset were purchased. (Leasing techniques are discussed in more detail in Chapter 8, "Leasing.")

SHORT-TERM DEBT

Long-term financing is designed to help a business handle large, sometimes irregular growth in capital needs that are planned for in advance. Short-term debt, on the other hand, is generally used to make up for the unplanned cash needs that long-term financing does not cover and that are difficult to plan for in advance—weekly and monthly fluctuations that arise from unexpected shortfalls or increases in sales or unforeseen increases in expenses. The major forms of short-term debt include the following:

- Revolving lines of credit for working capital

---

* Source: Brealy and Meyers

- Accounts receivable financing
- Inventory financing
- Revolving line of credit

Borrowing Working Capital

Working capital is defined as the excess of current assets over current liabilities, sometimes referred to as general operating funds. Not having an adequate level of working capital can hamper your company's ability to grow by limiting the amount of inventory you are able to buy or the amount of sales you can make on credit. Working-capital loans are often used to provide the necessary funds to finance inventories and receivables. Working-capital loans are particularly useful in helping companies smooth the effect of seasonal business fluctuations, when you may need to build inventory for sales in later periods. They can also help weather the effects of troughs in business cycles.

Working-capital loans are usually short-term (up to one year) and can be secured or unsecured. Borrowers with strong operating histories and cash-flow positions can generally borrow without collateral. Banks may require a pledge of assets as collateral when repayment is less certain, such as with young companies or those that are highly leveraged, in a high-growth mode, or experiencing seasonal needs. If the business's assets are insufficient, the bank may require personal assets pledged individually by the principals of the company and/or personal guarantees. These loans are unlikely sources of start-up capital unless the owners can pledge the necessary collateral from personal assets to assure repayment. Even then, banks are reluctant to make loans to a business without an operating history.

There are three main types of working-capital loans:

1. Secured accounts receivable financing, including factoring
2. Secured inventory financing
3. Unsecured revolving line of credit

Accounts Receivable Financing

If your receivables are of good quality with regard to age, collectibility, and diversification, a bank or finance company may lend against them. As goods are shipped, funds are advanced on the basis of a predefined percentage of eligible accounts receivable.

In return for pledging your receivables as collateral, banks are normally willing to lend you up to 80 percent of their value. Customers are usually not notified that their accounts have been used as collateral, and they pay your company directly, not the financing institution. Typically, banks will finance receivables based on a monthly borrowing-base calculation. Finance companies, however, may allow for daily borrowings and paydowns. When the receivable is collected, a payment is made to the bank reducing both the loan balance and the borrowing base until additional sales are used to recalculate a new borrowing base. This form of borrowing requires continuous recordkeeping to track the collateral and is costly to both borrower and lender. Thus, the rate of interest is usually higher and there may be additional service charges on the loans.

Accounts Receivable Financing with Factoring. Factoring is another form of receivables financing, though typically more costly because the lender assumes the credit risk of the borrower's customers and administers collection of the receivables. Factoring involves a continuing agreement under which a financing institution purchases your receivables as they arise, assumes the risk of default on any of these accounts, and is responsible for collections. Factors also perform credit checks on all customers.

Factoring can be valuable to small and medium-sized companies by allowing them to take advantage of some of the economies provided by full-scale, professional credit management (the lenders) normally associated only with larger firms. Such arrangements allow smaller companies to avoid establishing a credit department until credit sales are large enough to justify the cost.

There are two general types of factoring. In one, the financing institution (the factor) does not perform a typical lending function. The company and the factor agree on credit limits for each customer and establish an average collection period for all receivables, typically adjusted quarterly directly to the factor. The factor pays the company on the basis of the agreed-upon average collection period, regardless of whether or not the customer has paid the factor yet. For example, if at the end of a normal 30-day collection period a customer has paid only $5,000 on an outstanding invoice of $10,000, the factor must remit the entire $10,000 (less whatever fee has been agreed upon).

The factor may place an interest charge on the $5,000 not collected but paid. The factor's commission normally amounts to .5 to 1.5 percent of the value of the invoice. This type of factoring arrangement is called maturity factoring and provides assistance mainly with collection and insurance against bad debts.

In the other form, called old-line factoring, the factor will perform a lending function by making payment in advance of collection. This makes funds available close to the time of sale instead of upon anticipated collection. Factors will usually advance 70 to 90 percent of the value of an invoice at an interest cost of 1 to 3 percent above the prime rate. The advance rate is dependent on the overall dilution of receivables, generally due to bad-debt allowance, slow turns, and so on. The advance rate is typically determined by adding 10 to 15 percent to the dilution rate and subtracting from 100. For example, a 5 percent dilution rate plus a 10 to 15 percent margin, subtracted from 100, would equate to an 80 to 85 percent advance rate.

Factoring arrangements can be either "with recourse" (the company is liable for any deficiencies, as described previously) or "without recourse," as is the case when the factor has full responsibility for collection of the receivables with no recourse against the borrower.

Through the use of a factor, a company can usually

- Increase the turnover of its working capital, reducing other financing requirements.
- Limit credit, collection, and bookkeeping expenses to a definite percentage of its credit sales, which is the percentage commission on those credit sales it pays to the factor.
- Protect itself against bad debts.

Factoring is an expensive way to finance receivables and is not commonly accepted in many industries. It can be especially costly when invoices are numerous and relatively small in dollar amount. At one time, factoring was considered an indication of a company's unsound financial position. This is no longer true and today many healthy firms engage in this form of financing.

Inventory Financing

Banks and finance companies also lend on the security of inventory, but are selective about the inventory they will accept. For example, hard commodities and nonperishable goods are best because they can be sold if a customer defaults on its payments. Finished goods can also be used for collateral depending on their liquidation value. Since inventory is less liquid than other current assets, a bank will seldom lend more than 50 percent of the value of the inventory.

There are several forms of inventory financing. Three of the most commonly used are described here. Procedures for financing the last two depend on who controls the inventory—the borrower (floor planning) or the lender (warehouse financing).

1. *Blanket Inventory Advance.* If inventory has a high degree of marketability, a bank will often advance against it, generally together with receivables. The bank will take an overall filing against all inventory (and other desired assets) and monitor the inventory based on reports submitted monthly.

2. *Floor Planning.* Under a floor-planning or trust receipt arrangement, the lender buys the inventory and the borrower holds the goods in trust for the lender in an area under its direct control, either at a public warehouse or on premises. A trust receipt is issued by the bank—and signed by the borrower—that identifies the assets being used as security. When the assets are sold, the proceeds are used to redeem the trust receipt. The lender makes periodic inspections of the inventory to ensure that the collateral is being properly maintained. Automobile dealers commonly finance their inventories in this manner.

3. *Warehouse Financing.* Warehouse financing is similar to floor planning, except that the goods being used as collateral are stored at a public warehouse with the receipt held by the lender. If that is not practical, a public "field" warehouse can be established on the borrower's premises.

When the goods are stored in a public warehouse, the warehouse company issues a warehouse receipt and will release the goods only upon the authorization of the holder of the receipt. Because the holder of the receipt controls the inventory, the receipt can be used as collateral for lending purposes. Lenders require that the goods be stored under bond in sealed storage, and that they must not be moved or the seal broken until the loan is repaid. The warehouse receipt serves as a guarantee that the material will remain secure. It is turned over to the lender for the term of the loan.

If you are unable to store your inventory in a large public warehouse, a field warehouse can be established. With this type of arrangement, a warehouse company leases space on the borrower's premises and is responsible for controlling and managing that space. They will secure the goods and release them only at the request of the holder of the warehouse receipt, in this case the lender. The warehouse company usually puts up signs stating that a field warehouse is being operated.

The costs of establishing a field warehouse are relatively high, which makes it somewhat impractical for a small company.

However, this form of financing does have several advantages. The amount of funds available is tied to the growth in inventories, which means the availability of funds automatically grows as your financing needs increase. A field warehousing arrangement also increases the acceptability of some inventory items as loan collateral. As a side benefit, the use of specialists in warehousing can often result in improved warehouse practices and procedures.

Revolving Line of Credit

If your company has a continuous or recurring need for short-term capital, you may be able to obtain a line of credit. This arrangement allows your company to borrow up to a preestablished limit at any time. Funds are drawn as needed and interest is paid on the outstanding balance only, not the total commitment. If unsecured, the principal outstanding may need to be repaid for up to 30 days during a 12-month period.

Generally, only the most creditworthy companies can take advantage of this financing arrangement. A revolving line of credit generally extends for two years and is reviewed by the bank's credit committee on the loan's anniversary date. You may be able to convert a revolving line of credit loan into a longer-running term loan at the end of the period. A revolver can also be secured by company assets.

Interest cost is normally tied to the prime rate, or bank-reference rate. Banks typically are paid in a combination of interest, fees, and compensating balances. Fees may be paid quarterly, such as .24 or .5 percent on the total commitment or on the unused portion of the commitment, and/or paid annually up front. Compensating-balance requirements will typically range between 5 and 10 percent of the loan commitment, and will be maintained by the borrower at the bank in a non interest-bearing checking account. The compensating-balance requirement may not be a cost to the company if the day-to-day operations require similar amounts to be kept in the company's operating accounts. Fee and balance deficiencies are typically converted to hard-dollar costs and billed to the company periodically.

Exhibit 5–1 compares the key differences among the various types of long- and short-term instruments.

Current Developments

According to a survey of middle-market business owners, the interest rate charged on a loan was the third most important characteristic in a banking relationship, ranking behind "Knows you and your business" and "Reliable source of credit." The qualities ranked least important were "Provides helpful business suggestions" and "Comes to you with ideas for improving bank services."* This suggests that the consulting aspect of a banking relationship is less important than the continuing availability of credit. These non price components do not come free, though; you can be sure that they are factored into the cost of your loans.

During the 1980s, most of the country's top 15 or 20 banks began establishing loan production offices (LPOs) through the country at an unusually fast rate. The purpose of the LPO is to generate loans in cities beyond the bank's traditional boundaries. Larger regional commercial banks with strong reputations for responsively serving middle-market clients are joining the largest banks by opening LPOs in major metropolitan areas throughout the country. Do not be surprised when a representative from one of these institutions comes knocking on your door trying to take your business from your current banker.

The larger banks have caught the entrepreneurial fever that has been spreading across the country in the last few years. Like many other businesses, they have begun to recognize the short- and long-term profit potential that smaller clients represent. Not only do higher rates of interest result in higher short-term profits, but the banks bring in new sources of business with the hope that the successful companies will grow and stay with the same institution to serve their expanding banking needs.

---

* Source: *The Bankers Magazine.*

EXHIBIT 5-1. Comparative Chart of Short-Term and Long-Term Instruments

Key Terms/ Conditions	Short-Term Instruments			Long-Term Instruments		
	Accounts Receivable Financing	Inventory Financing	Revolving Line of Credit	Capital Loans	Term Loans	Leases[a]
Uses	Provide working capital	Provide working capital	Provide working capital	Finance capital equipment	Finance expansion, finance Large working-capital needs	Finance capital equipment
Secured	Yes	Yes	Yes or no	Yes	Yes	Yes
Compensating balance[b]	Usually no	Usually no	Preferred, usually up to 10% of line	Usually no	Varies	No
Repayment period	One to two years	One to two years	Two to three years	Five to seven years	Three to seven years	Varies
Points[b]	Up to 2%	Up to 2%	Up to 2%	Up to 2%	Up to 2%	1%
Commitment fee[b]	.25%–.5%	.25 %–.5%	.25%–.5%	Usually none	Usually none	.25%
Prepayment penalty[c]	Usually none	Usually none	Usually none	Varies	Varies	Varies
Admin/legal fees[b]	.5%–2%	.5%–2%	.5%–2%	.5%–2%	.5%–2%	.5%–2%
Other	May borrow from 75% to 85% of accounts receivable value	May borrow from 25% to 50% of inventory value	May have an option to convert line to a term loan		Interest cost that is tied to the prime or fixed rate	

[a]Refer to chapter on leasing.

[b]Many loans contain a combination, but usually not all, of these terms and conditions.

[c]Generally applicable to fixed-rate loans.

Commercial banks, as compared with finance companies and thrifts, provide the lion's share of small business's debt financing, accounting for 90 percent of their short-term needs and 70 percent of long-term requirements.

Many of the more sophisticated cash management, pricing, and capital-market products mentioned in Chapter 1 are available to middle-market companies, subject to pricing thresholds.

Bankers' Acceptances. A bankers' acceptance is a draft drawn by the vendor on the customer's bank requesting payment for merchandise. Bankers' acceptances are used when the customer's credit with the vendor is not adequate. The customer's bank releases the funds to the vendor, in effect lending the money to the customer. Terms of repayment are usually up to 180 days. Acceptances can be secured by the merchandise purchased or other collateral, or can be unsecured based on the business's creditworthiness as assessed by the bank.

Bankers' acceptances are an efficient way to overcome suppliers' credit concerns. Historically, they have been available only for international transactions, but are now available to U.S. companies selling to customers 25 or more miles away.

"Selling" Accounts Receivable. One additional development involves the pledging of accounts receivable. Under accounting standards, accounts receivable may be pledged to raise capital without the transaction being reflected on financial statements as a liability. This may occur if the transaction is structured as a sale. Receivables transferred to a "lender" with a guarantee will be considered a sale, not a borrowing/liability, when (1) your company surrenders all economic benefits from the receivables pledged and (2) you give a reasonable estimate of any obligations you may have concerning the pledged receivables, except under special prestipulated conditions. This ruling is detailed in Financial Accounting Standards Board Statement No. 77.

DEBT VERSUS EQUITY: ADVANTAGES AND DISADVANTAGES

When you wish to expand your business but cannot do so without additional financial resources, and are unwilling or unable to provide the additional equity investment yourself, you have two avenues for raising the additional money needed—debt or equity. Equity investors receive ownership in the business with their share of stock. Debt, on the other hand, is a way of financing growth without giving up ownership and control.

Advantages of Debt Versus Equity

- A lender has no direct claim on the future earnings of the company. No matter how successful your company becomes, the lender is entitled only to the repayment of the agreed-upon principal plus interest charges.
- Debt does not dilute the owner's interest, since the lender has no claim to the equity of the business.
- Interest on debt can be deducted on the company's tax returns. This, in effect, lowers the real cost to the borrower.
- Interest and principal payments are, for the most part, a known amount. Therefore, they can be forecast and you can plan for them. Variable-rate loans eliminate some of this advantage, since the interest payment changes as interest rates change. However, interest rate protection products, discussed in Chapter 1, can minimize interest rate exposure.

Disadvantages of Debt Versus Equity

- Interest is a cost of doing business and therefore raises a company's break-even point. High interest costs during a financial crisis or merely a financially unstable period can increase the risk of insolvency. Companies that become highly leveraged (that have large amounts of debt relative to equity) and have high debt service costs often find it impossible to remain profitable enough to grow and prosper.
- Cash flow is required for both principal and interest payments and must be planned for. Payments of principal are not tax-deductible.
- Debt is not permanent capital with an unlimited life; at some point, it must be repaid.
- Debt instruments may include restrictive covenants, limiting management's future actions with regard to financing and managing the company.

TABLE 5-1. Company'sFinancial Performance Assuming

	No Debt	Some Debt	More Debt
Equity invested	$1,000,000	$ 600,000	$ 200,000
Debt	–	400,000	800,000
Total debt and equity	$1,000,000	$1,000,000	$1,000,000
EBIT	$ 10,000	$ 100,000	$ 100,000
Interest expense	–	56,000	112,000
Earnings before taxes	100,000	44,000	(12,000)
Tax expense	(25,000)	(11,000)	–
Net earnings	$ 75,000	$ 33,000	$ (12,000)
Debt to equity	-0-	.67 to 1.0	4.0 to 1.0
Return on equity	7.3%	5.5%	–

- A business is limited as to the amount of debt it can carry. The larger the company's debt-to-equity ratio, the more risky the company is considered and the less a creditor will be willing to lend.
- Debt often requires pledging assets in addition to the personal guarantee(s) of the owner(s).

Obviously, the way a company is financed can significantly affect its future financial performance and its options with regard to growth and profitability. The following section outlines how a company's financial performance can be affected by different levels of debt and equity financing.

Debt/Equity Example

The Acme Company had earnings of $100,000 before interest and taxes (EBIT). Its average tax rate was 25 percent and it paid an average of 14 percent interest on any debt outstanding. How would the company's financial performance vary if its total liability-to-equity ratio changed? (See Table 5–1.)

As you can see, the net earnings and return on equity are significantly affected by changes in the debt/equity mix.

6

OBTAINING A LOAN

Chances are the banks have been thinking about you. Despite the "credit crunch" of the early 1990s, their business is still making loans. To do so successfully, banks keep a watchful eye on companies that have a look of success about them. Such companies make choice borrowers for a bank because (1) success breeds growth, (2) growth requires capital, and (3) successful companies are good risks to repay loans on time and in full.

It seems like a match made in heaven.

But it is not a cut-and-dried proposition. Your needs are different from other companies', and a loan must be tailor-made. Nobody knows this better than the banks, finance companies, and other financial institutions that make business loans.

Accordingly, two things happen when you open discussions. You and the bank begin an intensive examination of each other—you to see whether the bank is your best choice for raising the needed capital, and the bank to satisfy itself that you meet its standards for a safe borrower. And then you tackle the question of what kind of loan the bank can offer. Perhaps nothing will surprise you so much as the wide choice of loan instruments the bank has devised. In the fierce competition for your business as a borrower, banks and other lenders have been remarkably imaginative in creating a vast array of instruments to match your special needs.

EVALUATING POTENTIAL LENDERS

Lender Characteristics

Surveys of entrepreneurs have indicated a number of desirable characteristics in a bank with which the entrepreneur has a relationship, including the following:

- Knows you and your business
- Knows your industry
- Knows your financial needs
- Is a reliable source of credit
- Provides helpful business suggestions
- Has one person handling all banking needs
- Offers an inexpensive source of money
- Affords easy access to loan officer
- Presents ideas to improve bank services
- Offers a wide range of banking services
- Is conveniently located

Although all of these characteristics are important, four were found to be the most important to entrepreneurs:

1. *Knows You and Your Business.* Ideally, your banker should think of you as a partner, not a customer. Services should be tailored to a business's individual needs, and banks should be as responsible to the needs of a small business as those of a larger one.
2. *Is a Reliable Source of Credit.* Does your bank stand behind you if you encounter temporary problems meeting your loan's current obligations? Is your bank willing to support your expansion plans with the capital you need? Reliability of credit is believed to be the second most desired characteristic of a bank. The continued success and growth of your business depends on your being able to depend on your bank to provide a sufficient amount of debt financing in a timely manner.
3. *Offers an Inexpensive Source of Money.* The cost of a loan, while not the highest-ranking consideration, is still an important one. Borrowers should be aware of so-called hidden costs like com-

pensating balances, fees, and float days, and take them into account when comparing the costs of borrowing.

4. *Affords Easy Access to Loan Officer.* Can you see your loan officer on short notice? Is your officer easily reachable on the telephone? Does your loan officer have few enough accounts that he or she has time to see you other than when you need to discuss a new loan? If the answer to all three of these questions is not yes, perhaps you should reevaluate your current banking relationship. If you are in the process of selecting a banker, you need to investigate these characteristics.

In general, factors relating to the consulting aspect of the banking relationship were viewed as less important than the continuity and availability of credit. However, you may want to keep them in mind while searching for a new banker or reevaluating your current banker.

Cost Considerations—The True Cost of a Loan

The true cost of a loan is going to be much more than the quoted interest rate. The ultimate cost is based on a number of factors that can be grouped into two categories: first, those that reduce the amount of capital available and, second, those that raise the overall cost.

Factors That Reduce Available Capital

1. *Compensating Balance Requirements.* Banks prefer that you leave a certain amount of funds on deposit, often in a noninterest-bearing or low-interest rate account. The amount of interest you lose by maintaining this account should be added to the cost of your loan. Sometimes you can use your normal "float"— the difference between book and bank balances reflecting uncleared checks—if that float maintains a fairly consistent level, and apply it to your compensating balance requirement, thereby reducing or even possibly eliminating it.

2. *Discounted Interest (In Advance).* Here the lender collects all interest and finance charges in advance, thereby effectively reducing the amount of money left for the company to use.

3. *Lags in Check Clearances.* A bank may take longer to credit your account (check-clearing float and holds) for checks received from customers, in effect, slowing the turnover of your receivables and increasing your cost of capital.

Factors That Increase Overall Cost

1. *Points or Fees.* Points or fees are costs usually quoted as a percentage of the total loan charged at the closing of the financing, and should be amortized over the life of the loan to derive the effective rate.
2. *Commitment Fee.* Commitment fees are charges for maintaining a committed line of credit—in other words, charges for agreeing to have the funds available to you for a specified period of time whether you use them or not. Often .25 to .5 percent is charged on the unused portion of a credit line.
3. *Prepayment Penalties.* With a good loan at an attractive interest rate, the lender is making money. Early repayment of such a loan reduces the lender's profits and, therefore, the bank or commercial finance company will usually charge a prepayment penalty—a fee for repaying the loan before it is due.
4. *Float Days.* Float days are generally charged by secured lenders and asset-based lenders. Float days represent the time between when the lender receives payment and when the company receives credit for making that payment. Typically, checks are submitted daily to pay down the line of credit. Although the company will be able to reborrow the funds, the interest expense is calculated as if the loan amount were not repaid for one to three days. For interest calculation purposes, the loan amount appears to be greater for the negotiated float days, even though the funds are made available to be reborrowed within the available borrowing-base formulas.

WHAT DOES A BANK LOOK FOR?

Your Ability to Repay

Before the bank will agree to your loan request, your banker will analyze the company's overall financial health and assess your ability to repay the loan. Your banker will evaluate not only your current ability to service the debt but also your future ability to meet the terms of the loan agreement. The banker will examine many sources of information to gain an accurate picture of your company and how it compares to the industry. The banker's intuitive assessment of the management team's experience, ability, and character is critically important.

Following are some of the other specific factors that will be evaluated.

Financial Statements. Once satisfied with the integrity and intentions of the people, the banker will also evaluate the company's financial statements, which provide a descriptive picture of your business. They detail how your company has operated over the past few years and project your future financial results. The key ones include the following:

- Historical and projected cash-flow statements
- Historical and projected balance sheets
- Historical and projected income statements

Your cash-flow projections are very important to the banker. They will indicate your ability to generate sufficient funds to pay both the accrued interest and the outstanding principal. They will also indicate any ability to prepay some of the principal or forecast the need for additional borrowings.

The balance sheet captures your business at a specific point in time. It details your business's assets, liabilities, and net worth. Because balance sheets are based on the historical cost of the assets and liabilities, not the market or liquidation value, bankers often require an additional assessment of the current market value of certain balance-sheet components. The balance in these accounts serves as a guideline for the amount of funds the banker will lend in general, and for the amount of funds available for receivable and inventory financing in particular. Balance sheets represent a company's leveraged position (total liabilities to net worth), which indicates the amount of net worth available to support debt obligations. The higher the leverage, the less cushion available.

The income statement presents your revenue and expenses over a period of time. This historical assessment provides the banker with an evaluation of past performance from which he or she can extract profitability trends. Based on your projections, the banker projects your ability to operate profitably in the future and to generate the cash flow necessary to repay the loan.

When applying for a loan, you should usually have financial statements for the past two or three years and projected operating results for the same length of time as the loan request. It is often helpful if the historical statements are audited by a certified public accountant acceptable to the lender. However, the American Bankers Association explained its exceptions in the 1967 publication *The Auditor's Report, Its Meaning and Significance*:

> The independent auditor is neutral with regard to any interpretation of the financial statements. The unqualified opinion is not a stamp of approval from a credit or investment viewpoint and should never be mistaken for one.

This entire "due diligence" investigation is critical to the bank's loan decision because different lenders may assess information, or exercise their judgment, differently. Therefore, each lender has an obligation to obtain an understanding of you and your company sufficient for *its* lending purposes, given the risks it is willing to accept and the rewards it stands to gain.

Financial Ratios. The banker will calculate certain ratios based on your financial statements. The results of these ratios influence the loan decision. These ratios, by themselves, do not provide the banker with much information. But by analyzing them over a period of time, the banker can chart trends in your business and management's ability to steer the company. In addition, the banker compares your ratios with industry standards or other companies in the same business as yours.

Some of the more important ratios include the following:

- *Receivable Turnover.* Net sales/average accounts receivable. This ratio is used to evaluate the quality of your receivables and their value. A high ratio is indicative of ineffective collections and possible cash-flow and collection problems.
- *Receivable Collection Days.* Accounts receivable/sales, multiplied by days in the period. This ratio indicates the average days required to collect receivables. The lower the number of days, the quicker on average receivables are converted to cash. A higher number can indicate difficulty in collecting receivables and/or credit collection problems.

- *Inventory Turnover.* Costs of goods sold/average inventory. The inventory turnover represents the number of times your inventory was sold and replaced throughout the year. Generally, inventory turnover gives some indication of the marketability of the products and the amount of inventory held in stock. If too much inventory is accumulated, this ratio will fall, indicating that your cash flow is being reduced because it is tied up in inventory that is not generating sales.

- *Inventory Turnover in Days.* Inventory/cost of goods sold, multiplied by days in the period. This ratio indicates the average days required to convert inventory into finished goods and produce a sale. The lower the number of days, the quicker on average inventory is turning to produce sales and, ultimately, receivables and cash for the business. A high number can indicate difficulty in converting inventory to finished products, perhaps due to shortage of component parts, inefficient production flow, obsolete inventory, or over-purchasing of inventory. A low number may indicate a perishable product.

- *Payable Turnover in Days.* Accounts payable/cost of goods sold, multiplied by days in the period. This ratio indicates the average number of days the company requires to pay its bills. The lower the number of days, the more internal funds are used to finance the working-capital needs of the business. Conversely, the larger the number of days, the more the trade is used to finance the business. A fine balance between a high and low number of days works best. Ideally, a company would like to collect receivables before trade payables are due. A high number of days can indicate insufficient cash available to service current needs due to decreased or increased sales, increased costs, and/or increased working-capital requirements.

- *Current Ratio.* Current assets/current liabilities. Sometimes referred to as the working-capital ratio, the current ratio measures the extent to which the claims of short-term creditors are covered by assets that are expected to be converted to cash in a period roughly corresponding to the maturity of the claims. To a banker, it indicates the amount of current assets that would be available, in an emergency, to meet immediate bills and obligations, including short-term bank loans.

- *Quick Ratio.* Cash + marketable securities + accounts receivable/current liabilities. Similar to the current ratio, the quick or "acid test" ratio measures liquidity. It assumes that inventory is a relatively liquid current asset and that you would not have it available to meet short-term obligations without waiting for the proceeds from the sale of inventory.

- *Percentage of Inventory to Cover Deficit in Quick Ratio.* (Current liabilities — noninventory current assets)/inventory. This measure indicates the percentage of inventory that must be sold in order to cover the current debt obligations in the event of an emergency. If you are borrowing against inventory, your bankers may limit the amount of financing they may make available by the amount of inventory needed to cover current liabilities.

- *Debt-to-Equity Ratio.* Current liabilities + long-term liabilities/ total equity. The debt-to-equity ratio indicates the extent to which your total funds have been provided by creditors. Lenders use this ratio as a rule of thumb for determining whether or not a company can afford to increase its borrowings.

- *Debt to Tangible Effective Net Worth.* Total liabilities — subordinated debt/total equity + subordinated debt — intangible assets. This ratio is used to determine the true leveraged position of a company. Subordinated debt may be defined as debt that is not repaid until the senior debt is repaid. Under some definitions, subordinated debt terms may allow for interest payments or possibly principal payouts, provided the company is in loan compliance with the senior lender. For debt to be considered subordinated to a senior lender and therefore considered "effective net worth," the senior lender must have the documented right to stop any and all principal and/or interest payments to the subordinated debt holder should the company be in default with the senior lender. The perception of effective net worth is money that comes into the company, and does not leave the company and therefore functions as equity. Subordinated debt serves to increase the total equity base and therefore decrease leverage.

  Intangible assets refer to soft assets or value given to assets that a lender cannot readily sell or liquidate. Intangible assets include such things as goodwill, covenants not to compete, and trademarks. This value is subtracted from the total net worth to leave only tangible net worth or those tangible assets included in net worth. The resulting ratio indicates total liabilities that must be paid, and the resulting true hard asset and net worth cushion available to service the obligations.

- *Interest Coverage Ratio.* Earnings before income taxes + interest expense/interest expense. This ratio measures your company's ability to meet its interest charges on a regular basis. Bankers will reduce the amount of the loan if this ratio is not high enough to meet their credit criteria.
- *Profit Margins.* The banker will be interested to know that your profit margins remain stable over time or, even better, improve over the life of the loan. A solid margin gives the banker the confidence that you will be able to continue regular payments on any loan you have outstanding.

Other Measures. Because the financial statements are only a starting point, the banker will also evaluate other quantitative and qualitative measures to gain an overall understanding of your business, your position in the industry, and your company's ability to repay its debt. A discussion of the major factors follows.

- *Company Age.* Companies with an established operating history are likely to be viewed as less risky for lending purposes than a new start-up company.
- *Term of Present Management.* In general, a banker will believe that the longer a management team has been with the company, the more likely the company's continued success. Depth of management and the company's historical ability to weather industry downturns are also important considerations to a lender. Furthermore, a low rate of employee turnover implies a well-run company and a greater commitment to the organization's success.
- *Years of Continuing Increases in Profits.* A history of increasing profits is indicative of strong operations. Companies that have been profitable in the past are more likely to be profitable in the future and are more likely to repay their debts on time. Bankers have learned to understand the cyclical economic impact on profitability.
- *Trade and Credit Reports.* Bankers will read trade and credit reports to evaluate the industry and answer questions like these for themselves: Is there a significant demand for this product or service? How does this company stack up against the competi-

tion? Is the product priced competitively? How long can this company continue to effectively deliver its product or service?

- *Z-Score.* The Z-score, developed by Edward Altman of New York University, at one time was used by some bankers to predict a company's future financial strength. It has been used as an indicator of potential insolvency for up to two years before bankruptcy. The Z-score formula for a public company is as follows:

(1.2 × working capital/total assets) + (1.4 retained earnings/total assets) + (3.3 × earnings before interest and taxes/total assets) + (0.6 × market value of equity/total liabilities) + (1.0 × sales/total assets)

Companies with a score of 1.81 or less are likely to file for bankruptcy within the next two years. Those with a score of 2.68 or above are likely to remain financially healthy, at least for the near future. A score between 1.81 and 2.68 is the "gray area" and requires further qualitative evaluation.

For privately held companies, the formula changes slightly:

(0.7 × working capital/total assets) + (0.8 × retained earnings/total assets) + (3.1 × earnings before interest and taxes/total assets) + (0.4 × book value of equity/total liabilities) + (1.0 × sales/total assets)

For privately held companies, Altman concluded that a score of 1.23 or less indicates potential for bankruptcy and a score of 2.90 or more indicates continued operations. Again, the middle gray area, which is larger for privately held companies, requires more detailed analysis and qualitative evaluation.

General Business Analysis—Your Future Plans

The banker will assess your overall business strategy to make sure the company's plans are realistic and well thought out. The banker will evaluate your business plans, including your marketing strategy, financial control system, management reporting system, and personnel utilization. A banker will want answers to such questions as the following:

- Planning:
  - Have specific objectives and courses of actions to achieve those objectives been clearly identified?
- Marketing:
  - Has the business clearly defined its marketing objectives and strategy?
  - What market need does this product or service meet?
  - Has the specific market been identified and analyzed?
- Finance:
  - Why is the company proposing to finance its growth with debt as opposed to equity?
  - How does this strategy translate to revenues, profits, and cash flow?
  - How do the projections account for this growth in comparison with historical performance?
  - Has the company identified opportunities to improve performance of its assets—improving the receivables collection period, increasing the inventory turnover, or disposing of unneeded fixed assets?
  - Have the merits of leasing versus buying been evaluated?
- Systems:
  - Have the proper financial and inventory controls been instituted?

  (A timely and accurate reporting structure will help safeguard the assets and assure proper recording of sales and purchases. Further, the results of operations should be analyzed periodically and variances with budgets should be explained.)
- Human Resources:
  - How does the company identify and retain qualified personnel?
  - Are current compensation and incentive plans appropriate and adequate?
  - Are key personnel leaving the company?
  - Are personnel being used productively?
  - Are key management positions filled by qualified people?

Ongoing Business Analysis—Signs of Trouble

Continually, the bank will monitor your company's operations to make sure it is in compliance with any covenants included in the loan agreement, and will look for warning signals of possible trouble in the business. A number of signals may indicate the potential for failure to meet the loan terms and the need for bank involvement:

- *Hesitation in Providing Financial Data.* Being late with providing financial statements may indicate that the company has something to hide. The banker's reaction may be to investigate the material thoroughly and to carefully question any ambiguities or irregularities.
- *Shrinking Bank Deposits.* If the amount of cash the company has on deposit at the bank declines significantly or steadily, the banker may question whether cash will be available to service the debt. If the cash is deposited at another bank, the lender may question the company's commitment to the lending bank and may evaluate further loan requests more skeptically.
- *Overdrafts and/or Returned Checks.* Overdrafts and/or returned checks indicate an inability to manage cash effectively and transfer additional credit risk to the bank. The banker may question the company's continued ability to meet its loan obligations.
- *Failure to Meet Other Obligations.* If the company or its owners fail to meet other obligations, including the personal debts of the principals, the banker may question the company's ability to meet its business loan obligations. Often, cross-default provisions are included in the loan agreement, which create a default with this lender when a default occurs on other obligations.
- *High Inventory Levels.* High inventory levels may indicate either weak purchasing controls or slower-than-expected sales levels. Having too much cash tied up in inventory may limit the company's ability to repay its loan.
- *Delinquent Loan Payments.* The bank will investigate any delinquent loan payments to determine whether they are one-time events or likely to recur.
- *Reluctance in Arranging for Plant Inspections or Meetings with Top Management.* Again, any action that suggests that the company has something to hide will likely be carefully scrutinized.

- *Legal Actions Against the Company.* Legal actions taken against the company have the potential of resulting in cash-flow problems and difficulty meeting loan obligations.

- *Growing Accounts Payable and/or Accruals.* Increase in accounts payable and/or accruals may suggest an inability to generate the cash necessary to meet obligations. On the other hand, it could imply that improved purchasing agreements are permitting the company to hold on to its cash longer. The cause of payables increase should be explained to the banker before he or she questions the ability to service the debt.

- *Slowing Turnover of Receivables.* Inadequate collection procedures may reduce cash flow and increase the chance of the company's defaulting on a loan payment.

- *Increasing Fixed Assets.* If the company is purchasing new assets, the banker will want to make sure that all assets are being used effectively and efficiently. The banker may conclude that a better use of cash would be to repay the loan rather than to buy new assets. Loan agreements often restrict fixed-asset expenditures.

- *Expansions through Merger or Acquisition.* In a merger or acquisition, the company must have the ability to fund the purchase and to assume the increase in liabilities and expenses. In addition, the personnel must have the ability to assume the increased responsibilities. The banker must be convinced that this expansion will not overburden the company and that all obligations will be met on time.

- *Increasing Debt and Debt-to-Equity Ratio.* If the debt has been increasing, the cash needed to service that debt also increases. The company's cash flow must be able to meet these growing demands.

- *Management Changes.* High turnover in key management positions may signify a lack of faith in the future of the firm or other potential problems.

Continuing communication is essential between your company and the bank. Bankers do not like to be surprised. They want to understand the issues affecting your company and want to be kept well informed. Maintaining good relations with your bankers increases their desire to accommodate your requests, whether they include extending the loan term, removing any covenants attached to the loan agreement, making the terms of deposit more favorable, or agreeing to future loan requests quickly and easily. For a summary of what banks look for, see Exhibit 6–1.

NEGOTIATING WITH A LENDER

You should approach the negotiating process with a bank or other lending institution just as you approach negotiating any business transaction.

You prepare for negotiating before meeting with a potential supplier, before agreeing on price and terms with a new customer, before meeting with labor unions, and so on. In each case, you have probably decided ahead of time what you hope to accomplish during the negotiations, as well as those points on which you are willing to make concessions and those on which you are not. It is even better if you have estimated the cost, in both dollars and convenience, of any concession you may be required to make.

The same principles apply when meeting with a potential lender. Be prepared to negotiate the best possible deal for you and your company. The following suggestions will give you the best possible chance of accomplishing this goal:

- Prepare a loan package that details your borrowing needs and objectives.
- Identify ahead of time those terms and conditions you believe are most critical to obtaining a workable loan agreement.
- Make full use of your business advisors, such as your lawyer and accountant, who can assist in organizing your loan-package request and can later review any agreements you enter into to help you understand the implications of any conditions to which you agree.

The Loan Package

While the banker will certainly want to see historical financial statements, he or she will also want to see information that relates much more directly to the loan application itself. For example, if you are applying for a term loan to purchase a new piece of machinery or

EXHIBIT 6–1. Summary of What Banks Look For

YOUR ABILITY TO REPAY

Financial statements
   Historical and projected cash flow
   Historical and projected balance sheets
   Historical and projected income statements

Financial ratios (calculated by lender)
   Receivable turnover
   Receivable collection days
   Inventory turnover
   Inventory turnover in days
   Payable turnover in days
   Current ratio (working capital)
   Quick ratio (liquidity)
   Percentage of inventory to cover debt
   Debt-to-equity
   Debt-to-tangible effective net worth
   Interest coverage
   Profit margins

Other considerations
   Age of company
   Term of present management
   Years of continuing increase in profits
   Trade and credit reports
   Z-score

YOUR FUTURE PLANS

   Marketing strategy
   Financial control system
   Management reporting system
   Personnel utilization

SIGNS OF TROUBLE (Ongoing analysis)

   Hesitation in providing financial reports and exhibits
   Shrinking bank deposits
   Overdrafts and/or returned checks
   Failure to meet other obligations
   High inventory levels
   Delinquent loan payments
   Reluctance in arranging for plant inspections or meetings with top management
   Legal actions against the company
   Growing accounts payable and/or accruals
   Slowing turnover of receivables
   Increasing fixed assets
   Expansion through merger or acquisition
   Increasing debt and debt-to-equity ratio
   Management changes

---

equipment, the banker will want to see the analysis—typically, the internal rate of return or do a pay-back analysis on the project you want financed—which you performed to cost-justify the purchase.

Specific Negotiating Points

Following are some of the specific negotiable items you will likely be able to address with your future banker. Make sure you understand and are happy with the implications of any and all terms and conditions.

Interest Rates. The interest rate is one of the obvious key factors of any loan agreement. Usually there is not a lot of leeway in negotiating interest; however, small concessions on the part of the bank can make a big difference to you over time.

When negotiating a variable-rate loan, you may want to try to get the bank to agree to a "ceiling" above which the rate will not go. To get such a ceiling, you may have to agree to a "floor" below which the rate will not fall no matter how far the prime rate drops. If you believe interest is not likely to drop over the life of your loans, agreeing to such a condition may be very attractive to you.

Collateral Agreements. One objective is to minimize the amount of collateral you pledge against the loan. If too many of your available assets are tied up with one loan, this may limit your ability to borrow in the future. Lenders tend to request all the collateral they can get. On the other hand, already having assets as collateral generally allows a lender to respond quicker to loan increase requests on the same collateral.

In addition to the amount of collateral pledged, also consider the type and nature. Keep in mind industry practices. If it is unusual to pledge inventory or receivables and agreeing to do so could limit your competitive edge, make the lender aware of this and try not to agree to such provisions.

When pledging personal assets against a business loan, try to set a reasonable limit and exempt certain assets rather than sign a general personal guarantee pledging everything you own. If you pledge your stock in the company, take a close look at the default provisions. You may find that the banker can, in effect, take control of your company.

Ask for collateral release provisions as you pay down term loans to avoid significantly over-collateralizing loans as they mature.

Personal Guarantee of Indebtedness. In certain cases, a lender will request a personal guarantee from the owner(s). The guarantee, in addition to supplying credit support for the loan, represents a commitment by the principals of the borrower to the repayment of the loan. The guarantee may or may not be for the full amount of the loan, depending on the overall creditworthiness of the company and the financial strength of the owner(s).

Bankers may view the guarantee as more of a psychological commitment than relying on it for repayment.

In some cases, the bank may require that the guarantee be collateralized with assets such as marketable securities or real estate. A collateralized guarantee generally gives the bank direct access to personal assets. An unsecured guarantee generally requires the bank to go directly to the guarantor(s) but not directly to personal assets. Ideally, a release of the guarantee(s) is negotiated up front and is based on the company's achieving certain performance targets.

Use of Capital and Payment Terms. Borrow all you can when you can for as long as you can is an adage subscribed to by many business owners. While it is an overstatement, having access to funds when you need them is vital. Seek repayment terms that you know you can live with; for example, sometimes you can delay repayment of principal for a specified period of time, such as one to two years, while keeping interest payments current.

Attempt to negotiate the ability to prepay all or any part of the loan. This will allow you to take advantage of the drop in interest rates should they occur or to refinance all of your loan agreements should that be advantageous.

Future Borrowing Constraints. Any covenants with regard to future borrowings should not be too restrictive. You do not want to be in a position where the bank can significantly curtail your future operating options. Bear in mind that opportunities to grow and expand may arise in the future, and you will want to be able to take advantage of them. Likewise, try to avoid severely limiting your ability to make major capital expenditures in the future.

Ratio Requirements. Lending institutions may insist that your company maintain minimum levels of some ratios discussed. They know that if certain ratios prevail, they have a very safe loan. Carefully review the implications of any ratio requirements to which you agree. What may not seem burdensome now could become so in the future. Be sure you have time to correct a ratio imbalance before the loan can be declared in default. Your accountant or other financial advisor can be particularly helpful in this regard.

General Guidelines

As you can see, negotiating a loan agreement is no simple matter. Nonetheless, business owners and senior management should actively participate in the process. Not only will it illustrate to the lender that you carefully evaluate all aspects of your business, but through the negotiation process you will make clear all of your needs to the lender.

Since lenders want their relationships with borrowers to be long-term, the negotiating process can serve as the first and sometimes most useful step in developing this relationship. Historically, many bank loans have been made without the presentation of all the detailed financial information and/or without certain other steps described in this chapter being performed by the borrower or required by the banker. Relationships between the banker and the business person have been the key ingredient of many bank loans. Because of loan failures and the general increase in business and banking sophistication in recent years, most bankers are now requiring the thorough analysis depicted in this chapter, even with longstanding clients.

While the relationship is still important, the better prepared you are to present your loan requirements, the more likely you will be not only to get the loan but to do so on favorable terms.

No matter what you ultimately agree to as a final loan contract, always remember to:

- Voice all of your objections. Once you sign, you decrease your negotiating position.
- Evaluate how the loan agreement will affect you and your business in the long run. You, not your banker, should be running your business.

- Get everything in writing. No matter how friendly you are with your banker, you are really dealing with an institution, not an individual.

FINANCING WORKOUTS

There are numerous business reasons why companies file for protection from creditors under Chapter 11 of the Federal Bankruptcy Code (formal proceedings) or conduct out-of-court negotiations with creditors to restructure debt (informal proceedings). Regardless of the specific reason, most troubled companies are no longer able to meet their obligations as they become due and, as a consequence, should anticipate receiving little or no additional credit from existing sources.

In these cases, the successful resolution of the company's business problems is usually contingent upon new financing. Absent new financing, the troubled company may have only two other options: the sale or liquidation of its business. Accordingly, financing of workout situations has been included in this book.

In order to obtain financing for a troubled company through formal or informal proceedings, it is essential that the causes of the problems be critically examined and analyzed. Are they the result of internal factors, such as the loss of key employees or manufacturing difficulties that have hurt deliveries and customer service? Or are they external factors such as technological obsolescence of the product or the impact of new or increased competition?

A clear understanding of the issues affecting the business is critical to determining the required business "fixes," the time and, consequently, the financial resources necessary to implement the turnaround. Assume for the balance of this section that a viable business plan has been prepared by management and reviewed by competent professionals. Now the company is seeking new financing. A number of financing alternatives may be available.

Asset-Based Lending

Asset-based lending (previously discussed) is a financing alternative that is used by both financially sound and troubled companies. The first step in a formal or informal proceeding is identifying the available collateral base, if any. Assume the company has unencumbered assets that may be pledged to the lender in exchange for a line of credit. The next step is negotiating the advance-rate formula and terms to be used by the lender advancing the funds.

Because the company has encountered financial difficulties, lenders often use a highly conservative value of assets (frequently based on discounted liquidation values) in determining the advance-rate formula. Accordingly, free assets such as accounts receivable and merchandise inventory may be discounted for collateral availability purposes to amounts significantly below their going-concern values. The obvious problem is negotiating a funding formula that is sufficient to cover the cash requirements during the periods when outstanding loans are forecast to be at their peak. There is no simple solution to this problem. Lenders may consider a seasonal over-advance if the company continues to meet or exceed its forecasted results of operations and cash-flow projections.

Factoring of Accounts Receivable

A variation of asset-based lending is the sale or assignment of accounts receivable to a factoring organization. Factoring (also previously discussed) is a common form of financing in the apparel and textile industries. In order for a troubled company to qualify for factoring, the existing merchandise inventory should be unencumbered. The accounts receivable generated from shipments of inventory are purchased by the factor on either a recourse or nonrecourse basis. The factor will advance funds to the company based on the amount of eligible outstanding accounts receivable and the agreed-upon advance rate. As with asset-based lending formulas, the advance rate will be significantly lower than the going-concern value of the receivable, and more restrictive credit policies may be required by the factor since credit losses are usually for the account of the factor.

Companies that are considering factoring as a financing alternative should understand that the assignment of an account receivable to a factor does not necessarily eliminate the other business risks of collection. Pricing, quality, or quantity disputes will result in a reduction in the eligible accounts receivable base, and ultimately be charged back to the company. Further, the advance rate will be adversely affected if such chargebacks exceed prior experience levels.

Debtor-in-Possession Financing

In the event that a company has filed for protection under Chapter 11 of the Federal Bankruptcy Code and is in need of financing, a form of financing referred to as debtor-in-possession (DIP) financing is available from various sources, including finance companies and certain bank lenders. Lending in such instances is done pursuant to court approval of the term and conditions, and is generally asset-based. Unsecured assets provide the primary lending base for such loans; however collateral can, with some degree of difficulty, be "created" through legal mechanisms that prime a pre-petition secured-lender's lien (discussed later in this chapter) or give a pre-petition secured-lender replacement collateral (the indubitable equivalent as determined by the court) in lieu of original collateral against which the debtor-in-possession lenders might be more willing to lend.

However, troubled companies often wait too long before they seek protection from creditors by filing Chapter 11 and it is not uncommon that substantially all of the company's assets have been pledged as collateral for existing indebtedness at the time of filing. It is much more difficult to obtain new financing under these circumstances.

Use of Cash Collateral

A form of financing that may still be available for companies that have filed Chapter 11 debtor-in-possession is referred to as the "use of cash collateral." Cash collateral includes cash, negotiable instruments, accounts receivable, deposit accounts, or other cash equivalents subject to the security interests of a lender. As the collateral is converted to cash through the debtor's normal collection process and then used for its operations, the lender must be assured of adequate protection such as periodic payments or replacement liens so its collateral position will not be diminished. A debtor-in-possession may use these cash equivalents only with the consent of the creditor or, absent such consent, with court approval.

Sophisticated lenders might agree to enter into such arrangements because they understand that an immediate liquidation (auction) of the debtor's assets will minimize the amounts realized and maximize their potential for having an unsecured claim. Accordingly, existing lenders will consider entering into use-of-cash-collateral agreements, usually for limited periods of time, in order to provide the debtor with additional time to explore alternatives that will be in the best interests of the lender, the debtor, and other creditors.

Priming Existing Lienholders

Priming existing lienholders is, at best, a complex process available to debtors-in-possession. The underlying concept is that additional funding may be obtained if a new lender is given a first (prime) position in collateral that secures existing debt. In order to prime an existing lender, the debtor must establish, among other things, that the value of the collateral held by the present lender is in excess of the related loan. It is not unusual to have valuation hearings in the bankruptcy courts and, through expert testimony, present evidence in support of that position. Lenders are very reluctant to being primed and will generally oppose this action. In addition, the debtor will have to demonstrate to the bankruptcy court that it has obtained a financing commitment from a reliable third-party funder and that the pre-petition lienholder's position will not be impaired.

Equity in Real Property

Equity in real property may also be used as a source of new financing in both formal and informal proceedings. The company may be able to obtain a real estate mortgage or enter into a sale/leaseback transaction. Proper planning is essential in order to close the transaction and obtain the needed funds in a timely manner. It should be noted that the financing available to a troubled company based upon real property will be lower than would otherwise be received in a non-troubled situation, given questions concerning the borrower's credit-worthiness.

Sale of a Division or Subsidiary

Troubled companies may also have subsidiaries or divisions that are performing well and are marketable. However, selling a profitable operation may be a short-term solution to a continuing problem. Therefore, unless the ongoing problems can be identified and resolved, it would not be prudent to sell a profitable operation simply to provide funding for operating losses that will continue.

In addition to identifying the continuing core business and those that should be offered for sale, implementation of strategic turnaround measures can also provide funds for a troubled company. Immediate involvement on the part of top-level management is essential. Virtually every aspect of the ongoing entity must be evaluated with a view toward improving cash flow and profitability.

Areas that should be carefully scrutinized include the adequacy of the existing financial information systems and the ability to monitor the ongoing results of operations on a timely basis; cash management procedures and controls; the profitability of existing product lines; merchandising strategies; methods of reducing working-capital requirements; policies regarding the identification and disposition of obsolete inventory; termination of nonessential personnel; salary and other expense reductions; identification and disposition of nonoperating (idle) assets; tax planning in order to maximize recoveries of prior years' income taxes; and waivers of contributions to retirement plans and alternatives, including termination of over-funded pension plans. This is not an exhaustive list.

The management of a company that has experienced financial difficulties will, by necessity, need to convince lenders that they have taken meaningful actions to solve its business problems. In many situations, the implementation of cash conservation programs can bridge the difference between a company's needs and available financing. In addition, lenders may take a more positive view of a situation if they believe that appropriate measures are being taken by the company to minimize its cash requirements.

7

JOINT VENTURES AND OTHER STRATEGIC ALLIANCES

OVERVIEW

Since the mid-1980s there has been an explosion in the number of joint ventures and other strategic alliances formed. Strategic alliances involve two or more companies that join together and pool risks, rewards, and resources in order to achieve specific but sometimes different strategic goals. These alliances, ranging from full ownership control to contractual control only, are outlined in Exhibit 7–1.

Industry sources estimate that the number of strategic alliances has grown from only 345 in the 1950s to more than 3,500 formed in 1991 alone. The rapid growth in strategic alliances is perhaps best evidenced by a wave of joint ventures in the automobile and computer industries. As recently as 1980, it would have been viewed as "un-American" for a U.S. company to consider aligning itself with a Japanese firm to build cars. But today the marketplace boasts "Toyota-Chevys" (Novas), "Chrysler-Mitsubishis" (minivan engines), and "Ford-Mazdas" (Ford owns 25 percent of Mazda).

The willingness of large companies to enter into alliances presents an opportunity for smaller firms seeking financing for growth. Small companies that are focused on niche applications of unique products are able to command high premiums from larger ones, which often have difficulties reacting quickly to emerging markets and products.

111

EXHIBIT 7–1. Spectrum of Strategic Alliance Alternatives

Full Ownership Control Only	Partial Ownership and Contractual Control	Contractual Control
Mergers (or acquisitions)	Operating joint ventures	Cooperative agreements
Internal ventures (and spin-offs to full business unit status)	Minority investments	R&D
		Cross-licensing or cross-distribution agreements

Source: Harrigan.

Although this chapter discusses several of the alternatives listed in Exhibit 7–1 as viable vehicles for financing growth, it focuses primarily on partial ownership alliances.

Which joint ventures and other strategic alliances are viable options for companies seeking financing for growth? Before entering into a strategic alliance, one must first understand the risks involved. Katherine Rudie Harrigan, author of *Managing for Joint Venture Success*, has estimated that more than half of the cooperative ventures forged since 1975 were ill conceived at birth, their objectives were unclear, owners' capabilities were poorly matched, or owners aspired to achieve more than was possible in the business in which their joint venture competed. Harrigan's conclusions are supported by her research, which indicates that over 50 percent of joint ventures last four years or less.

To a company considering a strategic alliance as a vehicle for financing growth, it is important to note that alliances are more than a source of financing. While it is certainly true that an alliance can provide both an immediate and long-term source of funds, if the purpose of the alliance is only to provide financing, more conventional sources should be explored first. Entering into an alliance is a strategic decision that involves ceding an element of control with the offsetting benefits of reduced risk, increased potential rewards, and/or reduced investment in resources. In fact, the reduction of future resources necessary to finance growth through leveraging a partner's development, operations, marketing, or distribution resources may greatly outweigh the immediate cash infusion provided by an alliance.

JOINT VENTURES

An operating joint venture may be defined as a separate entity (partnership or corporation) that has two or more companies as owners. The partners contribute capital to the joint venture in the form of cash, inventory, distribution networks, manufacturing processes, fixed assets, or intellectual property such as technology patents and trademarks.

When considering joint ventures as an alternative for financing growth, consider the positions of all potential venture partners. The partner seeking financing is, presumably, a small or mid-sized company, perhaps one without access to more traditional sources of funds. Conversely, the other partner is likely to be a larger company with greater access to and availability of cash. It is also likely to have the operational capacity, such as distribution networks or manufacturing capabilities, to support the product of the smaller player. Operational capacity is important—sometimes even more important than cash—to the smaller company seeking to expand.

When does it make sense to enter into an operating joint venture rather than into a minority equity investment?

Generally, an operating joint venture makes sense when the large company is interested in a segment—but not all—of the smaller company's business. For example, a large company could be interested in a specific product line, market segment, customer application, or production operation of a smaller company. In such cases it may be logical to create a joint venture around the area of interest, with both companies maintaining ownership positions.

Another example of a situation that may be appropriate for a joint venture would involve a small company that has developed a technology or a capability outside the scope of its main business. For example, a manufacturing company may have developed software to control its production process. A computer hardware manufacturer may view the software as a viable product to market to other manufacturing companies. Thus, a joint venture could be created to which the larger computer company contributes development and marketing assistance, as well as cash, while the smaller manufacturing company contributes its proprietary software.

Crystal Technologies Corporation, a union of Jones Engineering and Waste Systems, Inc., is an example of a joint venture that was used as a vehicle for financing growth. Jones Engineering, which was founded by a group of engineers, is a general engineering services company whose primary business was chemical engineering consulting. Over the years, Jones Engineering expanded its scope and began developing freeze crystallization technologies for its clients. Freeze crystallization is a physical process that separates the components of a liquid solution by freezing them and separating their crystals from the remaining liquid.

After several years of researching and developing the technology, Jones Engineering decided to analyze the potential of freeze crystallization as a stand-alone business. Market research convinced company management that the most profitable and easiest market for the technology to enter would be the hazardous waste field.

Jones Engineering searched for hazardous waste companies with which to develop a strategic alliance, and it formed a joint venture with Waste Systems. Waste Systems provided the funding necessary to demonstrate the technology and to build the first commercial unit for hazardous waste remediation activities. Jones Engineering contributed the technology.

The joint venture was a logical financing vehicle for the situation; Waste Systems was interested only in the freeze crystallization technology, not in Jones's consulting business. In addition, while Jones Engineering recognized that the freeze crystallization business had significant cash needs, the company had no such requirements for its core engineering-consulting business.

MINORITY EQUITY INVESTMENT

A minority equity investment occurs when one company buys less than 50 percent equity interest in another company. The minority equity investment is frequently used by smaller companies to finance growth and is prevalent in high-technology industries. Large companies use this vehicle to spread out their research and development activities, as well as their investment risks. Large companies also use the minority equity investment vehicle as a way to obtain interest in a product or service line that is complementary to their businesses. The minority equity investment is often accompanied by supporting production, distribution, and/or marketing agreements.

A minority equity investment generally makes sense when a large company is interested in all of the smaller company's businesses or in situations where the area of interest is inextricably tied to the small company's total business. The minority equity investment is often an attractive alternative to creating a separate operating joint venture.

Minority equity investments often have structures that involve more than common stock ownership by the larger company. Many traditional financing elements can be present in minority structures. Financing instruments can include convertible preferred stock, convertible debentures, and debentures with warrants or options, as well as common stock ownership.

LICENSING

In licensing, one company grants the right to another company to produce a particular product or service, or to use a proprietary process, technology, trademark, or other intellectual property. The licensee compensates the licensor—generally through cash payment—for these rights. Licensing, therefore, can be an attractive financing vehicle for a small company with a proprietary product or technology.

Generally, a licensee pays royalties to the licensor over time, as products are marketed or technology is used. However, it is prudent for the company seeking financing for growth to challenge the arrangements traditionally made, and to seek a greater percentage of the royalty payments in advance. In the end, the licensor may find it advantageous to accept a lower overall royalty payment if the disbursement is skewed toward cash today. License agreements can be structured as "exclusive" or "nonexclusive." An exclusive licensing arrangement allows the licensee the sole right to market or to use the products, whereas the nonexclusive arrangement may involve a number of licensees.

An example of the use of a licensing agreement as a financing vehicle is Progressive Diagnostic Systems (PDS). A technology-based company, PDS had developed patents, trade secrets, and other proprietary technology relating to high-speed medical imaging. It had operated as a development corporation for five years and had not yet manufactured or sold products. The company was nearing the end of its second round of financing and needed additional financing to survive.

International Technologies Corporation (ITC) had developed a large installed base of medical diagnostic-imaging equipment in the

United States. Both ITC and PDS believed that a program of mutual cooperation could significantly advance the development and exploitation of high-speed imaging technology, with the product to be manufactured by ITC as the technology progressed.

International Technologies Corporation made a significant up-front cash payment to its partner and also provided PDS with some research and development equipment. In addition, the agreement called for ITC to make royalty payments to PDS when products were manufactured and sold. The up-front cash payment provided PDS with the financing needed to continue development of the product; ITC's large cash payment was offset by reduced royalty payments when the product was manufactured.

APPROACH FOR CONSIDERING STRATEGIC ALLIANCES

The first step when considering strategic alliances is to rigorously define your own company strategy. It is necessary to understand thoroughly your company's strategic core as well as the elements of the business that must be protected from encroachment by competitors. An alliance represents a compromise in which a company gives up a measure of control or autonomy to obtain something of greater value.

The next critical step in the strategic review process is to determine your company's strengths and weaknesses. An honest self-appraisal can help determine whether or not an alliance will yield beneficial results, as well as what type of alliance makes the most sense, and will assist in identifying potential partners.

As an example, Condor Computers, Inc., was a manufacturer and marketer of portable computers. Condor had established a subsidiary several years earlier that was developing software to provide a valuable communication link with mainframe systems. The subsidiary was in urgent need of financing to sustain its prospects for growth.

Condor clearly understood its strategic strengths and weaknesses. Its strengths included the development work completed to date on the integrated system product, an established market presence in a number of industries, and the quality and performance of its portable computers. Condor's weaknesses included a lack of marketing strength necessary to promote a product that differed from its traditional line (a software vs. a hardware product), a significant cash need at the subsidiary level, and insufficient field support for an integrated system product.

Condor's careful analysis of its strategic position helped it to understand the viability of various strategic alliance possibilities. Condor identified a major computer hardware/software manufacturer as the most appropriate potential partner with the cash, operating capabilities, and marketing wherewithal necessary to compensate for its weaknesses.

Finding a Strategic Partner

When narrowing down potential alliance partners whose strengths complement your company's weaknesses, try to consider categories of potential partners. When Condor began its search, it considered U.S. computer hardware manufacturers, foreign computer manufacturers, computer software companies, direct competitors, and even a professional services company that was organized according to industry sectors.

After a partner category has been selected, the process of identifying and contacting the most appropriate partner begins. At this stage, one should begin analyzing the mechanics, as well as the specifics, of the potential venture. Such analysis would include a preliminary financial analysis, market and competitor analysis, and analysis of the potential venture's impact on its parent companies. Appendix E contains a checklist of areas to consider when analyzing a joint venture or other strategic partnership.

Negotiating the Alliance Agreement

Once a potential partner has been identified and contacted, the process of negotiation begins. Negotiators should strive to complete a letter of intent and eventually a definitive agreement for the joint venture. It is important to remember that a win-win strategy must be employed in a strategic alliance, which may be different from strategies used in outright acquisitions. Appendix F contains an outline of the issues and sections in a typical definitive agreement.

A critical business issue to address during negotiations is the interaction between the venture and its parents. The alliance may either receive product from or supply product to its parents. In such cases, the interaction between the partners and the joint venture will involve transfer pricing issues. The mechanism for setting transfer prices should be determined during the negotiation stage.

Similarly, the procedures and charges for any administrative or operational function handled by one of the parents must be addressed during negotiations. If one partner is given responsibility for the accounting and personnel functions for the alliance, mechanisms for allocating overhead costs to the venture need to be clearly defined.

Another key negotiation issue is that of capital contributions. Two points regarding contributions should be decided during negotiations: the initial value of contributions and the guidelines for ongoing contributions.

Initial contributions may appear in many forms. Cash, machinery/ equipment, land/buildings, and technology/management know-how all represent potential contributions. In general, fair market value is the determinant in setting the amount for capital contributions. However, setting the value of technology and management know-how is always difficult. The worth of such intangible contributions must be estimated and negotiated. Furthermore, U.S. companies should recognize the potential tax liabilities incurred when transferring technology whose value exceeds its tax basis—although with proper planning any potential tax liability may be avoided.

As negotiations proceed, the partners must collaborate with one another to develop a business plan for the joint venture. The development of such a business plan often involves the active participation of a number of task forces that analyze potential operations; financial, tax, and accounting matters; and personnel issues. In addition, each partner should conduct its own financial analyses.

One of the key business issues addressed during negotiations is that of control. One must differentiate between management control and ownership interest. Ownership interest relates to the value of the contributions from each partner. While management control generally follows ownership interest, there are certainly situations in which a minority partner retains management control through a management agreement. It is our experience that ventures in which one parent has clear management control, generally are more successful and operate more efficiently than 50-50 joint ventures without a definitive management agreement.

To ensure that the minority partner is involved in the fundamental decisions affecting the joint venture, the joint venture agreement usually will grant blocking rights to that partner. Blocking rights cover areas or actions that require unanimous consent before the venture can proceed. These rights (outlined in Appendix F, Section 12) typically address selling or otherwise disposing of major assets, altering in any way the agreements that underlie the venture, appointing and retaining key management personnel, and pledging the venture's material assets.

Other blocking rights involve borrowing over some pre-agreed-upon limit and adopting the annual budget. They also address deviating materially from agreed-upon budgets to guard against exceeding, to any measurable degree, the capital expenditure allocation. Blocking rights could also involve changing other authorized capital (to preclude the majority partner's unilaterally altering the venture's capital structure), and distributing income. The minority partner should insist upon having a voice in the distribution of profits.

Conflict resolution is another key business issue to discuss during the negotiations. Blocking rights, as just described, present one way for the minority partner to exert some control over the process. But what happens when unanimous consent is not achieved regarding a matter of major importance? Most joint ventures have several mechanisms for resolving conflicts when consent of the joint venture board cannot be reached.

One effective mechanism is the coordinating committee. A coordinating committee made up of senior members from both companies has broader powers than the joint venture board. The coordinating committee's members are removed from day-to-day operations of the joint venture and meet routinely—perhaps twice a year, or more if needed—to resolve conflicts. Because the coordinating committee's perspective is broader than that of the joint venture's board, it is able to look past the day-to-day issues to the larger picture. And, as a side note, the coordinating committee mechanism is also an ideal way to keep the senior management of each partner informed about the joint venture's current status and operations.

Other conflict resolution mechanisms may be triggered if the coordinating committee is unable to resolve a conflict. One such mechanism is the so-called Chinese auction, in which one partner makes a bid to purchase the interests of the other. If the partner does not accept the would-be purchaser's bid, that partner is required to purchase from the first company at the bid price.

Arbitration is another mechanism. Arbitration involves an objective arbitrator who reviews both sides of the conflict and then issues a resolution. If arbitration is to be used, decisions about how the mechanism would work must be made during negotiations. Such decisions include who will be the arbitrator, where the arbitration will occur, and what circumstances will trigger this mechanism.

Due to the high percentage of joint ventures and other alliances that fail within the first four years, it is important during negotiations to consider the termination process. Clear identification of management's responsibilities, streamlining of policy and operating decision-making, and effective conflict-resolution mechanisms will go a long way toward avoiding termination. If the joint venture does terminate, all partners should concentrate on cost minimization.

Although it is not often utilized, reverse business planning is one mechanism for achieving cost minimization. Reverse business planning examines the same factors as regular business planning: markets, product competition, and operations. The goal of reverse business planning is to identify strategies that will enable the partners to achieve the greatest overall economic value from the venture's liquidation. Such strategies may include selling portions of the venture back to the partners or other investors, selling or otherwise disposing of assets, and selling technologies that were developed during the alliance. Although termination can often lead to confrontation, it is important to remember that both parties are more likely to benefit if the liquidation is approached in a positive, constructive, and cost-minimizing way.

8

LEASING

Leasing as a creative financing tool dates back to before 2000 B.C., when priests acted as lessors in land transactions with farmers. Since then, leasing has evolved to include land, buildings, equipment, and almost anything you can imagine, including nuclear power complexes and battleships. Since the 1950s, leasing has grown by leaps and bounds in the United States, with an estimated total leased equipment pool of $107.9 billion in 1987, and growing almost 7 percent a year.

The popularity of leasing has grown because it is a simple financing transaction. It provides the advantages of low cash outlays to lessees and, many times, off-balance-sheet financing. The ease of use, however, is offset by the complex nature of the factors behind the decision to lease or buy. Leasing requires an understanding of tax, accounting, and financial factors as well as legal, credit, and asset-management factors.

The basic concept of leasing has not changed since the earliest transaction; one party offers to rent land, a building, equipment, or virtually anything to a second party for a specific period of time. The first party gains income in the form of rental payments; the second party gains use of the property at relatively low cost, avoids a large outlay that purchasing the property would require, and saves cash for other financing needs.

Imaginative people in business have been refining the simple lease for generations. The feature of simplicity remains, but experts have discovered that the lease can be surprisingly flexible. New advantages for both parties are constantly being created to help entrepreneurs like you manage your funds wisely as you pursue growth.

TRADITIONAL LEASES

Characteristics

The traditional lease, also known as an operating lease, has been around for as long as businesses have been renting real property for office space, production facilities, and farm lands. It has the following characteristics:

- The lessor owns the property and, depending on the lease, may be responsible for maintaining it and paying the costs associated with it (such as property taxes and insurance). In net leases, the lessee pays some or all of these costs.
- The lessee has use of the property for a specific term and a fixed obligation to pay for its use.
- As owner of the property, the lessor benefits by any capital appreciation of the property during the lease term, and likewise stands the risk of any depreciation in value.
- The owner typically enjoys the tax benefits associated with owning property, such as deductions for depreciation and cash expenditures including interest and property taxes, as well as tax credits for rehabilitation of real property.

Advantages

A traditional lease offers the lessee some significant advantages over other types of financing, including the following:

- Your short-term needs can be met without significant capital investment for such items as temporary space, phone systems, office equipment, and automobiles. Virtually any nondepletable and nonspecialized/noncustomized asset can be used for a period of time and returned under a traditional lease arrangement.
- Traditional lease arrangements may not be subject to restrictions applied by lenders or other financing parties, allowing traditional leases to be executed simply and without loss of time. Some traditional leases can be arranged using a standard form supplied by the vendor. Because the obligations under the lease are both clear and measurable, you can at times execute a lease without the need to consult your professional advisors and without the fear of assuming great risks.

- Traditional lease arrangements leave the risks (and rewards) of ownership with the lessor, thereby insulating you from the risks of obsolescence or changes in needs.
- Traditional leases are treated in financial statements as executory contracts—no assets are recorded and no liabilities are shown, except payments as they become due—thus reflecting lower liabilities and lower expenses to your company, especially in the first, low-cost years of the lease. This generally presents a more favorable view of your financial condition and results of operations.

MODIFIED LEASES

Collateralized Loans (Capital Leases)

In recent years, lenders have come to realize that the traditional lease can be modified in any number of ways so as to resemble a collateralized loan, usually called a financing or capital lease. These modifications might include the following:

- As the lessee, you become responsible for payment of insurance, property taxes, and other executory costs.
- The term of the lease may be set for an extended period of time or consume the economic life of the property, or option periods may be added that guarantee you the right to use the asset for as long as you wish.
- Purchase options may be added so that you are entitled to purchase the asset at the end of the lease or prior to its term for fair market value, an agreed-upon stipulated price, or one dollar.
- Provisions can be added requiring you to purchase the property at the end of the lease term for a fixed amount or fair market value or, alternatively, to pay the difference between the fair market and a stipulated amount based on the end of the lease term.
- The rental payments may be set as a percentage of the underlying cost of the property. The property on which the percentage is based need not be identified in the lease terms, thereby allowing even more flexibility.

- The rental payments may be variable, based upon volume factors such as sales or production, or upon interest rates (creating a floating-rate lease).
- The rental payments may be increased over the term to reflect inflation, or they can be reduced dramatically to provide you with a significant cash-flow increase.

Advantages. As a result of modifications and combinations made to a traditional lease, the two parties can sign a lease that is, in substance, a collateralized loan or a capital lease. This offers several advantages:

- One of the most pervasive reasons for equipment leasing is to help lessees avoid some risks of ownership, including obsolescence. For example, a computer expected to have a 20 percent residual value in five years could be worthless in three years. Leasing the computer would pass those risks to the lessor. Many lessors allow for takeouts, rollovers, or upgrades for technological changes so the lessee can keep up with the state of the art. Lessors can find new lessees who need less state-of-the-art equipment to take the initial equipment.
- The flexibility of lease arrangements offers you and the lessor the ability to make a deal that meets each party's objectives.
- Lease arrangements can be structured so that either the lessor or you are treated as the owner.
- Leases can often be written for longer terms and usually provide for a lower down payment (often just two months rent) than an equivalent collateralized loan.
- Since the lessor maintains title to the leased property, it is easier for the lessor to obtain the rights to the property in the event of default.
- Leases provide a certain flexibility in the pricing of the arrangement related to the value of the property at the end of the lease term. This "residual value" is estimated at the beginning of the lease and may be assigned to the lessor or to you, or split in some fashion. Since the estimate of the residual value has an impact on each party's cash flow, and thus the pricing of the lease, the estimate of its value is an important feature in leasing. "Shopping" for a price may be productive.

See Exhibit 8–1 for an outline of basic modified lease considerations.

Venture Leases

Nontraditional leasing has spawned a new category of leasing to development-stage companies and research and development partnerships. Lessors who see the opportunity for large gains from owning equity interests in a company that may not pass their credit standards will provide leased equipment at normal or enhanced terms when they can negotiate equity interests through either warrants or stock ownership. These arrangements came into being in the 1980s. They provide another way to use this financing tool.

Master Leasing Real Estate

New real estate construction, including manufacturing and distribution facilities, can be financed through a master lease. Under this structure, an independent third-party entity (lessor) is formed to finance the acquisition and construction of real estate for the purpose of leasing the real estate to the tenant. Financing for the construction of the real estate is arranged through the commercial paper market and secured by a bank letter of credit. Upon completion of construction, the lessor continues to finance the debt through the commercial paper market, secured by the tenant's long-term lease. Although leasing the property, the tenant maintains control over the operation, maintenance, sublease, and sale of the real estate. The transaction can be structured as an operating lease so neither the property nor the associated liabilities appear on the tenant's balance sheet. A footnote may be required to disclose the required rental payments over the term of the tenant's noncancelable lease.

ACCOUNTING FOR LEASES ON THE FINANCIAL STATEMENTS

The almost endless list of modifications to lease agreements have left accountants debating for several decades the question. When is a lease a lease? While the answer has been elusive, the standards-setters have reached agreement on some basic guidelines. They have categorized leases into two basic types: the operating lease and the capital lease.

EXHIBIT 8-1. Basic Modified Lease Considerations

Modified Lease Agreement

Rental payment	Estimated residual value	Length of term	Allocation of associated costs	Ownership	Option to purchase
Variable payment possibilities	Assignment of residual value	Renewal option		Allocation of tax benefits	Required purchase stipulations
Escalating or declining payment options	Estimated value of risk protection and guarantees	Amount of down payment			Purchase price

The operating lease can be equated to the traditional lease—the payment of rent for temporary use of the owner's property. At the other end of the spectrum is the capital lease whereby you, the lessee, have obtained most of the rights and risks of ownership.

For practical purposes the standards-setters have developed tests, each of which must be met to qualify as an operating (traditional) lease. In general, a lease will fail to meet the operating-lease tests if, at the origination of the lease, (1) the property subject to the lease will likely be transferred to you, the lessee, at the end of the term; (2) the lease term is for more than 75 percent of the economic life of the asset; (3) the lease contains a bargain purchase option that would be so favorable that its exercise would be reasonably assumed at the inception of the lease; or (4) the present value of the rental payments is equal to at least 90 percent of the fair value of the property at the inception of the lease.

Financial Statement Presentation

The characterization of a lease as either operating or capital becomes important because they are treated differently on financial statements.

An operating (traditional) lease is treated as an executory contract—no assets are recorded and no liabilities are set up (except to record the payments as they become due), and the expense is measured by the amount of rent actually paid (or payable).

On the other hand, a capital lease is recorded in financial statements as (1) the purchase of assets and (2) the incurring of liabilities (both at the present value of the total future payments). The expense is then measured as both depreciation on the property and interest on the obligation. Although by the end of the lease term, the balance sheet and the income statement will be the same for both an operating lease and a capital lease, during the lease term the capital lease will serve to increase assets and liabilities (generally as the lease progresses, the asset will diminish faster than the liability resulting in a greater liability than asset) and will generate larger expenses at the beginning and smaller expenses at the end of the lease. Thus, the capitalization of a lease will appear to make your company's balance sheet look weaker and its income appear lower. This is the same result that would have occurred had the property been purchased with a mortgage.

Exhibit 8–2 shows the approximate effects on your financial statement of leasing property under an operating lease versus a capital
lease. The following comparisons may be noted:

- Although the equity is the same at the beginning of the lease for
  both types of lease, the debt/equity ratio is 1.15 to 1 under the
  operating lease compared with 4.23 to 1 under the capital lease.
- At the end of year one, the debt/equity ratios are 1.03 to 1 and
  3.56 to 1 under the operating and capital lease, respectively.
- Additionally, although not as significant, the income statement
  shows $5,000 greater income under the operating lease than un-
  der the capital lease, reflecting the difference between operating

EXHIBIT 8–2. Comparative Balance Sheet

	Operating Lease	Capital Lease
Summarized balance sheet— initially:		
Current assets	$ 700,000	$ 700,000
Leased property	—	1,000,000
Total assets	$ 700,000	$1,700,000
Liabilities	$ 375,000	$ 375,000
Obligation under capital leases	—	1,000,000
Total liabilities	375,000	1,375,000
Stockholder's equity	325,000	325,000
	$ 700,000	$1,700,000
Income statement—Year 1:		
Revenues	$1,000,000	$1,000,000
Expenses before rent, amortization, and interest	850,000	850,000
Rent	110,000	—
Amortization	—	100,000
Interest	—	15,000
Income before tax	$ 40,000	$ 35,000
Balance sheet—End of year 1:		
Current assets	$ 740,000	$ 740,000
Leased property (net of $100,000 amortization)	—	900,000
Total assets	$ 740,000	$1,640,000
Liabilities	$ 375,000	$ 375,000
Obligation under capital leases	—	905,000
Total liabilities	375,000	1,280,000
Stockholder's equity	365,000	360,000
	$ 740,000	$1,640,000

rentals and the sum of interest and depreciation. This excess will reverse itself sometime after halfway through the lease term; the debt/equity ratios will become equal at the end of the lease term.

TAX REPORTING

The tax authorities are just as interested in proper reporting of leases as is your accountant. A capital lease tends to lower the reported income on your books just as its tax equivalent, the conditional sales contract, lowers your net taxable income. As the term "conditional sales contract" implies, the tax rules generally attempt to determine whether the agreement to lease is actually an agreement to sell by the lessor.

Determining a True Lease

To determine whether an equipment lease qualifies as a "true lease" in advance, the lease must pass four tests that can be summarized as follows:

1. *Minimum Investment.* The lessor must maintain an investment of at least 20 percent of the cost of the property at all times during the lease. The lessor must represent that it is reasonably estimable that, at the end of the lease, the property will have a useful life of the longer of one year or 20 percent of its originally estimated useful life.
2. *Purchase and Sale Rights.* The lessee may not have the right, nor can the lessee be required, to purchase the property from the lessor at a price less than fair market value.
3. *Lessee Investment, Loan, or Guarantee.* The lessee cannot fund (either through purchase, loan, or guarantee) any part of the cost of the property or improvements of the property.
4. *Profit Requirement.* The lessor must demonstrate that it expects to receive a profit on the transaction exclusive of the tax benefits.

These same types of considerations must be evaluated in determining if real property leases are leases or sales.

The four tests are promulgated by the Internal Revenue Service for advance rulings that a leveraged lease is a true lease for tax purposes.

Generally, these transactions are "net leases" involving a lessor, a lessee, and a lender to the lessor.

While these rules are similar to the financial accounting rules, they are not precisely the same and thus some leases will qualify as operating leases for tax purposes but be conditional sales contracts for accounting purposes.

Personal Leasing

Prior to the 1986 Tax Reform Act, equipment leased by an owner of a corporation to his or her company produced significant tax advantages to the individual. The lowering of tax rates, the repeal of the investment credit, a complicated set of passive-activity rules, and more stringent at-risk rules implemented by the 1986 Act have eliminated many of the tax advantages of an individual's leasing equipment to his or her corporation. If real estate is involved, it may still be advantageous; by holding real estate outside the corporation only one level of tax will be assessed when the real estate is sold. To the extent you consider this type of transaction, you should seek professional advice.

PRICING A LEASE

The cost of a lease to you is a direct result of the cost of that lease to the lessor. The lessor views the lease as a cash outflow to acquire the property and a stream of cash inflow represented by the rental payments and the residual value. The rate the lessor is willing to accept is a function of his or her costs—primarily the cost of capital (usually a combination of borrowed funds and equity), overhead costs, and the risks associated with the lease. These risks can generally be divided into two portions: the risk that the user will default on payments (the credit risk) and the risk that the estimated residual value will not be realized. The credit risk is generally evaluated the same in a lease transaction as it is in a collateralized debt arrangement. The residual-value risk, however, is often viewed quite differently by different lessors.

Residual-Value Determination

The lease agreement, for example, may provide for a residual value guaranteed to the lessor by you. Thus, the residual-value risk becomes an extension of the credit risk. In other arrangements, such as an operating lease, the residual value may be the largest item of cash inflow, and estimation of the amount of the inflow is critical to the pricing. In these situations, the nature of the property, its marketability and alternative uses, the cost of refurbishing and relocation, and the historical price movements of similar property come to bear. In the case of real estate, the lessor will likely estimate a high residual value in pricing the lease and accept lower current rents as a result. In the case of computer equipment, the lessor will usually have a low estimate of residual value and price the lease accordingly. Alternatively, the lessor may request that you guarantee a specified residual value, eliminating the lessor's downside risk (but retaining his or her upside potential), and thus lower the pricing to you. If the lessor is affiliated (by ownership or by contract) with the equipment manufacturer, he or she is more likely to accept a higher risk and higher estimate of the residual value than other lessors.

Tax Advantages

Another key consideration in the pricing will be the tax advantages. The lessor will be willing to pass these deductions back to you in the form of lower lease payments—but only if the lessor can use the tax benefits. Leasing companies that have a limited appetite for tax benefits often structure deals that result in the lessee's either being treated as the tax owner of the property or becoming involved in brokering the lease by selling it to third parties. On the other hand, some lessors can readily use the related tax benefits and therefore may price the lease very competitively.

LEVERAGED LEASES

One novel third-party financing technique is the so-called leveraged lease. A leveraged lease provides you with the equipment under a lease that is a capital lease for accounting purposes, while the property is "owned" for tax purposes by a third-party investor who can use the tax advantages afforded by the property and who has purchased the equipment using funds borrowed from the leasing company. The "owner's" investment generally becomes negative in the early portion of the lease (taxes saved are less than his or her cash outlay) with most of the cash flow going to pay the debt. Thus, the total cash return on such an investment is small. Because the cost of structuring a leveraged lease can be quite high and because the owner of the property has a small percentage investment in the property, the total value of the property generally needs to be quite large—as in the case of a commercial airplane, tanker, or large specialized complex—for the transaction to be attractive.

SALES AND LEASEBACKS

This form of financing is used to raise capital when companies have underfinanced property or equipment that is not financed, and allows a company to raise money while maintaining control of its productive assets. Normally, purchase options to buy back the assets are available from the buyer (lessor). A few leasing and commercial finance companies specialize in these transactions. On real property, rates can be very competitive, and on equipment, depending on its type, rates can be fair to high. Most often, sale and leaseback is done in connection with recapitalization or a management or leveraged buyout of current owners. The tax and accounting issues can be very complex, and generally you should have your advisors help you recognize and avoid any traps these transactions may involve.

9

GOVERNMENT FINANCING

It comes as a surprise to many business people that the government, often cast as antibusiness, slow moving, and awash in regulations and red tape, turns out to be one of the principal benefactors of businesses in need of capital. Through a variety of federal, state, and local programs, government throughout the United States is the largest single source of funds available to business for growth and expansion. It is important that you understand the range of programs and services government provides, what government's aims are, and whether government financing is the right or wrong source for you.

However, understanding government programs is rarely easy for the business executive. Programs and the philosophies behind them frequently change as the leadership changes and as old programs are phased out and new ones make their appearance. To keep abreast, it is essential for you to stay in touch with the people who administer these programs in your area and to get help from your banker, accountant, attorney, and specialists who make a business of tracking these programs.

Getting money from the government is not likely to be anyone's first choice as a means of raising capital. Government will usually impose the same conditions as a bank or other lending organizations, but with political provisos added. In many cases, government will lend you money only after a bank or private source has turned you down—a last resort—or will guarantee the repayment of most of your loan and thus make it safe for the bank to go ahead.

Whatever the nature of your transaction with government, you can count on one invariable fact: it will be a paper-intensive, time-consuming procedure, and more than once you will wonder whether it is worth the bother.

In short, it takes patience. But it may pay you handsomely to take the trouble to understand why government acts as it does. To begin, let us examine three basic reasons why government offers financial help to private businesses.

1. *Supporting the Economy.* The first reason government lends money to business is to help make the economy strong and give companies like yours a better chance to realize their ambitions. The entire political, social, and economic structure of this country rests on the expectation that private business will prosper, innovate, and expand; this concept underlies government's commitment to hold out a helping hand. One of the clearest examples is the Small Business Administration (SBA), created by Congress in 1953. Most Americans believe the government has a legitimate role in making certain the private sector remains independent and vigorous. One way to do this is to offer loans and other financial assistance.

2. *Creating Jobs.* A second reason government lends money to private business is that growth and expansion usually leads to more jobs, and that goal is dear to the hearts of government leaders. Nothing is more fundamental.

Moreover, in a private enterprise system like ours, it is usually more sensible for government to help the private sector create jobs than to try to absorb the unemployed into government work projects that might be inefficient and temporary.

There are also humanitarian motives. Government often uses its support to encourage business to create jobs where the need is especially urgent—in specific communities, for example, and among certain ethnic groups. One example of this job-related support is the Urban Development Action Grant (UDAG), administered by the U.S. Department of Housing and Urban Development (HUD).

3. *Supporting Special Situations.* The third reason for government involvement is to supply funds for projects of great importance that private lenders might find too risky. For example, certain government loan programs encourage investment in research and development for critical technologies in defense, science, and agriculture.

IDENTIFYING GOVERNMENT FINANCING TOOLS

Governments at all levels—federal, state, and local—provide financial assistance to businesses. Most resources are provided by the federal government; some of these funds may be "passed through" and made available by a local or state organization. But before reviewing these federal financing tools, local and state financing mechanisms should be briefly discussed.

LOCAL GOVERNMENTS' PROGRAMS

Many cities and counties have established industrial development authorities to issue tax-exempt Industrial Revenue Bonds to promote new and expanding businesses. Some communities have also established downtown development authorities responsible for tax-exempt notes to be used for commercial revitalization. Business people seeking financial resources should contact their city or county governments to see if such organizations are in place and may be able to provide assistance.

Some areas have established locally operated revolving-loan pools controlled by city or county governments. Although this tool is not available in most places, if your business is operating where such a lending institution is functioning, it is worth investigating. Often such pools of money are the result of federal grants or pass-throughs, but they may be locally controlled.

The use of tax-exempt financing through local development authorities has been controversial in recent years. The tax advantages associated with "private activity" bonds have been reduced, and legislation is under consideration that would phase out such authority to grant tax-exempt financing by the end of this decade. As a result, it may be only a few years until many local governments are completely out of the business of providing financing. Recent legislation puts a ceiling on the amount of bonds that each state can issue.

STATE GOVERNMENTS' PROGRAMS

Just as local policies and resources vary widely from place to place, different states have diverse resources to offer in the area of financing.

Some states have committed money to a statewide business development corporation with money to lend to healthy enterprises. Other states are utilizing Community Development Block Grant (CDBG) funds from the Department of Housing and Urban Development to promote economic development and business investment. Many of these programs are aimed at creating jobs for low- and moderate-income individuals, and therefore have a great many restrictions on how the money is used for business growth.

To find these potential lending resources, contact your state office of economic development or state office of commerce. Once again, your banker, accountant, or business analyst may be able to bring you up to date on state programs. Ernst & Young has co-authored a series entitled Starting and Operating a Business in (State), which can be extremely useful.

Through various state agencies, financing programs are offered to businesses that are operating, expanding, or locating in their state.

State financing programs typically appear in the form of direct loans for fixed-asset purchases, construction or renovation, inventory or working capital, and infrastructure improvement. They are normally not available for contingency funds or debt restructuring. State agencies do not serve as primary lenders. Instead, they act as participating lenders in a conventional financing package. In other words, they provide financing for a percentage of the total project cost, with banks and equity providing the remainder.

Demand by companies for state financing programs usually exceeds the availability of funds. As a result, there is often strong competition among companies to receive funds. The major criterion used in selecting companies to finance is the creation or retention of jobs. The application process can be long and arduous. State agencies usually review applications on a monthly or quarterly basis.

Financing programs vary from state to state, yet there seem to be certain basic similarities. Businesses should contact state government officials to find out what sort of assistance is available in their particular state. The "Blue Pages" in the local telephone directory and the state department of commerce are good places to start.

State loan and grant programs frequently change in terms of funding availability, program requirements, and eligibility criteria. It is essential that businesses keep in close contact with the state agencies' representatives to monitor the status of the various programs.

THE FEDERAL GOVERNMENT

Most government loans and loan guarantees come from federal agencies. This chapter goes into detail on the variety of these programs and their requirements. No one agency on the federal level is aware of what all, or even most, of the other agencies also involved in making business loans are doing. Do not expect coordination or cooperation among the agencies. In addition, there will be some important requirements, noted in this chapter in detail, about limits on the use of federal funds from different sources.

WHAT TO EXPECT FROM A GOVERNMENT LENDER

The basic approach in requesting a loan from a government entity is similar to that used with a private lender.

There are also important differences. A lending officer for a bank or similar financial institution is concerned primarily about the loan he or she is about to make, and asks: "How does this look in the bank's portfolio? Will the loan be good? Can we collect? Is the collateral sufficient? Is this a creditworthy client?"

The government lender may ask some of these same questions, but another concern will be: "Are all the forms complete and filled out properly? Do we have all the information required by law and regulation?" It is this additional set of questions that leaves many business people shaking their heads after an encounter with a government lender.

Your banker may be able to make a loan based heavily on one of the "three Cs"—character, collateral, and credit. Some bankers place special importance on the character of the client. Most government loan organizations do not have that option. They will depend almost entirely on what is presented to them in the loan application—and all the correctly completed forms.

With that in mind, the entrepreneur should always ask the question, "Is it worth my investment of time to secure this government financing?" Although not all public-sector loan programs require a great deal of time, many contain a set of complex steps not present with other lending institutions.

Government loan programs have often been seen as the "lender of last resort," a resource to be utilized when all other possible financial institutions have already turned down a request for a loan. That is one valid perspective in understanding how the government as lender works. Government funds should not usually be considered the first alternative in seeking business financing. Several government loan programs require an applicant to have been turned down by a commercial lender before it can be considered.

Another perspective on government's role in providing loan funds can be seen in the "but for" test. Often government funds are loaned in order to make a project viable (i.e., but for this loan a project would not be workable). Government financing can also be used to improve a financial package by improving the rate or the term of a loan. The Small Business Administration and other government agencies may be able to offer a better term or even a better interest rate to make a business loan easier for you to repay.

While there are a multitude of government agencies with the capacity to make loans, many are dependent upon appropriations or regulations in order to exercise their loan capacity. One test you can use before beginning the loan application process with a government agency is this: Ask about the number of applications submitted and the number of loans made in the last year. If there have been relatively few loans considering the number of applicants, it may not be a good investment of time to seek these funds.

TYPES OF FINANCING PROGRAMS

Government financing programs can be divided into six types: direct loans, guaranteed/insured loans, project grants, insurance, direct payments, and equity participation.

Direct Loans

In a direct loan, a government agency gives the money directly to a business and expects repayment directly to the agency. In this instance, the government functions like a commercial lender—setting interest rates and terms and establishing the mechanism for repayment. These types of loans are becoming increasingly scarce as a means of government financing and are often available only to specialized groups. Many experts, including some government loan officers, believe these loans will soon be completely phased out.

In the case of a direct loan, you deal with the government agency just as you would any other lending institution. The loan officer for the government entity will discuss with you the nature and purpose of the loan to see if it meets the agency's eligibility criteria. After this initial contact, you should receive the proper forms, which must be filled out correctly and completely. You may want to work closely with your accountant, lawyer, or other professional advisors to be sure the information is complete and accurate. Government agencies generally will not process any loan request until all required information is provided. The loan request is reviewed by the agency's loan officer and, if complete, sent on to the agency's loan review committee.

Guaranteed/Insured Loans

Guaranteed/insured loans are the most common form of government financial assistance. These loans are made by a commercial lender with no advancement of government funds. Government participation is in the form of a guarantee, and funds will be advanced only if the loan goes into default. The commercial lender will expect repayment of the loan from your company and therefore will apply its usual tests for repaying. Guaranteed loans are advantageous to both you and the bank. Your business may receive approval of a guaranteed loan more readily than a conventional arrangement with a lending institution. The bank, while retaining first position on the loan, has its potential liability greatly diminished by the government guarantee and can show these loans in its portfolio at only the "nonguaranteed" portion, thus improving its potential loan volume.

With guaranteed/insured loans, you generally have very little contact with the government entity and deal mainly with the commercial lender. Typically, you would go to your bank to apply for a loan. Many lenders are familiar with available government financing tools and can assist in completing the forms. If the banker determines that a government guarantee or insurance is necessary for the bank to make the loan, the banker should discuss the requirements in detail, including why the guarantee is necessary, which federal agency might be able to make the guarantee, and the legal requirements of the agency for its involvement. Again the information must be complete and accurate. The loan request is reviewed by the lending institution's committee and, if approved, forwarded to the government agency with a positive recommendation. The loan will then depend on the approval or denial of the government agency involved.

Project Grants

Project grants are generally financial awards tied to a particular project. Most government project-grant programs require that the applicant invest a reasonable amount of his or her own capital, or that the grant be matched by private funds. Utilization of government-grant funds requires fairly stringent accounting records for the grant project, as well as periodic audits of management and control systems to ensure that the conditions of the grant are consistently being met.

Grant programs may have annual deadlines and specified formats for applications. It is best to work as closely as possible with representatives from the relevant agency to ensure that all grant-related paperwork is on time and in order.

Direct Payments

Direct payments are similar to project grants in that they are generally intended for a particular project or for a specific use, although a few payments are made for unrestricted use. Direct payments differ from grants in the governmental accounting procedures that track these two types of disbursements. This form of assistance sometimes requires cost-sharing as well—the recipient may have to invest a portion of the necessary funds. Direct payments are often used to encourage conservation, pollution control, or other types of public-welfare projects.

Insurance

Government assistance with insurance refers primarily to export insurance, which protects exporters against the failure of foreign buyers to honor their credit obligations. Designed to reduce risk at low cost, this type of insurance can cover both commercial and political risks. As with other types of insurance policies, export insurance has a fee and premium structure dependent upon the amount of coverage and often requires a deductible.

Equity Participation

Although government's role in equity participation is comparable to that of any other investor, there are usually regulations dictating that the percentage of a project's total financing supplied by the government must be under 50 percent. Generally, emphasis is placed on pioneering or innovative entities developing new projects or processes. As with private investors, the government requires repayment of its investment from the sale of the newly developed product or process. Before taking an equity position in any concern, the government agency thoroughly evaluates the viability of the concern, including the capabilities of management and the probability of success.

Enterprise Zones

At the present time, Congress is considering legislation that would create approximately 150 enterprise zones in various urban and rural areas across the United States. The purpose of this legislation is to offer financial incentives for businesses to locate in neighborhoods that have the most immediate need of economic development. The legislation would offer preferable tax rates or tax abatement for capital investments in the defined neighborhoods. In addition, new economic development programs would be established to promote job creation. Many of these new programs would be administered by the Department of Housing and Urban Development. The proposed programs include direct loans, interest-rate subsidies, and loan guarantees for businesses that move into the enterprise zone. Locating in an enterprise zone would also make the borrower eligible for loans that have been earmarked for local lending to ensure bank compliance with the Community Reinvestment Act. Some states have already created local enterprise zones and make investment capital available through similar programs. Check with your state's economic development office for details.

FEDERAL FINANCING PROGRAMS

The federal government offers a variety of financial assistance programs, primarily through three agencies: Small Business Administration, Farmers Home Administration, and Economic Development Administration. One federal program involves several different agencies and can be an important source of funds for start-up companies—the Small Business Innovation Research (SBIR) program. (See Exhibit 9–1 for a summary of these programs.)

EXHIBIT 9–1. Federal Domestic Assistance Programs

	Direct Loans and Guaranteed/ Insured Loans	Guaranteed/ Insured Loans	Insurance	Direct Payments	Project Grants
Small Business Administration Telephone: (202) 653-6500	Offers direct loans and guaranteed/ insured loans to establish, preserve, and strengthen small business. Types of loans include loans to businesses owned by minorities, persons with disabilities, and veterans; disaster relief loans; loans to investment companies.	Offers guaranteed loans to small businesses that are unable to obtain financing in the private credit market and to state development companies that lend to small businesses.	Guarantees surety bonds issued by commercial surety companies for small contractors unable to obtain a bond without a guarantee.		Awards project grants to provide management and technical assistance to small businesses.
Farmers Home Administration Telephone: (202) 690-1533	Offers direct loans to help lower-income rural families obtain or repair housing; to accelerate resource conservation, development, and utilization, to	Offers guaranteed/ insured loans for farm capital and operating expenses; for the proper use of soil and water resources, to enable Native American tribes to obtain		Awards direct payments to reduce rents paid by low-income families.	Awards project grants to provide low-rent housing; to improve rural water and waste facilities; to provide technical and supervisory assistance in the rural areas, to

	improve rural water and waste facilities, to improve watershed areas, to improve overall rural services, to improve business facilities.	finance rural industrial sites and stimulate industry in rural areas.
	loans; to help rural families obtain housing; to stimulate industry in rural areas; to assist family farms when they are short of cash, to reduce the interest rate for qualified applicants.	
Economic Development Administration Telephone: (202) 482-5113		Awards project grants to state and local governments to promote economic development in areas of economic distress.
Small Business Innovation Research programs Telephone: (202) 205-7777		Awards project grants to stimulate technological innovation in the private sector and strengthen the role of small businesses in meeting federal research and development needs.

The federal government agencies often work with state and local government to provide a package of financing assistance using funds from different sources. In particular, Small Business Administration and Export-Import Bank programs tie in closely with each other, as well as with state and local government programs. Your agency contacts will be able to help with understanding and coordinating the array of financing options to maximize the aid that is available to you.

The Small Business Administration

The largest single agency with responsibility for making business loans is the Small Business Administration. This organization, based in Washington, D.C., with offices in most major American cities, should be considered one of the primary resources for the entrepreneur interested in government financing.

First, a quick look into the background of the SBA.

Defining Small Business—Size, Eligibility, Need. One of the tasks given to the SBA when it was created by Congress in 1953 was to decide what constitutes a small business. Since then, the definition has changed as inflation has risen and manufacturing and distribution patterns have changed. Unfortunately, there is still not a universal definition of small business. The following general guidelines may prove helpful, but the best course is for you to ask the SBA whether your company is eligible before proceeding with the application process.

Generally, a small business must meet the following criteria:

1. It cannot be dominant in its field.

2. It must be independently owned and operated, and not an affiliate of a larger business.

3. It must meet size standards based on the number of employees or annual receipts. These two benchmarks vary for different industries, although as a rule of thumb a small business has fewer than 500 employees.

The SBA also has rules against making loans or loan guarantees for uses such as these:

- Paying unsecured creditors or principals
- Speculation, such as wildcatting in oil or dealing in commodity futures

- Nonprofit institutions
- Newspapers, magazines, and book publishers
- Gambling
- Lending or investment
- Acquiring real or rental property held primarily for sale or investment
- Monopoly
- Pyramid sales plans
- Relocation of business under certain conditions such as movement to nullify a labor contract or a move that would result in significant unemployment or a substantial loss from an existing lease

If a business meets the requirements of size and eligible activities, the next important test has to do with the appropriateness of an SBA loan. Generally, the SBA will not be the lender of first choice. No loan application will be considered if

1. Financing is available from a commercial credit source at reasonable rates and terms;

2. The business has assets not essential to growth or operations that could be liquidated for additional capital;

3. Collateral is insufficient to meet the value of the loan; that is, an SBA loan cannot be used for what has been referred to as a bailout; or

4. The loan proceeds will be used for payment to owners or shareholders in the business.

Increasingly the SBA is applying the same credit standards—adequate collateral and appropriate creditworthiness—that commercial lenders use. The difference is that, in some instances, the SBA is able to finance a business with different terms or rates, or may be able to provide a loan or guarantee when a more cautious private-sector lender would not make capital available.

Any entrepreneur planning to approach the SBA for a loan should be prepared to provide the following information:

- History of the business
- The last three years' historical financial statements

- Signed personal financial statements
- A complete description of the use of funds being requested
- Business projections
- Pro forma financial statements
- Aging of receivables and payables
- Details of debt and lease commitments

SBA Loan Programs

The 7(a) Program. The largest of all SBA loan programs, the 7(a) program, like most SBA loan programs, takes its name from the section of the Small Business Act that has granted this authority and created the parameters for its operations. The 7(a) program has become almost exclusively a loan-guarantee program. The law does provide for direct loans for persons with disabilities, veterans, and specialized small business investment companies (SSBICs).

Eligible activities under 7(a) loans include the following:

- Acquisition of borrower-occupied real estate
- Fixed assets such as machinery and equipment
- Working capital for expansion

The guaranteed portion of the loan cannot exceed $750,000. The SBA will generally guarantee up to 85 percent of the loan for the bank, and in some situations as much as 90 percent of the loan for loans less than $155,000.

The term for 7(a) loans is related to the life of the assets, the cash flow of the business, or the use of the funds. Real estate loans, by statute, can be for a term up to 25 years, and fixed assets may be financed for the effective life of the asset, typically 3 to 7 years but not more than 25 years. Working-capital terms are usually 7 years. In all cases the maturity of the loan is consistent with the time required by the applicant to make repayment; the term of the loan is in direct relation to the cash flow of the business.

The interest rate for all 7(a) loans is pegged to the prime rate. The law requires that the interest rate may not exceed 2.75 percent over prime, or 2.25 percent if the terms are under seven years. The rate may be floating or fixed as determined by the bank. If the rate is floating, it may be adjusted monthly, quarterly, semiannually, or annually.

These 7(a) loans can be used for financing up to 100 percent of the total capital needs for expansions of existing businesses. A typical start-up can expect to borrow 70 to 75 percent of the capital needed.

The credit and collateral criteria for these loans is usually stringent. As the potential borrower, you must be able to demonstrate that cash flow will be sufficient to repay the debt. Having passed this credit test, you should be prepared to offer as much collateral as possible to make this loan more attractive to the SBA and the commercial lender.

Typically, the collateral required includes a general security agreement and a lien on all assets of the business. Personal guarantees from the business principals will also be required. The SBA will expect to be named as beneficiaries of life insurance in an amount equivalent to the outstanding balance of the loan in case of the death of a principal in the business.

A 7(a) loan may be used in conjunction with other federal loan programs, but may not be used to guarantee a tax-exempt revenue bond. It is common to package a 7(a) loan with other federal loans in order to provide working capital for a business expansion. It is important to remember that the maximum amount the SBA may guarantee for any small business is $750,000.

Overall, the 7(a) program is not designed to offer incentives to the borrower such as a reduced rate or improved terms, but should be viewed instead as a financing tool in instances where the overriding issue is obtaining capital. To qualify for a 7(a) loan, you must demonstrate that you have been turned down by a commercial lender.

An example: Company A needed additional working capital after expanding its product line and machinery and equipment. In order to meet the demands of its heaviest season, the company needed an additional $250,000 to purchase inventory and finance existing receivables. After being turned down for a line of credit and a working-capital loan by its bank because of its current level of debt, the company approached the Small Business Administration in its hometown. It applied for the $250,000 loan under the 7(a) program and received approval in the form of an 85 percent loan guarantee. With the SBA guarantee, the bank was willing to make the loan.

The business gave the bank a lien on all available assets, as well as a general security agreement, and received the working capital it needed to make the inventory investment and fund its receivables. Under the loan agreement, the company paid 1.5 percent over prime for three years in monthly installments. At the end of three years, having successfully satisfied all requirements of the loan, the bank established a revolving line of credit for the company to use in similar situations involving inventory and cash-flow cycles.

Frequently, it is unnecessary to approach the SBA directly. The bank will usually recognize situations where the SBA might be helpful and bring that to your attention.

The 502 Program. Another SBA loan program, also named for a section of law, is the 502 program, designed to help the entrepreneur with the acquisition of fixed assets only and not working capital or inventory.

While the previously described 7(a) program exists to serve the entrepreneur when the question of credit is the primary problem, the 502 program is designed to meet problems related to terms and collateral for a particular project. For example, you need to acquire a piece of equipment that will have a life of, say, 15 years, and wish to amortize the loan over the effective life of the equipment. The commercial lender may not be willing to make the loan for that long. The 502 program, by providing longer terms for the acquisition of property, plant, and equipment, assists the entrepreneur in meeting his or her financing needs.

The acquisition of fixed assets under the 502 program is accomplished through an arrangement among the SBA, a Local Development Company (LDC), a commercial lender, and your business. An unusual feature of a 502 loan is that your project must be in an area served by an LDC. Local development companies are usually formed by local governments or citizens whose aim is to improve the economy in their area. Your local SBA office or commercial lender can advise you on this feature.

In such a situation, the LDC acts as the legal borrower on behalf of your small-business concern. The acquisition of fixed assets under the 502 program is actually a lease purchase agreement between an LDC and your company, with the SBA acting as the loan guarantor and a commercial lender acting as the funds originator. Loan procedures under this program can be somewhat complex but valuable if you need long-term asset financing with minimum collateral.

Through 502 loans, the SBA and the LDC accomplish their goal of supporting local business. In addition, as with all government-guaranteed loans, the commercial lender benefits by having its potential liability greatly reduced.

In the 502 program, the maximum amount the government guarantees is $750,000. The SBA will generally make a 90 percent guarantee to the local lending institution through an LDC. The term for this loan, which is usually the key factor, is the life of the asset not to exceed 25 years. Once again, interest rates are pegged to the prime rate, with a ceiling of 2.75 percent over prime. The loan can be at a fixed or floating rate.

In structuring all 502 loans, the SBA requires a minimum of 10 percent local capital investment be made in the project. This money can come from the entrepreneur, a local bank, the LDC, or almost any other source. The remaining 90 percent of the project cost can then be financed through a commercial lender and an LDC with SBA guarantee. Usually, personal guarantees and life insurance will be required to cover the debt.

An example: Company B, a manufacturing concern moving into a new product line, needed to acquire $400,000 worth of machinery. Although the equipment would have a useful life of ten years, the bank was unwilling to make a loan for more than five years. Management saw the need to lengthen the terms in order to meet the debt-service requirements and match the company's funds to the effective life of the equipment purchase.

Working through an LDC and a local bank, the company obtained a $360,000 SBA 502 program loan for ten years at 1.25 percent over prime. Management made an additional equity investment of $40,000 to meet the loan requirements. The company is presently making the monthly installment payments to retire the debt.

The 504 Program. In 1980, Section 503 of the Small Business Act was passed, and updated in 1989 by Section 504. The 504 loan program operates in much the same way as the 503 program did, but the law was altered to specify the utilization of private funds as opposed to federal financing. This program is similar in many ways to the 502 program. However, the 504 program can accommodate a far larger total project size.

The structure of a 504 loan involves a commitment of 50 percent of total project costs from a private-sector lender (nonfederal funds), a 10 percent equity investment from the development company or the small-business concern being assisted, and 40 percent participation by the SBA. Under such agreements, projects exceeding $1 million can be financed using the 504 program.

Unlike other SBA loan programs, 504 loans must meet criteria that demonstrate a positive impact on the local economy. The normal guideline is the creation of at least one new job for every $35,000 worth of debt secured by the government's 40 percent share in the loan package. While these requirements are not rigid, the better the job-creation ratio the stronger the loan request.

The structure of the 504 program also requires participation of a Certified Development Corporation (CDC) to act as agent for this loan. Any community served by an existing CDC is eligible for the 504 loan program, and many businesses outside a local CDC area have been able to secure financing through a statewide CDC. Contact the SBA office in your area or state to find out how your area is being served.

As in the 502 program, the proceeds from a 504 loan can be used only for fixed assets, including the following:

- Acquisition of land, land improvements, and buildings
- New construction, renovation, modernization, or conversion of existing facilities
- Machinery and equipment with useful life of at least ten years

Working capital cannot be financed by a 504 loan.

Financing under the 504 program can have two different interest rates: one set by the bank for its portion, and the 504 portion at 1 percent above United States Treasury bond rates of similar maturity at the time the debentures securing the loan are sold.

The tests of credit and collateral are similar to those of the 502 program, with the primary criteria being cash flow to meet debt-service requirements and adequate collateral to secure the loan. Personal guarantees and life insurance will usually be required, but individuals are normally not required to invest or pledge their total net worth as collateral if the project has a substantial economic development impact on the community.

Lending institutions are usually interested in participating in this type of loan guarantee arrangement because they are in first position to acquire and liquidate all assets in case of default, even though their liability is only 50 percent. The SBA usually holds second position in such an arrangement for its 40 percent share in case of a default.

The 504 loan program is a complex but valuable tool for the entrepreneur. Not a good source of funds for business start-ups, refinancing, or turnaround business ventures, this approach to government financing is most appropriate for the expansion of an existing business with strong credit and collateral in search of better fixed-asset financing.

An example: Company C, a fish processing plant in New England, was ready to open an additional location nearer a port that served local fishermen. With a strong business history and a stable pattern of growth, this company could demonstrate its potential. It needed $1 million for an expansion project that included the acquisition of an existing building, renovations to that building, and the cost of machinery and equipment for fish processing. The bank was unwilling to loan the entire amount, but working with the local CDC, the company put up capital of $100,000, the bank made a direct loan of $500,000, and the SBA guaranteed an additional $400,000. The new location was opened and 82 employees were hired. Through this vehicle, the company financed the real estate acquisition for 20 years and the remainder of the project for 15 years.

Other SBA Programs. There are approximately 18 smaller and targeted programs that can provide both loans and loan guarantees to specific groups of small-business people. The availability of these special funds can best be ascertained by contacting the SBA. Examples of special loan programs include, but are not limited to, the following:

- Handicapped assistance loans for small-business people with physical disabilities
- Energy loans to companies and firms involved in manufacturing and installing energy-saving devices and technology
- Disaster assistance loans for businesses and homeowners
- Pollution control financing for small-business people

Small Business Innovation Research Program

A different approach to providing government financial support to entrepreneurial activities is provided by the Small Business Innovation Development Act of 1982, designed to include small private businesses in federally supported R&D. It differs from other programs discussed in this chapter in that it is a hybrid between a loan or grant program and a new pattern of contracts for procurement of services.

Recognizing that much private-sector R&D paid for by the government was done primarily by the nation's larger businesses, the Small Business Innovation Research program was created to ensure participation by smaller businesses in these activities. Rather than creating a new agency, the SBIR initiative spreads the responsibility among other agencies. Each is responsible for committing a certain amount of its R&D funds to small businesses through the SBIR program. The SBA oversees the program, while each agency establishes its own programs and contract criteria.

The participating agencies include the following:

- Department of Defense
- National Aeronautics and Space Administration
- Department of Health and Human Services
- Department of Energy
- National Science Foundation
- Department of Agriculture
- Department of Transportation
- Nuclear Regulatory Commission
- Environmental Protection Agency
- Department of the Interior
- Department of Education

These agencies, each with an R&D budget in excess of $100 million, direct some of their R&D work to small businesses.

Cooperative Research and Development Agreements

Cooperative Research and Development Agreements (CRADAs) are R&D projects undertaken between various governmental laboratories and industry. Research funding and staffing commitments are usually shared between parties with the specifics of the research commitments detailed in the CRADA.

CRADAs offer a unique opportunity for industry or academia to collaborate with the United States government. CRADAs present the best of both worlds to the industry partner, who obtains the funding it needs for R&D as well as rights to technology developed by the government in advance. This is possible because all patents or inventions developed in the CRADA are owned by both parties. The government then issues an option for the exclusive license for the products of the CRADA. CRADAs have most often been used in the biotechnology industry, but may be used for any R&D project.

The Farmers Home Administration

Another federal agency that aids business is the Farmers Home Administration. An arm of the U.S. Department of Agriculture, the Farmers Home Administration focuses on providing assistance and loans to the nation's rural areas. Businesses in urban areas are ineligible to receive assistance under the Farmers Home Administration program.

Recent changes in the federal budget have had a great impact on the loan and loan-guarantee activities of this agency. You would be well advised to investigate the number of loans and loan guarantees made locally by the Farmers Home Administration before pursuing the application process in any detail.

Defining Rural Areas. The Farmers Home Administration works within closely defined parameters for rural areas in making loan decisions. A rural area may be defined as any area that is not a town or city with a population of 50,000 or more. Also excluded are those areas adjacent to urbanized areas with more than 100 persons per square mile. Priority is given to projects in rural communities and cities with a population of less than 25,000.

Types of Farmers Home Administration Loans. The Farmers Home Administration provides credit for a variety of uses in rural areas. It has participated in rural housing development lending as well as lending for public facilities in small towns and less populous counties. These programs would not generally be of interest to the small business executive, although they may be used as a tool for housing or infrastructure development to enhance a business expansion.

The Farmers Home Administration has provided two primary types of assistance that could benefit the entrepreneur. The first is agriculture and agricultural production loans; the second, business and industry loan guarantees.

Agricultural Loan Programs. The agricultural loan programs provide credit assistance to applicants who are operating family-sized farms or cooperatives made up of family-sized farms. These loans include the following:

- Farm ownership loans
- Farm operating loans
- Loans to limited resource farmers
- Specialized loans, such as aquaculture loans
- Economic emergency loans
- Nonfarm enterprise loans
- Disaster loans
- Soil and water loans

The terms and conditions of these loans will vary from program to program, although generally they are loan-guarantee programs that depend on a local lending institution making the loan with a Farmers Home Administration guarantee of up to 90 percent. These loans apply specifically to the business involved directly in agricultural production. For detailed information on these loans, you should contact the nearest state office of the Farmers Home Administration.

Business and Industry Loans. The Farmers Home Administration is also active in guaranteeing loans through commercial lenders for the creation and expansion of industry in less populous areas. In recent years, however, allocations for these loan programs have been reduced. In some areas, loan activity has been severely restricted.

Having met the basic conditions of a rural area, the applicant must meet a number of other stipulations. These loans may not be used for any of the following purposes:

- Payment to a creditor in excess of value
- Payment to owners or shareholders or other equity owners
- Projects involving agricultural production
- Transfer of business ownership unless such transfer prevents a closing with subsequent loss of jobs
- Guarantee of lease payments
- Financing community antenna television services or facilities
- Guarantee of loans made by other federal agencies (such as the SBA)
- Projects of over $1 million or over 50 employees where such projects will result in the transfer of operations with a significant impact on the labor or demand of existing markets

Loan guarantees are available for the following business activities:

- Acquisition of buildings and land
- Renovation of buildings or new construction
- Acquisition of machinery and equipment
- Working capital for inventory and cash-flow needs

The terms vary depending upon the nature of the loan, with maximums of 30 years for real estate, 15 years for machinery and equipment, and 7 years for working capital. The term of the loan is generally consistent with the use of the proceeds.

These Farmers Home Administration loans generally require a commitment of at least 10 percent of total project cost in equity. The amount of equity required of a new business or start-up can be as high as 25 percent.

Credit and collateral are important considerations in the approval process. Your business must demonstrate a capacity to meet debt-service requirements with cash flow, and the collateral must match the value of the capital used to acquire it.

The interest rate is determined by the local lending institution and the Farmers Home Administration, and is usually set at an increment above the prevailing Treasury bond rate of similar term. The rate may be either fixed or variable, depending upon the nature of the participation by the commercial lender.

The Farmers Home Administration may require unconditional personal guarantees from owners and partners making the application. Life insurance may also be required of the applicant. In instances where the loan request exceeds $1 million, a feasibility study is required.

The Farmers Home Administration business and industry loans do not include the precondition that an applicant has been turned down by a commercial lender before a loan guarantee can be granted by the agency.

In many rural areas, business and industry loans have provided significant financial incentives to the creation of jobs and the investment of capital. It should be apparent, however, that the number of specific prerequisites may make this fund source unavailable to many entrepreneurs.

The Economic Development Administration

The Economic Development Administration (EDA), an arm of the U.S. Department of Commerce, was created in 1965 to promote industrial and commercial development. Since its inception, this agency has supported business development with grants to state and local governments.

Much of the infrastructure necessary for the development of new industrial parks and sites has been undertaken with the assistance of the EDA in underdeveloped areas in the country. In the last few years, the amount of money appropriated for EDA activities has steadily diminished.

The EDA has regional offices in Philadelphia, Atlanta, Chicago, Austin, Denver, and Seattle. For further information, check with your nearest regional office.

Research Grants and Contracts. As previously stated, the SBIR program provides grants and contracts for R&D activities. Small businesses compete for the awards to develop and refine ideas over a period of years. The process includes the following phases:

Phase I. Research grants of up to $100,000 for projects that will evaluate the technical and scientific merits as well as feasibility of ideas (solicited or unsolicited, see following explanation) that fall within the scope of the participating agency.
Phase II. Awards of up to $750,000 over a two-year period to develop the most promising ideas.
Phase III. Public-private partnership to support and bring this innovation to the marketplace. This will generally involve follow-up production contracts from the federal agency that supports the original research and development.

Any U.S. for-profit business with 500 or fewer employees is eligible to participate in the SBIR program. Specific requirements vary somewhat from agency to agency, depending on priorities for R&D activities. Generally, the greatest problem for entrepreneurs is to identify the R&D needs of various agencies and show that their company has the capacity to carry out such activities.

To help mitigate this problem, the SBIR program allows two levels of response by small businesses.

You can contact the SBA's Office of Innovation, Research, and Technology and put your company on the semiannual presolicitation announcements, which lets you know about requests for proposals (RFPs) from any participating agency.

Small businesses may also submit unsolicited proposals for R&D activities to any agency. Before such a proposal is submitted, the small business should determine the following:

- Does the agency fund unsolicited proposals?
- Is the proposed research and development appropriate to this agency?
- Does the work duplicate previous research or research-in-progress?
- Is the proposal technically sound?
- Do the key investigators have the capacity to undertake the proposed research?
- Is the cost reasonable?
- Are the funds currently available?

Obviously, good information is a key in gaining access to the benefits of the SBIR program. The SBA is a valuable information resource. In addition, you should make full use of the National Technical Information Service (NTIS), a government clearinghouse of technical information and publications. (Telephone: 703/487-4650.)

For the entrepreneur involved in research and development, the highly specialized SBIR program offers some new resources and potential business development, as well as additional funding opportunities. The terms and availability of resources under this program, however, vary greatly from agency to agency.

10

BUSINESS COMBINATIONS AND DIVESTITURES

BUSINESS COMBINATIONS—CATEGORIES

The alternatives for raising capital considered by the entrepreneur or fast-growth company generally do not include business combinations, since this usually results in a dilution of business control and return on investment for one of the parties to the transaction.

However, a business combination may not only foster financial support from a new combined entity, it may also lead to qualitative benefits such as executive and management talent; manufacturing techniques; administrative infrastructure; additional distributing and sourcing channels; research and development expertise; and complementary products.

The objective of the business combination is to raise capital to create a stronger and more profitable combined entity compared with continuing as separate entities. This interaction is known as synergy and is a characteristic that can be found in all successful business combinations. Business combinations are generally accomplished using one of three methods: statutory merger or consolidation, asset acquisition, or joint venture.

Statutory Merger or Consolidation

A statutory merger or consolidation occurs when, pursuant to state authority, one entity is merged into another to create a new third entity, or when the separate existence of the acquired entity is consolidated with the acquirer.

Asset Acquisition

An asset acquisition is the acquisition of the assets, liabilities, and business of a target company by the acquirer.

Joint Venture

A joint venture is formed when a new entity is created with the contribution of assets of a business by two or more separate entities. The entity operates as a separate business, apart from the corporate owners' operations, for the benefit of the owners.

BUSINESS COMBINATIONS—THE PROCESS

To successfully enter into a business combination, a company must ensure that the substantive steps of the proper process are developed creatively and performed diligently. The process involves several phases and generally requires patience, tenacity, and experience. The steps in the business combination process are as follows:

- Self-assessment
- Identification of targets
- Selection of strategy and targets
- Creation of interest
- Negotiation of deal parameters and structures (letter of intent)
- Due diligence
- Finalization of deal terms (definitive agreement)
- Closing of deal
- Implementation, transition, and monitoring

Self-Assessment

The decision to pursue a business combination must be based on an in-depth self-assessment, which should answer three main questions:

- Why do you want to combine your business with another?
- What are your expectations of a combined business?
- What characteristics would a target company possess?

The answering of the questions will facilitate a successful combination, and therefore the process should be performed diligently with extensive research. A discussion of each question follows.

Why do you want to combine your business with another? The most common answer to this question is expansion and growth. However, the underlying problem that restricts expansion and growth is the lack of available capital. A problem all too common in business today is that a business will grow very quickly but cannot finance this growth; that is, as sales increase so does the purchase of inventory. This purchase of inventory needs to be financed and can result in severe financial difficulties. A business combination may be an alternative to raising capital that allows you to reach your objectives.

What are your expectations of a combined business? The expectations will be similar to your reasons for a combination, except they should be more specific. For example, an entity may want growth but this growth should now be identified in specific areas. An example is an entity wishing to increase its sales. The entity should specifically identify how to achieve this growth, such as combination with a competitor or with an entity with wider distribution channels and complementary or more diverse products. The more precise an entity can be regarding its expectations of growth, the easier it will be to identify a target company for combination. A number of precise expectations should be identified and analyzed before moving on to identifying a target company.

What characteristics would a target company possess? The characteristics will be based on prior analyses and expectations of business combinations. Examples of specific characteristics of a target company are as follows:

- *Working Capital Availability.* This can be in the form of a cash-rich business with a high value of current assets but no significant growth expectations. Using the liquid assets of the combined business will facilitate growth of a combined entity.
- *Improved Debt Capacity.* An entity that has a low level of debt, a high uncollateralized asset base, and a strong financial performance may have a substantial borrowing base to benefit the combined entities.
- *Access to Capital Markets.* As with the debt capacity, a stronger balance sheet will assist an entity's access to capital markets.

- *Physical Facilities.* A target company may possess facilities that are more beneficial to a combined entity. Some examples are excessive warehousing space and underutilized office buildings, plants, or equipment. Since such facilities are underutilized, they may be acquired at a very competitive price and prove to be more valuable after the combination is consummated.

Intangible Assets

Examples of intangible assets are licenses, trademarks, and patents. It may be that the acquiring company can more effectively exploit these assets. A description of other intangible assets follows:

- *Technology.* An entity that has a strong customer base but does not have the technology to expand its product line may look to a target company to improve its technology. This is especially pertinent to manufacturing companies.
- *Distribution Channels/Market Access/Market Share.* An entity may have a strong customer base and strong financial position, but this may all relate to a local business. An ideal target would be an entity with an established reputation in another area to allow a geographic expansion of operations. This kind of expansion avoids the risk of investing in unknown markets. Instead, the established expertise of a target company can be used.
- *Talent/People.* A common reason for a business combination is to acquire from a target company its people, who bring their special skills, technology, know-how, management style, reputation, and customer base to a combined entity.

On completion of the self-assessment, a business is in a stronger position to merge, acquire, or jointly venture in order to expand and grow while avoiding the need to raise capital.

The self-assessment should be performed with assistance from outside professionals due to its importance to the whole process of a business combination.

Identification of Target Companies

Using the self-assessment details, the target entity should be identified to match your requirements. Generally, the target entities will be one of the following:

- Investment funds
- Merchant bankers
- Corporate partners
- Technological partners
- Suppliers of products or services
- Customers
- Competitors

Investment funds and merchant bankers—or financial partners—typically provide only cash, investment oversight, and independent management advice. Corporate partners often include asset-rich and growth-poor companies. These companies can contribute physical facilities, people, licenses, distribution channels, cash-flow stability (debt capacity), management, or management systems.

Technological partners often include major domestic or foreign companies that desire access to the company's products or technology. Suppliers of products or services may be interested in protecting product distribution or in vertical integration. Customers of the company may need to protect product supply or their very existence. Competitors can be a source of gross margin improvement, distribution efficiency, plant capacity, or critical mass.

Many commercial databases are available to perform searches for target companies. However, target companies identified through bankers, attorneys, and accountants often provide more viable targets. Another way to identify targets is to engage an intermediary who will pursue suitable candidates through utilization of their extensive networks and knowledge of the field. This can be extremely important if your timing does not allow for the development of a contact network.

However, before engaging any intermediary, satisfy yourself as to his or her knowledge of your field, and experience and success rate in situations such as yours. An intermediary's services should include (1) developing a confidential memorandum explaining the company's history, business, customers, financial situation, and so on; (2) developing a buyer list including strategic and financial buyers; (3) approaching all buyers on a highly confidential basis on behalf of the seller; and (4) managing the sale process to maximize the price, minimize disruption to the selling company, and meet the overall time schedule for combining the businesses.

Another advantage of using a professional intermediary is that the search is the intermediary's principal job and it will be pursued relentlessly. If time is an important factor, you probably should not conduct the search yourself. Operating your company should take precedence, and a company seeking capital for a specific growth opportunity usually cannot afford the luxury of a lengthy search process. A professional intermediary will normally charge as a fee a percentage of the transaction price, which usually runs between 1 and 5 percent and is negotiable.

BUSINESS COMBINATIONS—THE DEAL

The remaining steps in the process are part art and part science. But if earlier steps in the process are focused, planned, and executed, the remainder will be manageable. The structure of the deal will be affected by legal, tax, and financial requirements.

The legal requirements of the deal are very important. First, the agreements should reflect the business deal and protect the interests of participants. Second, state and federal regulations (such as the Hart-Scott Rodino Act) have to be adhered to. Finally, the agreements should be written to reflect the tax and accounting structure of the transaction. If the legal form of the transaction is not in accordance with the desired tax structure, the tax cost of the transaction can be devastating. Assistance and advice from the company's tax consultant is critical to minimize the tax cost of the transactions.

Control of the combined entity will be one of the crucial negotiating issues in the acquisition/combination process. It is unlikely that control in the true sense of the word will vest totally with either merger partner. The business combination must be a win-win result for both merger partners for maximum success of the joint effort.

Due Diligence

Due diligence or preclosing investigatory procedures of a target entity is a fundamental step. Both parties to the transaction will need to gain assurance through their own investigations that representations and reported facts are supported by convincing evidence. Usually due diligence procedures will be performed by professionals and are based on specific instructions from the acquirer and acquiree.

Due diligence procedures will usually include the following:

- Reviewing the accuracy of the target's financial statements
- Reviewing the accounting policies to ensure that they appropriately represent the financial condition of the targets
- Interviewing the target's independent financial and tax consultants and reviewing their work papers, management letters, and other reports
- Analyzing historical data to uncover and explain fluctuations in performance
- Reviewing assets and liabilities to uncover overstated assets and understated or unrecorded liabilities
- Reviewing capital expenditures and future requirements so future needs can be gauged
- Reviewing working-capital requirements as compared with expansion prospects
- Evaluating projections of future results based on historical data gathered during reviews
- Identifying liabilities that are beyond the scope of the balance sheet such as environmental issues, pension plans, litigation, and termination penalties
- Analyzing other operating statistics such as market share, product demand, economic trends, and competition

The aim of the due diligence procedures is to help parties to the transaction learn and observe the business to gain needed comfort to consummate the transaction.

Closing the Deal and Implementation

Closing the deal is really the easiest part of the process. Although the closing may be emotional and hectic, the larger challenge is implementing the combination. This transition period will determine the success of the business combination. Issues of expansion must be identified and an implementation plan devised. Production schedules, employee policies, research methodologies, management style, marketing focus, and many other issues will require careful analysis to maximize the benefit of the capital or capital-in-kind from the partners in the transaction.

The implementation of new structures and policies is essential to the success of the combination, and therefore any changes should be implemented with care and monitored extremely closely.

Divestitures

Divestitures as a source for raising capital, as with business combinations, can be complex and include numerous structures. Taxable, nontaxable, asset, division, and subsidiary divestitures, as well as split-ups and spin-offs, are but a few of the choices. The aim of the divestiture is to make available to the company additional equity capital, debt capacity, or earning capacity. As with planning for the business combination, the divestiture should begin with a thorough self-assessment, transaction positioning, process planning, and execution.

TRANSACTION POSITIONING

Posturing for the divestiture can involve different steps than posturing for the business combination. Accumulating data, preparing operations summaries, analyzing financial performance, and preparing financial forecasts are only part of this procedure. In addition to these ministerial duties, many techniques can be employed to maximize value upon disposition. Limiting capital expenditures and intercompany leasing of fixed assets, transferring administrative functions and personnel, limiting pay increases, and decreasing working capital are but a few of the techniques. However, perhaps the most important aspect of transaction positioning is timing and time. If adequate time is allowed for implementation of successful posturing techniques to create a higher profit history, the value upon divestiture can be significantly improved. Of course, the time for transaction positioning is ultimately dependent upon the early identification of the company's future capital needs.

11

RESEARCH AND DEVELOPMENT

INTRODUCTION

As an entrepreneur, you know firsthand that nothing is more exciting, or potentially more profitable, than an idea that can be developed into a major new product. Exciting is not the only word for it. It can also be costly and enormously risky.

Raising the money for research and development (R&D) often seems to require as much imagination as inventing the product. Promising as the new-product idea is to your expert eye, everybody knows there are unanswered questions that represent risks for investors. Will the product be as good as you expect? Will it fill a genuine market need? Will it outperform the competition? Will the costs of production and distribution allow you a fair profit? Does your staff have the expertise to market this kind of product?

As the executive of your business, with a new-product idea full of promise, you will probably ask yourself these questions:

1. How can I raise the necessary R&D capital and still keep control of my product?
2. How can I protect the rest of my company's operations from the risks inherent in the process of researching and developing this new product that may, or may not, prove successful?
3. Should my company finance and carry out the R&D itself? Or should I give up some of the control and rewards, and reduce the risks, by bringing in outside investors and/or contracting the R&D to an outside organization?

American business has been remarkably imaginative in creating R&D funding arrangements to fit virtually every set of circumstances, probably including yours.

Business Considerations

Research and development arrangements have been used to develop a wide variety of new products, from the mundane to the exotic, from such high-technology fields as biotechnology, medical diagnostics, and computers to the long-established aircraft and small-firearms industries. And, as might be expected, the terms of R&D arrangements vary as widely as the products, reflecting the trade-offs between the parties involved.

Initial Steps

Generally, before a corporation establishes an R&D arrangement, it needs to complete two basic steps:

- Your company should already possess the basic technology needed for developing the product. To be attractive to investors, R&D arrangements, should "accentuate the D and avoid the R" because many investors believe that arrangements to finance basic research are too risky.
- Your company should develop a strategic plan that describes in detail the technical feasibility of the product to be developed; the R&D to be done; the anticipated demand and profitability of the product; the competition the product will likely encounter; the time and costs of completing the R&D work; and the possible tax effects, return on investment, and exit strategies for potential investors.

TYPES OF R&D FUNDING ARRANGEMENTS

The most common R&D funding arrangements are as follows:

- Strategic alliances in which technology and related rights are traded for up-front cash payments, milestone payments, and/or royalties

- Acquisitions, of either 100 percent or lessor amounts of the R&D company, to retain the entrepreneurial environment
- Seed-capital rounds followed by venture capital, mezzanine financing, and then one or more public offerings
- Designer preferred stock (usually as part of the venture capital process)
- Government grants, including the SBIR program
- Spin-offs and carve-outs
- 50-50 joint ventures
- Special-purpose corporations
- Foreign R&D arrangements
- Limited partnerships and R&D partnerships

Most of these financing arrangements are described at length in other chapters of this book. The remainder of this chapter focuses on those aspects of the arrangements unique to deals involving R&D.

Strategic Alliances

Strategic alliances, attractive because they can be structured to suit a wide variety of needs, are one of the most common methods used to raise capital for R&D. Strategic alliances take many forms and occur between a wide variety of partners, but some basic patterns have emerged:

- Alliances between young technology-rich companies needing funds and larger companies attempting to add to their product line or to gain a window on new technologies
- Alliances between companies attempting to complement each other's technologies or product portfolios
- Alliances for the purposes of obtaining manufacturing facilities, outsourcing manufacturing, or utilizing unused manufacturing capability
- Alliances to obtain marketing and/or distribution rights
- Alliances to enhance credibility, since strong strategic alliances have been shown to increase the market value of technology companies

Alliances between Technology-Rich Companies and Larger Corporations. Due to their complementary interests, start-up companies and more established corporations with a need for new products account for a large percentage of technology-related strategic alliances. Young technology-rich companies usually need funds and may get them in the form of up-front cash payments, milestone payments based on the success of research, and/or royalty payments based on product sales. Typically, the young company can negotiate for a greater amount if it accepts a smaller up-front cash payment and larger royalty payments than if it requests a larger amount up front and smaller royalties.

In addition to cash payments in return for technology rights, strategic alliances frequently also include some of the marketing and manufacturing dimensions discussed in sections that follow. A general rule of thumb, and a starting point for negotiations in strategic alliances, is that the technology aspect of a product accounts for 50 percent, the marketing aspect 30 percent, and the manufacturing aspect 20 percent of total profits.

Alliances between Companies to Complement Technologies. When technology companies of a similar size enter into strategic alliances, it is frequently for the purpose of exchanging rights to overlapping intellectual property or to pool resources on technological projects with a similar end product. When these alliances are entered into strictly to resolve intellectual property disputes, they often do not involve anything other than the exchange of rights to conflicting claims; however, they may encompass other dimensions as well.

Alliances for Manufacturing Purposes. Since the manufacture of high-technology products is often complex and the establishment of manufacturing facilities represents a large commitment of time and capital on the part of a start-up high-technology company, strategic alliances are frequently entered into for the purpose of either outsourcing manufacturing or obtaining manufacturing rights for another party. In certain industries, such as foods and pharmaceuticals, the manufacture of goods comes under strict regulatory guidelines, giving small companies another incentive not to undertake the entire project themselves. This may be particularly true when manufacturing will occur in a foreign country.

One critical aspect of the negotiation of manufacturing-related strategic alliances is the question of how much of the total profits from the product's cycle to allocate to the manufacturing process (and reflect in the transfer price of completed goods). As mentioned previously, the manufacturing process should generally account for 20 percent of the total profits generated from the product's sales. When foreign countries are involved, the establishment of manufacturing strategic alliances and the division of profits through transfer prices have significant tax implications and should be discussed with tax advisors in advance.

Alliances for Marketing and Distribution Rights. One of the most common targets of large companies in strategic alliances is the marketing and distribution rights to products developed by smaller technology-rich companies. This often works to the small company's advantage because it can be quite costly to develop its own marketing and distribution infrastructure. When bargaining over the rights to market a product, the technology company often finds it to its advantage to divide the marketing rights into geographical areas and product uses. For example, a drug company might consider the rights to a particular drug to be divided among the geographic areas in which the drug will be distributed, and within those geographic areas divided among the diseases the drug will be used to treat.

This gives the technology company greater flexibility in structuring strategic alliances, for it may find that marketing rights for the same product for different uses and in different geographical areas have markedly different values to different potential partners. Similarly, the larger strategic partners may find they want to pay only for those rights that fit their own strategic focus particularly well. Alliances for marketing and distribution rights are usually embedded in strategic alliances with other dimensions and may include up-front, milestone, and/or royalty payments to the technology company.

Enhanced Credibility through Alliances. In a recent study, Ernst & Young compared the market valuations (as determined by IPO price) of technology companies with strong strategic partners, with the market valuations of similar companies without partners, and found that the companies with partners received markedly higher valuations. Young companies benefit from the credibility associated with entering into an alliance with a strong partner, in terms of both market valuation and attracting additional strategic partners, and in some cases customers.

In today's global economy, strategic alliances are becoming increasingly important in staying abreast of market opportunities and tax optimization. Companies are entering into them at earlier and earlier stages of their existence, and are finding them to be a critical element of their overall business strategies.

Selling or Acquiring Technology

One way for large companies to obtain the technology they need for strategic purposes is simply to purchase entire small technology-based companies that fit into their strategic plans. While on the surface it might appear to be an ideal situation for both parties, there are dangers lurking on both sides.

Probably the largest danger for the acquiring company is the possible loss of many of the key scientific personnel shortly after the deal is completed. This is not an uncommon occurrence, particularly when the scientists are accustomed to, and enjoy, the relative freedom of working for a small enterprise. For this reason, many acquirers attempt to obtain employment contracts from key employees prior to finalizing the deal; still, demoralization of the small company's employees may detract greatly from the original perceived value of the transaction.

From the small company's perspective, the risks of accepting a 100 percent buyout include possibly receiving a lower valuation than might be achieved in a public offering, as well as the risk that the large company will simply take the technology and divest itself of the rest of the small company, including its employees.

Primarily for the purpose of allowing the acquired organization to retain some of its culture and retain the feeling of some control over its autonomy, a new paradigm of acquiring technology companies has emerged recently—the "60 percent paradigm." In this scenario, the acquirer obtains approximately 60 percent of the acquiree initially, allowing the remaining 40 percent to be publicly traded or owned by employees to continue to provide them performance incentives. It is not uncommon for the parent to obtain some type of option for the remaining 40 percent, which will be effective at some future time. The jury is still out on whether the 60 percent paradigm is effective in achieving its goal of allowing the parent to obtain the technology

of the acquiree while the acquiree retains its culture and key employees, but the very emergence of this paradigm underscores the
importance of the need to carefully manage the acquisition of technology-based companies.

The Seed, Venture, Mezzanine, Public-Offering Financing Model

Entire high-technology industries have been built around the power
of venture capitalists to quickly form companies that are able to com-
mercialize late-stage technology in a relatively short time (two to five
years). The founders of these companies are usually technical people
from large corporations or universities who have rights to a particular
piece of technology. They generally begin by raising a "seed round"
of a few thousand to a few hundred thousand dollars, either from
friends or from the venture capital community. Typically, the venture
capitalists fund the next several million dollars of equity which, depending on the industry, may be enough to prove the concept the
founders started with. Often additional rounds of financing are raised
from venture capitalists, mezzanine players, and/or institutions before the company achieves liquidity for its investors through an initial
public offering. Once public, it is relatively easier for the company to
access the public equity and debt markets. For many technology companies that have committed themselves to a venture capitalist's program, it is more a question of when than if the investors will require
an initial public offering.

Since technology companies on a venture capital, initial public offering track grow rapidly (up to $100 million or more in revenue in
five years), the decision to accept each new round of financing provides both challenges and opportunities. If a company is able to attract
investors, it must decide when and how much capital to receive during
each round and what percentage of the company to sell. Generally,
the longer the company waits for new capital during growth periods,
the higher the valuation it will receive; however, if it waits too long
and runs low on funds, it will be in a weak bargaining position and
may have to accept a lower valuation. Critical also to a technology
company on this track is securing the intellectual property rights to
its technology at an early stage (usually prior to formation). Experienced investors will usually not invest in technology companies with
weak or uncertain intellectual property positions.

Designer Preferred Stock

A key aspect of the seed, mezzanine, IPO method of raising money is designer preferred stock. Designer preferred stock has key advantages over both debt and common stock as a source of growth capital. Emerging technology companies usually have not yet achieved profitability or positive cash flow, so obtaining funding through a debt instrument bears risk that is often too high to be viable. Since profitability is low or has not yet been achieved, preferred stock offers added protection over common stock to the investor, as any available assets will first go to satisfy the claims of the preferred holders before those of the common holders. The liquidation preference is normally specified as part of the stock purchase agreement.

Not only can preferred stock offer added protection to the holder, it can contain features that allow for flexibility in many other areas as well. For example, the dividend rate may be specified or left to the discretion of the board of directors. The claims of preferred stockholders to those dividends must be satisfied before any dividends are paid to the common stockholders. In addition, if the preferred stock bears cumulative dividend rights, the dividends in arrears must also be paid first. Dividends in arrears are the amounts that would have been paid to the preferred holders had such dividends been declared on a timely basis.

Another feature that can make preferred stock attractive is its convertibility into common stock. Convertible preferred stockholders will not only enjoy preference over the common as to both dividends and proceeds (should the company liquidate) before conversion, they will also be able to participate in the earnings along with the common stockholders after conversion. Conversion can occur at any number of events. The preferred can be convertible at the option of each individual holder, or all the preferred may convert upon the vote of a specified percentage of the preferred holders, such as two-thirds. Conversion can be automatically triggered by an initial public offering, although usually both the price per share and aggregate proceeds of the offering must exceed certain targets before conversion occurs. Additionally, conversion can be either permitted or required upon the attainment of certain product development, operational, stock performance, or other goals. The conversion rate is normally on a one-for-one basis at the time the preferred is issued and will adjust to maintain that relationship in certain events, such as a split of the common stock or other dilution.

As additional rounds of preferred are sold, the previous investors may be offered (or may demand) the right to purchase additional shares so that their ownership percentage is maintained. This is of particular interest to investors in the event that subsequent offerings are made at per share values less than that paid by those previous investors; if the previous investors do not, or are unable to, participate, their interest will be diluted.

The process whereby the company reacquires the preferred stock for cash is known as redemption. Redemption can be either mandatory, normally at a given date, or at the option of the company. If the mandatory redemption amount is in excess of the carrying value of the preferred stock at issue date, the company will need to increase the carrying value over time to the redemption amount by charging retained earnings. It is important to note that the SEC requires preferred stock whose redemption (or liquidation) is outside the control of the company to be classified outside of the stockholders' equity section of the balance sheet for public companies.

The voting rights of the preferred stock may also be adjusted to fit the needs of the investor. Normally, the preferred stockholder has the right to vote on the same basis as if conversion had occurred.

When companies require recurring capital infusions, as they do when they are in the development stage, the preferred stock is usually issued in series so that the price per share can be adjusted with each subsequent round and so the company does not have more cash than it needs for some reasonable operating period. Each series of preferred stock is senior to the previous issue and may have different features from the prior series; when those features are similar, the details may vary. For example, the liquidation preference will vary (it is normally the original purchase price), the voting rights may be the same, and one issue could have cumulative dividends while the others are non-cumulative. The ability of the company to vary the amount, terms, and timing of the issuance of preferred stock affords it a very powerful tool in its efforts to raise capital.

Government Funding

Many technology companies have gotten started with grants from the Small Business Innovation and Research program (described in Chapter 9), which disburses as much as $500 million a year to technology companies, or with direct grants from agencies like the Department of Defense or National Institute of Health. The primary advantage for small companies of government grants as opposed to other types of financing is that the government does not usually retain any equity in the company. This allows the company to use the government financing to fund its activities until it is large enough to obtain more conventional types of financing (like bank loans or an IPO) at favorable valuations.

The primary disadvantages for small companies of obtaining government financing are the sometimes burdensome reporting requirements of the government and the long time periods and inflexibilities typically associated with the application and approval process for receiving grants. In some high-technology industries, for example, a product cycle may be as short as a few months; in a fast-paced environment like this, the waiting period for government funding is prohibitive. Government programs are also subject to arbitrary termination due to changes in political sentiment or changes in areas of scientific interest for the government, and both the application process and the record keeping required after the funds are received can be burdensome and difficult to understand. Thus, if a high-technology company desires to fund itself through the government, it must structure itself so that its capital needs can be met by this relatively inexpensive but equally unpredictable source.

Spin-Offs and Carve-Outs

A carve-out is the process whereby a company sells shares of its subsidiary to the public in an initial public offering, whereas a spin-off results when the parent distributes the shares to its own shareholders.

Spin-offs and carve-outs are both ways companies can divest themselves of lines of businesses or activities not compatible with their primary corporate objectives. The businesses might have been acquired along with another business that is compatible; the parent company may have changed or redefined its strategic plans; or part of the company may have simply evolved to the point that it now conflicts in some way with the goals the company has set for itself.

With high-technology companies involved with R&D, what can often happen is that some facet of the original technology shows great promise but competes in some way with the other technologies being developed. Alternatively, the technology may require additional capital to be developed to the point of commercial feasibility, and attracting that capital is easier to do if the technology is placed in a stand-alone legal entity. A third possibility is that the new technology may appear to have a much shorter path to market than other technologies because it is simpler, is already fully developed, or may be brought to market without the regulatory burden that is present in the core business. In this case, the parent can use that short-term promise to reward its own investors or, perhaps at the same time, sell that promise and use the proceeds to fund its own, sometimes more protracted, development efforts.

A parent often contributes some capital itself to assist the subsidiary achieve commercialization. Also, it is not unusual for the parent to transfer some of its management to the subsidiary to provide for continuity of operations and to assure that the subsidiary develops in a manner that remains beneficial to the parent. The parent will also typically retain some ownership interest in the subsidiary so that it can reflect the successful results of the subsidiary in its own financial statements. If the subsidiary is profitable, the parent can sell its shares in the market in the case of a carve-out. When a spin-off occurs, the subsidiary must complete an IPO so the shares can be publicly traded. The shares registered in that IPO will often be those originally distributed, those the subsidiary may wish to sell to new investors, or those that were retained by the parent at the time of the original spin-off.

Fifty-Fifty Joint Ventures

A vehicle for funding sales activities and R&D projects when two companies with mutually attractive capabilities are involved is the 50-50 joint venture. The legal structure of the joint venture may be a partnership or a corporation, depending on the various structural and tax needs of the parties. The premise underlying a 50-50 joint venture is that the two parties essentially share the risks, costs, and rewards of the enterprise equally. In a technology setting, one company may contribute technology to the enterprise while the other contributes manufacturing, marketing, or other expertise. Cash may be contributed by either party to make up for the perceived difference in value. Generally, the contributions are accounted for at fair market value, although assigning a value to contributed technology may not be allowable under Generally Accepted Accounting Principles.

Fifty-fifty joint ventures are appealing in their ability to spread risk and meet complementary goals. But at times they fail to live up to expectations because neither party is willing to contribute as much time to a 50-percent-owned project as they are to a 100-percent-owned project. This may be particularly true in a technology setting if one party believes, in hindsight, that its contribution to the joint venture is more valuable than the other party's. Thus, the management and control issues in 50-50 joint ventures are perhaps even more critical to their success than they might be in other forms of partnering.

The R&D Corporation

A corporate variation on the R&D limited partnership theme has been developed by the investment banking community. It is attractive because you obtain the necessary R&D financing, and shareholders are permitted to participate in stock appreciation. The R&D corporation is structured as shown in the following example.

Your company incorporates a new R&D corporation (Newco). It has nominal capitalization, and its officers and directors are appointed by you. Your corporation licenses its technology to Newco, and an R&D development contract that provides that your company will perform research and development for Newco is executed. Newco will pay your company for this work.

Newco also grants your company an option to repurchase Newco's technology or stock for cash, stock, royalties, or some combination. In return for this purchase option, your company will grant to Newco shareholders warrants convertible within a specified time at a specified premium. Newco also grants a manufacturing and marketing option in return for royalty payments to Newco that you will exercise if the research and development efforts are successful.

To fund Newco so that it can pay your company for its R&D, your company will grant to your shareholders a "right" to an investment unit that consists of a warrant (or fraction thereof) for your stock and a warrant (or fraction thereof) for Newco stock. The actual terms, conversion ratio, and price should be determined by negotiation between you and the investment bankers prior to completing the R&D, so that you avoid any misunderstandings with the investors. For example, you may negotiate the exercise price to be $9 in cash and require the exchange of eight rights for each share of Newco and warrant for your stock.

If the Newco offering is not fully subscribed by your existing shareholders, you may sell the units to the public through an underwriting managed by the investment bankers. This transaction will also be facilitated by having your company contribute the required warrants for its stock to Newco and agree that if the public-offering price is less than $9, the original investors receive a rebate on their purchase price so that all investors will pay the same price for the Newco stock.

If structured properly, Newco will be an independent entity that may fund R&D at your company. Although this is similar to the R&D limited partnership, the corporate form of organization poses some significant tax issues. There is the possibility that when you grant your existing shareholders the right to acquire a warrant and Newco share, the IRS will contend that this grant should be treated as a dividend to the extent of your earnings and profits. If your company decides to purchase the technology, there may be an issue of whether and over what period of time the purchase price may be amortized for tax purposes. You may want to consider obtaining an independent appraisal to value and determine a useful life for the purchased technology.

Alternatively, if you acquire Newco's stock, Newco's net operating loss carryovers (if any) would be subject to Section 382 of the tax code, which limits the annual deduction amount. Other rules may also apply, which may limit the source of income that may be offset by the available net operating losses after application of Section 382. The availability of the R&D credit may also be limited (see "Tax Aspects" in this chapter).

From a financial accounting standpoint, your acquisition of Newco will be accounted for as a "purchase." The purchase price is allocated among the various assets based on their relative fair market values. You also need to be concerned about the level of "related-party" investment in Newco—that is, your company, your 5 percent shareholders, your directors, and your officers—because related parties may not own more than 10 percent of Newco and still obtain the beneficial contract accounting treatment (see "Accounting Treatment" in this chapter).

Although the R&D corporation is a viable structure and investment bankers have encouraged its use, its overall complexity and potential tax issues may limit its utility in some situations.

Foreign R&D Arrangements

Over the past few years, companies have begun to explore the possibility of obtaining R&D funding from, and actually conducting research and development in, foreign countries. In addition to the language and cultural impediments to such arrangements, U.S. tax law also hampers this form of R&D funding.

The transactions are typically structured as follows. Your company has the basic technology. A foreign investor has cash. In addition to locating the potential funding, you wish to access the foreign market, engineering talent, local management, and eventually manufacturing and distribution. After you evaluate potential investors and determine the appropriate participant, your company and the investor form a joint venture, organized in the foreign jurisdiction as a corporation.

The following example illustrates a possible capital structure—the price per share and terms of which must be negotiated. You will contribute the basic technology in exchange for 100 percent of the joint venture's common stock or its equivalent. The foreign investor invests $1 million in cash in exchange for 100 percent of the joint venture's preferred stock or its equivalent. In some parts of the world, including most of Asia, business practice and custom require that all participants hold identical interests in the joint venture. Although this is a cultural and not a legal requirement, the foreign investor may not be willing to accept preferred stock, and thus may not participate if the arrangement is structured in this manner. Assuming the investor accepts the preferred stock, you and the joint venture then enter into a contractual R&D cost-sharing agreement whereby you each agree to actually share the R&D costs and any resulting technology developed by the joint venture.

These joint ventures frequently provide for geographic exclusivity with respect to market exploitation. The foreign joint venture often has exclusive rights to its country, and the U.S. joint venture has exclusive rights to the rest of the world. The joint venture should also enter into a royalty-free license agreement with you that permits you access to any enhancements to the basic technology free of charge within geographic areas other than those covered by the joint venture agreement.

The license of the basic technology will be subject to the "super-royalty" provisions of U.S. tax law. This provision permits the IRS to impute royalty income in excess of that agreed upon with the joint venture if it concludes that the original royalty rate does not reflect a reasonable return on the technology that has been made available to the joint venture. This imputed royalty generally will not be deductible by the joint venture in computing its taxable income, and any cash royalty paid will generally be subject to foreign withholding taxes. Finally, the U.S. R&D tax credit will not be available for research and development activities that occur outside the United States.

The foreign investor's preferred stock should include terms that require dividend payment in an amount that approximates the cash royalty rate so that the actual cash return to both parties is effectively equalized. Alternatively, the foreign investor may require you to receive an amount equal only to the U.S. tax liability on the royalty income so that no dilution occurs.

The foreign investor may also wish to charge the joint venture for services actually rendered, or for other tax-deductible items, if the payment of preferred dividends is not deductible in computing the joint venture's taxable income. The terms of the preferred stock, such as liquidation, conversion ratio, and redemption preferences, should also support the valuation ratio (i.e., 10 : 1) when compared to the common stock value. (The 10 : 1 ratio referred to is a general rule of thumb that does not have technical support under IRS, SEC, or judicial pronouncements. The actual ratio should reflect the fair market value of the contributed technology, which may be more or less than 10 : 1.)

You should consult your accountant and attorney when negotiating and structuring these arrangements because they are obviously very complex. You should also retain a foreign attorney, accountant, or representative in these matters. Expenditures that would qualify as research and development in the United States may not be construed as such in the foreign jurisdiction, and such expenditures of the joint venture may not qualify for either tax or financing incentives in the foreign jurisdiction.

THE LIMITED PARTNERSHIP

Research and development arrangements have been historically organized as limited partnerships, which used to offer numerous tax and business advantages over other forms of organization. Limited partnerships are also commonly used for business activities other than R&D where the limited liability provisions are attractive to certain investors—the concepts discussed here apply equally to limited partnerships organized for these other activities.

Since the Tax Reform Act of 1986, tax benefits available to individual investors from this structure have been significantly diminished. Recent adverse court decisions have also diminished the attractiveness of this form of investment vehicle to individual investors. (These tax issues are discussed in the "Tax Aspects" section of this chapter.) Because of the diminished tax benefits relating to R&D partnership arrangements, they are now formed and structured on a basis more closely related to the economics of the project.

Assuming the investors are able to use the tax benefits that accrue from the limited partnership form of organization, a typical structure of an R&D limited partnership is as follows. The investors are limited partners, while your corporation, a subsidiary, or another affiliate is frequently the general partner. Exhibit 11–1 displays a typical R&D limited partnership structure.

Limited partners typically consist of a group of investors who are seeking an attractive investment, which may or may not include tax benefits. Limited partners usually look for a significant after-tax annual rate of return—40 to 50 percent—from the project, commensurate

EXHIBIT 11-1.   A Typical R&D Limited Partnership Structure

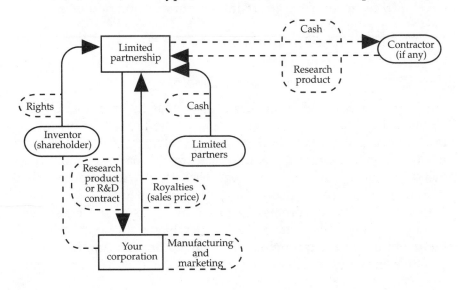

with the high risks inherent in this type of investment. In some cases, especially for start-up companies, the limited partners may be company affiliates. As discussed in the "Accounting Treatment" section of this chapter, if affiliates own a significant portion of the limited partnership, your company may well have to account for the R&D arrangement as a borrowing.

To permit the investors to achieve the desired rate of return, recent limited partnerships have been structured as follows. In return for their equity investment, the investors receive a limited partnership interest. Additionally, the investors issue and exchange an option that permits the general partner corporation to acquire their limited partnership interests in return for a warrant to purchase stock in the general partner corporation. The option to purchase the limited partnership interests may be exercised after a period during which the partnership exploits the technology that has been developed. The option price is usually defined as cash royalties for a certain term, or general-partner stock.

The limited partnership enters into a cross-license agreement with the general partner that permits it to use the general partner's basic technology necessary for its R&D. The limited partnership also enters into a development agreement with the general partner that provides for the general partner performing R&D for the limited partnership. If the general partner's efforts are successful, the limited partnership and general partner agree to form a joint venture that will exploit the developed technology for a certain minimum period of time as specified in the agreement.

An explanation of the specific elements of this structure follows:

The Basic Technology

Your corporation normally makes available, as its investment in the R&D partnership, the basic technology for the product or process to be developed. When you license the technology to the limited partnership, you will want to retain access to the basic technology to avoid having to buy the technology back for use in products other than those being developed through the partnership.

One way for your corporation to retain access to the basic technology is to give the partnership a nonexclusive royalty-free license limited to use of the technology in the R&D project. Another way is to enter into a cross-licensing agreement with the partnership whereby you make the technology available to the partnership, royalty-free, for use in an R&D project in return for a royalty-free license from the partnership enabling you to use the technology in other applications. A third way is to license the technology to the partnership for use in developing a specific product. Under this method, your corporation would retain all other rights to the technology.

The R&D Contract

Your corporation ordinarily performs the R&D work for the partnership under contract. One advantage of this is that the development work is usually being performed by the people who developed the basic technology and who are, therefore, most familiar with the project. Another advantage is that it enables your corporation to manage and control the project. Both of these advantages should enhance the likelihood of success. Frequently, the partnership's payments to your corporation for performing the development work are limited to reimbursement costs you have incurred. In other cases, the partnership may compensate your corporation on either a fixed-fee basis or a cost-plus basis.

An R&D partnership usually works best if its R&D project is clearly separated from your corporation's other R&D projects and if the R&D contract clearly defines exactly what is to be delivered at the conclusion of the contract work if it is successful. This helps minimize the likelihood of disputes between the partnership and your corporation.

Development work is performed on a best-efforts basis, and the contract does not guarantee the project's success. Frequently, an R&D arrangement does not specify the course of action to be taken if the partnership's funds prove to be insufficient to complete the project. In some cases, the limited partners may be obligated, within limits, to invest additional funds to complete the project. In other cases, your corporation may or may not be obligated to complete the project. If you are not obligated, but wish to continue the project, you will have to raise the necessary funds or use funds on hand. Also, many R&D arrangements have been silent about the manner in which any royalties will be divided if additional funds have to be raised to complete the R&D project. One method of handling this is to provide that subsequent royalty payments will be adjusted pro rata to reflect the additional investments.

After the R&D Project is Completed

The limited partnership ordinarily has the rights to the basic technology (under the nonexclusive royalty-free license agreement or the cross-license agreement) and to the results of the R&D project when it is completed (see "Legal Aspects" section). If the project is not successful, the partnership will usually disband because it is not likely to be able to sell, or otherwise benefit from, the R&D work. If the project is successful, you will want to enter into a joint venture with the partnership to exploit the product. After a reasonable period of joint venture operations, you will acquire the limited partnership and its technology.

Methods of Compensating Limited Partners

If the R&D project is successful, the partnership may be compensated in several ways. During the period of joint venture operations, the limited partnership will participate in the joint venture's profit or losses and cash distributions based on an agreed-upon percentage. Upon conclusion of the joint venture, you will have the opportunity to acquire the limited partnership or its products.

Your payment for the partnership or its products may consist of a lump-sum cash payment, stock in your corporation, royalties, or a combination of these. Regardless of the form of payment negotiated, you must make sure that it will provide the desired rate of return to the investors as well as be affordable by the company. If you conclude not to exercise your option to acquire either the partnership or its products, the partnership will be entitled to continue marketing and manufacturing the products, to license any or all of its rights, or to sell the technology to a third party.

The structure of the partnership's compensation will be influenced by several factors. The first is the nature and character of the income to be reported by the investors. During the operation of the joint venture, the income allocated to the partnership should be taxable as ordinary income and, if the investors are individuals, trusts, estates, partnerships, or closely held corporations, reported as passive income on the investor's tax returns. The gain from the sale of the partnership or all rights, title, and interest in its products may be taxable as a capital gain to the investors.

The second factor relates to the timing of product sales that generate the income, and the estimated period of market domination (i.e., before saturation occurs or significant competition enters the market). If the market window is relatively short, you will be required to pay a large portion of the total compensation during the early years.

Some R&D arrangements contain a provision that the limited partners' compensation will be based not only on the product's success, but also on the success of any competing products that may be developed by your corporation at about the same time. An R&D arrangement may contain such a compensation provision when your corporation desires to continue performing R&D on other products that may serve purposes similar to those served by the product being developed under the partnership arrangement. Such a compensation provision protects the limited partners in case your competing products displace the partnership's product in the marketplace. If such displacement were to occur and the limited partners were not compensated, they would find that the company whose R&D they were helping to fund was competing with them. The possibility of such an occurrence might make an R&D arrangement too risky to attract investors.

In any case, all partnership compensation provisions should contain objective measures of the following:

1. Whether the products developed under the R&D arrangement are successful

2. The purposes to be served by the products to be developed under the R&D arrangement and any competing products

3. The methods of determining the compensation to the limited partners

Without these objective measures, your corporation likely could not account for the R&D arrangement as a contract for the performance of R&D. (See "Accounting Treatment" section.) Contract accounting cannot be used unless the limited partners do bear the risks of loss if the products developed under the R&D arrangement are unsuccessful. They would probably not bear this risk if they were assured of payments on competing products.

Trade-Offs

Many of the specific features of an R&D arrangement result from trade-offs between the potential risks and rewards to both the investors and your corporation. For example, the greater the likelihood that a marketable product will be developed, the lower the potential returns need be. Similarly, if the R&D arrangement can be structured so as to provide tax benefits, the gross returns to the investors can be less than if the arrangement were not tax-advantaged investment.

Some investors try to reduce the risk of total failure by investment in an R&D arrangement that involves more than one R&D project. In return, they are willing to accept potentially lower rewards. In addition, a proposed R&D arrangement involving a corporation with a history of R&D successes is more likely to attract investors while offering potentially lower rewards than would an equivalent arrangement involving an unproved corporation.

Additional Types Of Partnership Arrangements

Research and development arrangements may take other forms to better meet the needs and objectives of the parties. One form involves R&D limited partnerships that are structured differently from those described. These are "equity" limited partnerships and may be particularly suitable for start-up corporations that desire to maximize the amount of funds they can raise by obtaining funds from different groups of investors whose investment objectives differ significantly.

Equity Limited Partnership R&D Arrangements

A start-up corporation with some promising ideas and/or technology is likely to need funds both for R&D and for working capital, fixed assets, manufacturing start-up, market research, advertising, and so forth. An R&D arrangement that has to spend significant amounts of funds for non-R&D purposes may not be particularly attractive to potential investors, because limited partners may be entitled to a tax deduction only for that portion of their investment spent on R&D. In addition, the structures of the R&D limited partnerships previously discussed may not be attractive to venture capitalists, who may not be particularly interested in the tax advantage but may desire a significant long-term piece of the action in the new business.

Operating Procedures. In situations like this, an R&D equity partnership may be attractive. This type of arrangement operates as follows (there can be many variations to fit particular circumstances):

- A start-up corporation is formed. The corporation issues convertible preferred stock to the venture capital investors and common stock to the founders/key employees.
- An R&D limited partnership is formed. The corporation transfers cash and the rights to use its basic technology to the partnership, and thus the corporation becomes the general partner. The corporation/general partner usually has more than a 50 percent interest in the capital and profits of the limited partnership, unlike those limited partnerships described previously, in which the percentage of interest is normally very small. The limited partners-investors interested in investing cash in an R&D arrangement contribute the remaining capital and receive the remaining profit interest.
- The partnership agreement specifies that virtually all the partnership's losses resulting from the initial R&D efforts will be allocated to the limited partners until the losses are approximately equal to the limited partners' capital contributions and the bases of their investments in the limited partnership have been reduced to nominal amounts. Thereafter, virtually all the losses will be allocated to the general partner (the corporation).
- The limited partnership is incorporated in a tax-free transaction if the R&D projects are successful but before the partnership becomes profitable. The limited partners receive a series of convertible preferred stock (with a very low basis) in this new company.

  Their interest in this newly incorporated company equals their former interest in the limited partnership. As the general partner, you receive another series of preferred stock in the newly incorporated company (which is distributed to your original start-up corporation's venture capitalists) and some common stock (which is distributed to your original start-up corporation's common stockholders, such as founders and key employees).

Investor and Corporate Advantages. This type of R&D arrangement offers to investors and to start-up corporations certain advantages over both other types of R&D arrangements and over a traditional new corporation, such as the following:

- More funds may be obtained because two different groups of investors with different investment objectives can be tapped.

- The cost of funds is reduced because of the initial tax write-offs that may be available to the limited partners.
- The founders/key employees may suffer less dilution of their holdings because their dilution is predicated upon the success of the R&D efforts and "roll-up" of the partnership into the new corporation.
- The venture capitalists' financing is supplemented by the limited partners' investment, thereby encouraging venture capital involvement.
- The venture capitalists may obtain a greater equity interest in the corporation per dollar of investment.
- The venture capitalists can be helpful to the founders/key employees in managing the company, since the latter may lack managerial expertise and experience.
- Your newly incorporated company may not have to buy out the limited partnership if the R&D project is successful, since all the parties to the R&D arrangement will become shareholders.
- The limited partners may have fewer difficulties in obtaining capital-gains tax treatment, since their income is likely to arise from selling their low-basis shares in the newly incorporated company rather than from operating income or from selling their rights to the results of the limited partnership's R&D activities.

The R&D equity partnership has some significant disadvantages in that (1) it involves numerous legal complexities, (2) management control issues can be difficult to resolve, (3) the limited partners can block the tax-free incorporation, and (4) the IRS is likely to scrutinize these R&D arrangements quite closely.

Pooled R&D Arrangements

Another variation of the R&D limited partnership involves two or more companies seeking funds for their own R&D projects through a single limited partnership. This multicompany pool offers investors the opportunity to invest in the development of a diversified group of products and may thus enable them to reduce the risk of total failure, even more so than if they had invested in a single-company R&D arrangement involving more than one R&D project.

These pooled arrangements are complex and usually involve unrelated companies. As a result, an investment banker ordinarily is required to bring the parties together and to market the partnership interests. This feature of pooled R&D arrangements often provides another advantage to investors: the presence of sophisticated management to represent them in evaluating and monitoring the R&D activities.

ACCOUNTING TREATMENT

Determining the accounting treatment for R&D arrangements generally depends on which of the parties has an investment at risk if the project should fail. Structuring R&D arrangements when the investors stand the risk of loss and yet giving the investors satisfactory returns for that risk is sometimes difficult.

In 1982, the Financial Accounting Standards Board (the accounting rule-making authority in the United States) issued Financial Accounting Standard No. 68, "Research and Development Arrangements" (FAS 68), which reiterated the historic premise related to "risk of loss" with much elaboration on how to determine the real substance of an arrangement. Under FAS 68, there are two key questions illustrated here as they relate to an R&D limited partnership: (1) Are the limited partners looking to the success of the R&D for their investment returns? and (2) To what extent is the corporate general partner obligated to repay other parties?

Determining the answers to these two questions is frequently not easy—FAS 68 elaborates on the many facets to be studied in making the determination. In some cases, part of the arrangement is accounted for as a loan and part as a contract for performance of R&D.

While a detailed explanation of proper accounting treatment is beyond the scope of this book, there are two matters that deserve attention.

First, when the investors in the R&D arrangement include parties related to your corporation, the likelihood of the arrangement being accounted for as a loan increases substantially. There are exceptions, but they must be carefully structured and usually prohibit material investment by any related parties.

Second, FAS 68 prescribes the following disclosure requirements for R&D arrangements accounted for as R&D contracts:

- The terms of significant agreements under the arrangements (including royalty arrangements, purchase provisions, license agree-

ments, and commitments to provide additional funding) as of the
date of each balance sheet presented.

• The amount of compensation earned and costs incurred under
  such contracts for each period for which an income statement is
  presented.

Elsewhere in your reports to shareholders, you may wish to present
detailed analyses of all your major R&D projects by describing them
and setting forth their progress and outlook. Such analyses should
differentiate between R&D financed by your corporation and R&D
performed under contract for others.

Under FAS 68, some transactions one accounted for as financings;
that is, the cash received by the corporation is recorded as a loan or
as additional equity, and the R&D costs are expensed by the corporation as incurred. Other transactions are treated as sales of R&D
under contract. The treatment under FAS 68 depends upon the specific
structure, facts, and circumstances and the true substance of the arrangement.

Given a choice, your corporation is likely to prefer the latter accounting method for the following reasons:

• It keeps the R&D expense out of current net income (especially
  for a young company, this could mean the difference between a
  loss and a profit).
• It keeps the financing off the balance sheet (thereby presenting
  a better debt-to-equity ratio).

Net income and debt-to-equity ratios are traditionally important
indicators in lenders' and investors' analyses of a company's financial
health. Thus, if two corporations account for similar transactions differently, the accounting may make a difference in the companies'
abilities to borrow or obtain equity financing, no matter how com-
prehensively the transactions are disclosed. Further, if two companies
account for very different transactions as if they were the same, one
of the companies may be gaining an advantage in the capital and
debt markets.

Accounting for the roll-up of the R&D arrangements at the conclusion of the research and development activities may also present
some technical accounting issues. The SEC and FASB require that
purchase accounting concepts be applied to the acquisition of the

entity, and its subsequent interest in or exclusive rights to the entire results of the research and development. Application of purchase accounting concepts to this transaction will result in recording an intangible asset (technology) whose value is equal to the fair market value of the consideration exchanged (usually stock) or fair market value of the assets received, whichever value is more clearly determinable.

The practical difficulty with this treatment is that you are required to value the technology, stock, or perhaps both in order to properly record this asset. This asset will be characterized as an intangible asset on your financial statements and must be amortized over its estimated useful life. Because the estimated useful life is not easily established given the inherent uncertainty regarding market acceptance, technical obsolescence, and competitors' products, your auditors will argue for a rapid amortization period (three to five years). Further, to the extent the acquired technology represents "in-process research and development" with no alternative future use, you will be required to immediately write off the value of the acquired technology.

This amortization expense will reduce financial-statement income and in some cases may generate a net loss from operations. For tax purposes, this amortization expense will not be deductible unless the roll-up was taxable to the investors. Taxable roll-ups are generally avoided because the income generated from a taxable disposition of the technology eliminates any benefit from the prior years' pass-through losses. Consequently, purchase accounting treatment may result in an expense for financial-statement purposes that is not deductible for tax purposes and reduces operating income at just the time you are attempting to demonstrate a positive trend in earnings.

LEGAL ASPECTS

Structuring, financing, and implementing R&D arrangements involve a careful analysis of myriad legal ramifications in addition to business, tax, and accounting considerations, such as the following:

Federal Securities Law

Limited partnership interests, if offered for sale, are considered to be securities under the Securities Act of 1933, and unless eligible for a statutory exemption must be registered with the SEC. For a more comprehensive discussion of public and exempt securities offerings, see Chapter 2, "The Going Public Decision," and Chapter 3, "Private Placements," respectively.

Blue Sky Laws

To protect investors, all 50 states have enacted some type of securities legislation, commonly referred to as blue sky laws. Generally, securities that fall under the federal securities laws will also be subject to blue sky laws. There are some exemptions from registration under the laws. The categories of exempt transactions are similar to those provided under federal law, but keep in mind these rules vary from state to state. Most state laws provide an exemption for an offering where the total number of offerees is less than a specified number. Additionally, most states provide an exemption for isolated transactions, depending on (1) the type of offer, (2) the number of units offered, (3) the manner of the offering, and (4) the relationship of the seller to the offerees. Unless the offering of the securities fits within a blue sky law exemption, state registration of securities will be required.

Prospectus and Private Placement Memorandum

Whether the offering is public or private, the antifraud provisions of the federal securities laws are applicable. To avoid liability you must achieve full disclosure through the proper documents. A well-prepared and complete prospectus or placement memorandum will also indicate to potential investors that considerable care and expertise were exercised in the formulation of the R&D arrangement. The prospectus or placement memorandum should answer the questions potential investors are likely to have, such as the following:

- What is the potential market for the products to be developed?
- How quickly can the new products be brought to market? Is government approval required? Are the products patentable? How vulnerable are they to rapid obsolescence?
- Is your corporation capable of manufacturing the new products in commercial quantities? Does it have the necessary facilities?
- What technological advances must be made to develop the products?

- Has an independent feasibility study been performed?
- How successful has the researcher been with similar products in the past?
- How successful have the corporation's prior R&D arrangements been?
- Will the corporation's fees for performing the R&D include an element of profit?
- What happens if the money runs out before the project is finished?
- What are the major risks?
- Is the projected rate of return reasonable in relation to the risks?
- What will the rate of return be if the R&D project takes twice as long to complete as planned?
- What will the rate of return be if sales of the new products are only half of those anticipated?
- What happens if your organization decides not to manufacture and market the new products after they have been developed?
- What happens if the project fails?
- What will the tax consequences be if your organization decides to invest in the arrangement?

In order to answer most of these questions, the prospectus or placement memorandum will need to be fairly detailed. The most important sections to the potential investor normally include the following:

- The summary of the limited partnership or R&D entity.
- The significant risk factors.
- Information about management experience; track record; financial participation in the project, if any; and proposed project responsibilities.
- Information about your corporation, including financial and other information about its business and its track record in developing other, often related, products.
- The description of the R&D activities to be performed, the products to be developed, and time frame within which this will be accomplished.
- The use of the proceeds to be raised. (In addition to funding the R&D, funds will be required for the underwriters, commissions,

organizational expenses, and working capital.) A potential investor should reasonably expect at least 85 percent of the proceeds to be allocated to the R&D.

- The anticipated market for the product to be developed, the marketing methods to be used, and the anticipated competition.
- If the R&D arrangement is in the form of a limited partnership, the percentage of the partnership's profits and losses to be allocated to the limited partners.
- The contract between the limited partnership and your corporation, setting forth the potential payments if a marketable product is developed.
- The potential cash flows and taxable income to the limited partners if the project is successful.
- The limited partnership agreement itself.
- The tax opinion that sets forth the probable tax consequences to the limited partnership and to the limited partners.

Proprietary Rights

In putting together the R&D arrangement, there are legal documents that need to be drafted in order to protect the proprietary rights of the respective parties. One of the most important rights to be protected is the right to the contracted—for technology.

In the case of an R&D limited partnership, all the proprietary rights to the developed technology, including any patents, patent applications, trademarks, and copyrights, generally rest in the partnership. Furthermore, the contracting party and the partnership need to agree on the party responsible for making any requisite patent filings. Usually the procedure is either to have the developer obtain a patent in the partnership's name or to have the partnership assume primary responsibility for filing with any necessary assistance from the developer.

The rights to the resultant technology should also be clearly delineated. It is common practice for an R&D agreement to provide that the products which result from the R&D work are considered the purchase of technology from the partnership. These products include inventories, improvements, designs, patents, technologies, and know-how, as well as any subsequent invention, discovery, or improvement made by your corporation (purchaser of the results) with respect to the resulting products. This provision prevents the purchaser corporation from using the resulting technology in direct competition with the partnership at no cost. The proprietary rights of parties in an R&D arrangement are affected by numerous considerations, not the least of which is the marketplace. Suffice it to say that care must be taken to address all the issues when structuring the arrangement.

TAX ASPECTS

The potential tax benefits or detriments of R&D arrangements are key factors to potential investors and corporations considering entering into such arrangements. The enactment of the Tax Reform Act of 1986 and subsequent tax legislation and judicial decisions have significantly diminshed potential tax benefits available to individual investors from the R&D partnership or S corporation.

Most tax-advantaged investments for individuals have been organized as either limited partnerships or S corporations because, unlike C corporations, these entities are not generally taxable. Income, deductions, and credits flow through to the individual investors, who include these items in their own personal returns.

For the limited partners to obtain the tax benefits potentially available as a result of the partnership's ownership of the technology developed under the R&D agreement, the form of the various transactions and agreements that constitute the overall transaction must be respected by the courts and IRS.

There are several substantive issues regarding this requirement that turn on the specific facts and circumstances of the transaction. The authorities may assert that the form of the partnership's transactions should be disregarded on the basis that the partnership is only providing financing, services, or some combination to the general partner. They may also assert that the partnership is really purchasing a profit interest in the technology rather than actually developing it through the R&D arrangement. The authorities could also assert that the activities of the partnership should be attributed to the general partner rather than the limited partners.

Finally, in order for the R&D expenditures to be available as a deduction to the limited partners, it is necessary that they be incurred "in connection with" the partnership's trade or business, and that there be a reasonable possibility that the partnership will actually engage or participate in a trade or business related to the developed product or technology.

The taxation of R&D arrangements is a complex subject. This section describes the most important concerns that individual investors and corporations should consider before undertaking an R&D arrangement. Further, this section does not consider the effects of state and local laws, which may be quite different from the federal income tax law and which may differ substantially from one state to another.

Investor Tax Goals—How to Structure an R&D Arrangement

Potential limited partners will want to address the following tax issues when considering an investment in an R&D arrangement.

1. *Will the investors be subject to the passive-activity loss rules?* In 1986, Congress enacted Section 469 of the Internal Revenue Code, which severely curtailed the tax benefits of R&D limited partnership arrangements for individual investors and therefore their use as funding vehicles. This section provides that the deductibility losses from trades, businesses, or investments will be limited if the individual investor is not a "material participant" in the activity. Limited partners, by definition, are not material participants because their involvement in the activity cannot be "regular, substantial and continuous" without risking their limited liability status.

    The partnership losses allocated to the limited partners will generally be available only to reduce "passive-activity income"—not salaries, interest, dividends, royalties, and so forth. To the extent that the limited partner does not have enough passive-activity income to absorb the losses, the excess losses will be suspended and carried over until the partner has passive activity in a later year or disposes of the interest in the partnership in a taxable transaction. Consequently, individuals will be interested only in an R&D arrangement if the "economics"— the probability of success and potential return—meet their investment requirements or they have sufficient passive-activity income to absorb the losses.

    Assuming that the investor will not be adversely affected by Section 469, there are other tax issues that may affect the current deductibility of the partnership losses.

2. *Will the partnership generate deductions (and credits) for the investor and will the partner's investment be recovered through ordinary deductions, or will some of the investment result in capital expenditures that are not deductible currently?* Generally, a partnership's expenditures are not deductible until the partnership begins "carrying on" a trade or business. However, there is an important exception to this general carrying-on rule for R&D expenditures, which may enable the limited partners to deduct these expenditures even if the partnership is not carrying on a trade or business at the time the expenses are incurred. Research and development expenditures may be deductible as long as they are incurred "in connection with" a trade or business, a less strenuous test than "carrying on" a trade or business. (See question seven, "Will the research and development expenditures be deductible?")

Other expenditures may need to be capitalized. Even if the partnership has deductible expenses, the limited partners will not be entitled to currently deduct the expenses if the expenses exceed their basis in the partnership, if the partners are not "at risk," or if they do not have passive-activity income that exceeds these deductions and all other passive-activity losses. (See question six, "Will the partner's deductions be limited?")

If the partnership is carrying on a trade or business, which is not the usual case in an R&D arrangement, the limited partners may also be able to claim an R&D tax credit limited in amount to the tax liability on income derived from the partnership. This credit equals 20 percent of a taxpayer's qualifying R&D expenditures in excess of a base-period amount. Qualifying expenditures include 100 percent of the cost of certain research expenses undertaken directly by the taxpayer and 65 percent of that undertaken by others on his or her behalf. A taxpayer who incurs R&D expenditures while performing R&D on behalf of others, such as under an R&D contract in an R&D arrangement, cannot include those expenditures when computing its credit. Note that the credit was extended with recent legislation to include amounts paid or incurred on or before June 30, 1995. However, current legislative proposals would permanently reinstate the credit retroactively to July 1, 1992.

In legislation enacted in 1989, taxpayers can claim the R&D credit on expenses undertaken directly by them if, at the time the expenses are incurred, the principal purpose of the taxpayer in making such expenditures is to use the results of the research in the active conduct of a future trade or business. Although the taxpayer may deduct the expenditures, provided they are incurred in connection with a trade or business, the credit is generally available only if the carrying-on test is satisfied.

One reason Congress imposed the stricter "carrying-on" test in order to qualify for the R&D credit was to bar the credit from R&D tax-shelter arrangements. However, the partners in an R&D tax-shelter arrangement may be entitled to claim the credit if the arrangement uses the product of the research in producing or providing a product or service (for example, as a credit against income generated by the joint venture that exploits the product or technology). Even when the credit can be claimed, it can be used only to offset tax attributable to the activity or business that generated the credit. In other words, the investor partner in an R&D arrangement cannot use the credit to offset taxes on income not related to the R&D project. Further, in situations where a taxpayer is eligible to both deduct an R&D expenditure and claim an R&D credit on such expenditure, the taxpayer must reduce the deduction by an amount equal to the credit unless an election to claim a reduced credit is made.

The only exception to the carrying-on test arises in the case of a research joint venture. In this case, the venturers may be able to claim the credit for the venture's R&D expenditures, even if the venture itself is not carrying on a trade or business, provided the venturers (such as two established corporations) are carrying on a trade or business to which the research applies and are entitled to the results of the research.

Obviously, the rules related to the deductibility of R&D expenditures and the tax credit are quite complex, and you will need professional assistance to enable you to take advantage of them.

3. *Will the partnership generate taxable income and, if so, will the income be ordinary income or capital-gain income?* The answer to this question depends largely on the partnership's role in developing the new products and its role after they have been developed, and on each individual partner's actions. For example:

- If the partnership has only a royalty interest in the new products, through a licensing or similar agreement, the royalties will be taxed as ordinary income.

- If the partnership manufactures and sells the new products or services, it will have sales and cost of sales that are taxed as ordinary income.

- If the partnership develops a patent that it uses in its business, the capitalized costs, if any, of the patent may be amortized over its useful life.*

- If the partnership sells the patent or all of its rights to the technology for which a patent has been applied, any gain on the sale may qualify for the capital-gain treatment (although some or all of any depreciation deductions taken previously would be recaptured as ordinary income).*

- If a partner sells his or her partnership interest, the gain or loss on the sale would generally be a capital gain or loss, except that the partner would have to recapture as ordinary income some or all of his or her share of any depreciation deductions.

---

* Section 1235 of the Internal Revenue Code provides long-term capital-gain treatment for the gain on certain dispositions of certain patents, regardless of the seller's actual holding period, and regardless of whether the patent qualified for capital-gain treatment in the seller's hands under other Code sections.

Code Section 1235 treatment is available only for sales by a holder of the patent to an unrelated buyer. A "holder" is defined as an individual who created the patent or who purchased the patent from its creator before the patent was usable. Treasury regulations make it clear that a partnership cannot qualify as a holder, but that the individual partners can qualify.

If Section 1235 treatment is unavailable, the partnership may wish to assert that the patent is a capital asset or is an asset used in a trade or business. To receive long-term capital-gain treatment in these cases, the patent must have been property held by the partnership—other than as an inventory item—for more than 12 months, or the patent must have been depreciable property held in the partnership's trade or business for more than 12 months and in either case must have been disposed of in a sale or exchange. If the partnership has held and depreciated the patent, then upon its sale (or upon a partner's sale of his or her interest in the partnership), the depreciation deductions will be recaptured as ordinary income.

Case law holds that in some circumstances Section 1235 is the only section under which capital-gain treatment is available for the sale of a patent. Therefore, it is possible that if Section 1235 is unavailable, a partnership's sale of a patent will not be treated as a capital gain.

4. *When will the limited partner's investment be deductible?* The Tax
   Reform Act of 1984 significantly changed the requirements for
   determining the proper timing of certain deductions by both
   cash and accrual-basis taxpayers. The economic-performance
   standard generally provides that otherwise deductible expenses
   can be claimed only when the services to which they relate are
   performed or, in the case of property, when the property is
   delivered.

   The timing of deductions may also be affected by the related-
   party provisions of the Internal Revenue Code, which require
   the matching of deductions claimed by the payor with the income recognized by the payee. Among the related parties subject to these rules are a partnership and any of its partners. As
   previously discussed, R&D limited partnerships are often structured with a contracting corporation to perform R&D and serve
   as general partner, so the related-party rules may be applicable.

   Although the economic-performance requirements and related-party rules will generally lengthen the period over which
   a limited partner's investment will be recovered, these provisions do not adversely affect the ability to claim deductions for
   R&D activities. Of course, any portion of the limited partner's
   investment that is not spent on R&D or other deductible or
   amortizable items will be recovered at the time the partner sells
   or otherwise disposes of his partnership interest.

5. *Will the investment entity qualify as a partnership?* For the R&D
   arrangement to achieve the benefits of being a limited partnership (i.e., the items of partnership income and loss flow
   directly to the partners and are included on their income tax
   returns), it must qualify as a partnership for tax purposes. To
   do so, the entity must lack at least two of the following corporate characteristics:

   • Indefinite life
   • Free transferability of ownership interests
   • Centralized management
   • Limited liability

   If the entity has more than two of these characteristics, it
   will be taxed as if it were a corporation rather than as a partnership. If that happens, the entity will usually be subject to

tax and the taxable income and losses will not be passed through to the shareholders (investors). As a result, the investors will not receive any tax deductions when the R&D expenses are incurred and they will be entitled only to take a deduction if they terminate their interest in the R&D arrangement at a loss. Therefore, from the investor's standpoint, it is essential that the arrangement be recognized as a partnership for federal income taxes, rather than as an association taxable as a corporation.

If the arrangement qualifies as a partnership, the IRS will honor the partnership's method of allocating profits and losses to the general and limited partners provided the method has "substantial economic effect" (i.e., the tax and economic effects are consistent).

6. *Will the partner's deductions be limited?* Even though an entity qualifies as a partnership, there are limits on the tax benefits it can pass through to its partners. In general, a partner's deductions from a partnership may not exceed their basis in the partnership. In addition, individuals and closely held corporations that are partners in an R&D limited partnership must be "at risk" and cannot deduct more than the amount they have at risk. A partner's basis in a partnership (1) includes their contributions of money and other property to the partnership, (2) is increased by their share of the partnership's income, (3) is decreased by their share of the partnership's losses, and (4) is decreased by the distributions the partner receives from the partnership. A general partner's basis in the partnership also includes their share of the partnership's "recourse liabilities" (liabilities to which the partner would be subject in the event of a partnership default). All partners (including limited partners) may generally include their share of the partnership's nonrecourse liabilities as part of their basis.

However, if the at-risk rules are applicable to the partner, the partner must be at risk in order to deduct their share of the partnership's R&D expenses, even if the partner has basis in an R&D limited partnership. Furthermore, the partner may not deduct more than the amount he or she has at risk in the R&D partnership. The meaning of "at risk" for tax purposes is similar to its meaning for accounting purposes. Thus, for a partner to be at risk, the R&D contract must make clear that the partners bear the risk of loss if the R&D is unsuccessful. Guarantees that the research will be successful or will have any particular economic utility, guaranteed minimum royalty payments, or guarantees that the partnership will be bailed out through a buyout arrangement if the R&D project is unsuccessful could result in the IRS denying a partner a deduction for some or all of their share of the R&D expenses.

A partner is considered to be at risk for the amount of cash and the tax basis of other property the partner has contributed to the activity as well as for their recourse borrowings with respect to the activity. Any tax losses incurred in an activity and any withdrawals from the activity will reduce a taxpayer's at-risk amount, while any income earned in the activity will increase their at-risk amount. Generally, a partner is not considered to be at risk for their share of the partnership's non-recourse liabilities.

7. *Will the research and development expenditures be deductible?* To be deductible as R&D expenses, expenditures must meet the following Treasury Department definition of research and experimental expenditures:

> Costs incident to the development of an experimental or pilot model, a plant process, a product, a formula, an invention, or similar property and the improvement of already existing property of the type mentioned.

Research and experimental expenditures do not include expenditures for the acquisition or improvement of land or depreciable or depletable property that is to be used in connection with an R&D project if the R&D partnership acquires ownership rights in the property. Similarly, research and experimental expenditures do not include expenditures for acquiring another's patent, model, production, or process. Thus, the R&D contract should provide that your corporation, not the partnership, will acquire any assets of these types that are required for use in the R&D project, and that the ownership rights in them will not be transferred to the R&D partnership. (If, however, the partnership does acquire assets of these types, depreciation relating to them may qualify as deductible R&D expenses.) The costs of producing, marketing, or quality-control testing of the products developed do not qualify as R&D expenses.

In addition to meeting the definition of an R&D expenditure under Section 174 of the Internal Revenue Code, an R&D expenditure must be paid or incurred "in connection with the taxpayer's trade or business" to be deductible.

While the types of expenditures that will qualify for the R&D deduction are usually reasonably easy to identify, the point at which a trade or business begins is not. The existence of a trade or business is a question of fact, as it depends largely on the actual intention of the taxpayer. If the taxpayer genuinely holds itself out as selling goods or services, it is generally considered to have a trade or business, but if its motive does not appear to be to make a profit, a trade or business generally will not be considered to exist.

The presence of gross receipts from an activity that are significant when compared to the activity's expenses is one indication that a trade or business exists. However, the landmark Supreme Court case *Snow et ux. v. Commissioner* held that the absence of gross receipts did not prevent the deduction of R&D expenditures when expectations of profits were high and the general partner was putting about one-third of his time into the research project. The question of whether a specific R&D limited partnership has incurred R&D expenditures in connection with a trade or business will continue to be decided on a case-by-case basis.

Even if the R&D expenditures are deductible for regular tax purposes once all of the other tests (e.g. basis, passive loss, at risk, trade, or business) have been met, the deduction may be revised in effect by the alternative minimum tax (AMT) system. Ninety percent of the R&D deduction is added back to income in computing the AMT.

Corporate Tax Concerns

Your corporation will be interested in many of the preceding tax issues in order to make the R&D arrangement attractive to investors. If your corporation is one of the limited or general partners in the limited partnership, it will be taxed on its allocable share of the partnership's income or loss, and it will receive its allocable share of any tax credits, just as the other partners do. In addition, it may have taxable revenues and deductible expenses from an R&D contract with the limited partnership.

If your corporation is in a tax-loss position, or if it is a start-up corporation without any taxable income, the R&D arrangement may enable you, in effect, to transfer the R&D tax deductions to the limited partners. This may enable your corporation to achieve a lower after-tax cost of funding its R&D program. However, if the R&D program is highly successful, the costs to the corporation may be greater than if it had obtained other sources of funds at the outset.

One tax disadvantage to your corporation of an R&D arrangement is that the R&D expenses it incurs under the R&D contract with the limited partnership will generally not be eligible for the R&D tax credit, assuming it is reinstated (per previous discussion). These expenses might be eligible for the credit if the R&D were funded internally or from debt or equity financing. This factor may slow the growth of R&D arrangements as some corporations may decide to employ more traditional means of raising funds for their R&D so that they do not lose a substantial R&D tax credit.

═══ 12 ═══

CASH MANAGEMENT

In recent years, more and more attention has been focused on what might be called the very best way to raise capital—doing a better job of managing your company's cash.

As obvious as that concept may be, it is often neglected because entrepreneurs underestimate how valuable it can be. They tell themselves that the company has been getting along quite well with a rather easygoing attitude toward cash management, and that it would be unnecessary and difficult to impose tighter controls. And management, busy at producing and selling a line of products, does not find it easy to pay attention to cash management.

There is another reason for neglect. Management suspects that while large corporations might realize substantial savings, the benefits for small to mid-sized companies are probably too insignificant to bother with. The facts suggest just the opposite.

Better cash management may be even more important for a growth company in its early stages than for the large, mature organization. The young, emerging company, bursting with ideas and energy though it may be, nevertheless has a limited track record, and sources of outside funds may be limited and expensive. With aggressive management of the company's cash flow, you can accumulate working capital, reducing reliance on outside funds and increasing profitability.

An extra benefit, as you will see in the detail of this chapter, is that sound cash management practices will earn respect from banks, suppliers, and customers that will pay off in countless ways. While various bank services can be useful in managing a company's cash, the greatest opportunities for improvement are typically internal. Commonsense procedures such as controlling the level of raw materials and inventory, dispatching bills on a timely basis, and paying bills no earlier than necessary can significantly improve both liquidity and profitability.

THE CASH-FLOW CYCLE

Most business managers are familiar with the revenue and cost cycles of their businesses. This information is typically presented in the income statement, which describes the economic performance/profitability of the business during the reporting period. While important to the long-term health of the business, profitability is not the primary contributor to liquidity. The key ingredient in managing business liquidity is the cash-flow cycle.

Simply stated, the cash-flow cycle is (1) the investment of cash in raw materials and product, (2) the sale of the product, and (3) the receipt of cash payment for the sale. Because of the order in which these business activities occur, the liquidity of the company is directly affected by the timing differences in cash transactions for each activity. Cash disbursements, inventory overhead expenses, and cash receipts occur at disconcertingly different times, resulting in the need for greater cash flow or other sources of funds (capital or borrowings) to support liquidity.

The relationship between your income statement and your actual flow of cash is accounted for on the balance sheet in the various elements of working capital. Increases in working capital must be financed by your business, and if not properly controlled may result in serious liquidity problems. Generally, business managers cannot pay raw-material suppliers, personnel, lessors, mortgagors, or service vendors without using working capital or borrowing unless they first collect funds for the products they sell. However, if everybody tried to collect for sales before paying vendors, nobody would get paid. Thus, business managers must focus on control of the cash-flow cycle.

Cash-Flow Cycle Example

Exhibit 12–1 presents a typical cash-flow cycle, segregated by the asset cycle and the liability cycle. The business purchases raw materials, which are held for an average of 30 days before conversion

EXHIBIT 12–1. Before Controlling Cash Flow

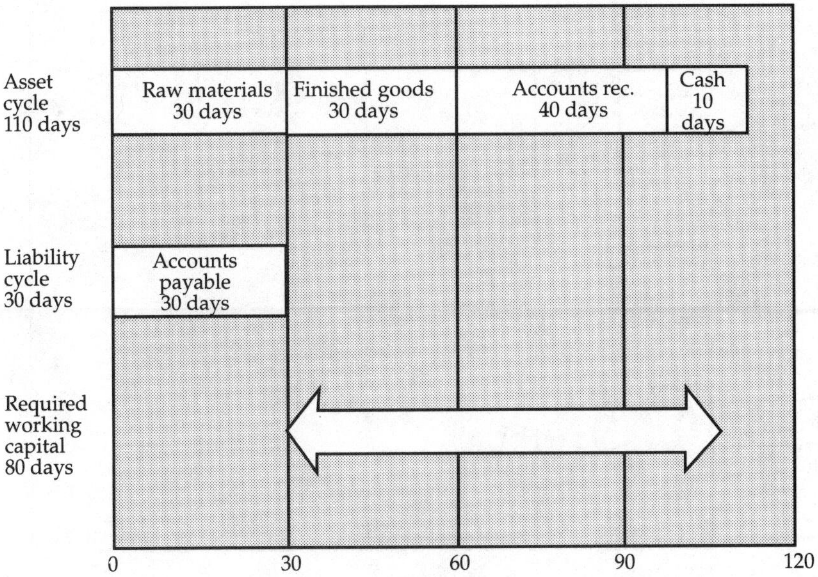

Asset cycle 110 days	Raw materials 30 days	Finished goods 30 days	Accounts rec. 40 days	Cash 10 days

| Liability cycle 30 days | Accounts payable 30 days | | | |

Required working capital 80 days

0   30   60   90   120

to finished goods. In this example, finished goods are considered held in inventory for 30 days prior to shipment to customers and conversion into accounts receivable.

The company's customers typically pay 40 days after shipment. The company also keeps a cash balance equal to approximately 10 days of sales, for bank compensation and operating purposes. In the liability cycle, accounts payable are deferred for 30 days. As a result, this business has 80 days (30 plus 30 plus 40 plus 10 minus 30) of sales value invested in net working capital. Therefore, 80 days worth of sales must be financed through loans, infusions of capital, or the retention of earnings.

Controlling the Cash-Flow Cycle

Exhibit 12–2 presents the desired effects of controlling the cash-flow cycle. Raw-material and finished-goods inventories have been reduced to 15 days each, and accounts receivable have been reduced to 30 days. Cash is controlled to eliminate idle balances. Accounts payable are deferred for an average of 40 days. Net working capital

EXHIBIT 12–2.   After Controlling Cash Flow

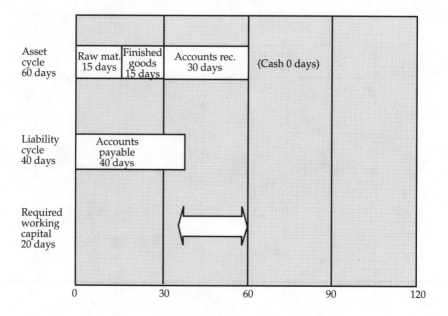

is reduced from a total of 80 days to 20 days, or a 75 percent reduction in the working-capital requirements.

Consider the actual financial effect of the working-capital restructuring in Exhibit 12–2 on a company with annual sales of $5 million. Before restructuring, the required net working capital for 80 days of sales would equal approximately $1,096,000 ([$5,000,000 ÷ 365] x 80). Through restructuring, the working capital required is reduced to 20 days of sales, or approximately $274,000 ([$5,000,000 ÷ 365] X 20). Where has the remaining $822,000 gone? The improvement does not typically show up in the balance of cash. Instead, good business people will take this opportunity to reduce expensive debt or reinvest in assets that support increased sales levels.

The economic benefit of a reduction in net working capital may be most dramatically seen in the example of debt reduction. To the entrepreneur or the manager of a high-growth company, external financing may be very expensive. An entrepreneur, whose only alternative funding source is often venture capital, may in fact have an effective annual financing cost of 12 percent or more. When this is applied to our example, the $822,000 reduction in working capital would reduce annual interest by up to $98,640 per year. Examined more directly, at $5 million in annual sales and 12 percent financing rates, each day's sales squeezed out of net working capital is worth up to $1,644 ([$5,000,000 ÷ 365] x .12). This quantification methodology can help the business manager determine whether changes in operating methods or procedures are beneficial when compared with the cost of making those changes.

Fluctuating Sales: Cash-Flow Effects

This cash-flow approach to cash management is particularly important in understanding the effects on your business of rapid expansion or contraction of the sales level. For example, Exhibit 12–3 presents the effects on a company with rapidly increasing sales for five months, followed by three months of significant contraction. Despite continuous profits through the entire period, this company has experienced significant demands for additional working capital during the expansion cycle, but generated significant extra, unallocated cash ("throw-off") during the contraction cycle. As Exhibit 12–3 demonstrates, a business may require large injections of additional capital to fuel rapid growth. Conversely, cash throw-off during sales decreases can be illusory because cash will be required later during the next expansion in business.

These cash-flow effects are particularly important for companies in seasonal markets, such as toys or construction. Reducing the net number of days of working capital can significantly reduce the size of your cash requirements or cash throw-offs in fluctuating sales situations. However, it cannot change the fact that additional working capital will be required for growth, and that cash throw-off will frequently occur during contraction.

APPROACHES TO CONTROLLING WORKING CAPITAL

The key to cash management is controlling the flow of cash through working-capital accounts, thereby reducing your investment in working capital. To effectively control working-capital accounts, the business manager must focus on the individual elements of working capital: inventory, accounts receivable, accounts payable, and cash-position management, including bank cash management services.

EXHIBIT 12–3. Income Statement Cash-Flow Example

	Monthly Statements							
	1	2	3	4	5	6	7	8
Income statement								
Sales	100	150	200	250	350	250	200	150
Cost and expenses (80%)	(80)	(120)	(160)	(200)	(280)	(200)	(160)	(120)
Net	20	30	40	50	70	50	40	30
Cash requirements								
Working assets:								
Minimum cash (15 days)	50	75	100	125	175	125	100	75
Inventory (60 days)	200	300	400	500	700	500	400	300
Accounts receivable (45 days)	150	225	300	375	525	375	300	225
Subtotal (120 days)	400	600	800	1,000	1,400	1,000	800	600
Working liabilities:								
Accounts payable (30 days)	100	150	200	250	350	250	200	150
Net working capital	300	450	600	750	1,050	750	600	450
Cash (required) throw-off	—	(150)	(150)	(150)	(300)	300	150	150

210

Inventory

For adequate inventory control, consideration should be given to reducing the lead times required for materials and services. Without good production and purchasing planning, overly long lead times can result, frequently causing significant overstocks of one or more products. Planning is the real key to the control of raw material, work-in-process, and finished-goods inventory levels. Inventory can generally be defined as those costs incurred but not yet sold to customers. In service companies, this would include labor or materials expended but not billed. Sound "inventory" control in service businesses is critical to liquidity.

The greatest single requirement for planning inventory levels, and thus production and purchasing lead times, is reasonable sales forecasts. Sales forecasting requires adequate anticipation of customer requirements. If close working relationships exist between your marketing personnel and your customers, it may be feasible to request long-term forecasts on orders from major customers. The availability of this information from customers may save a great deal of additional interest and obsolescence costs. If this requirement is presented to customers in terms of better service and cost control, customers will frequently be willing to assist you in planning your production.

In planning lead times from your company's suppliers, the converse may be true. If you can supply vendors with an estimate of your anticipated purchases over an extended period of time, it may be easier for those suppliers to assure shorter lead times on orders from them. A continuing dialogue with suppliers can also be a significant source of information on future problems in your supply channel. Thus, changes in vendor lead times and the availability of their products can more frequently be included in your company's planning process.

Improved management information systems (MIS) in sales forecasting, production planning, and purchasing can often convert good sales forecast data into timely, meaningful information on departmental production loading, material requirements, and labor requirements. With good MIS, changes in any variable can quickly be reflected in inventory and production plans.

Business managers frequently analyze the number of inventory turns per year, or the average number of days of inventory. This information assists in controlling the overall level of inventory. However, additional improvement in inventory levels may be realized if individual products or raw materials are evaluated in relation to their usages or customer shipments. This can frequently assist you in identifying slow-moving or obsolete inventories, as well as other areas in which purchasing or production planning could be improved.

Accounts Receivable

The investment in accounts receivable and related risk of customer default is typically minimized by those companies that maintain close working relationships with their customers. Payment terms, credit limits, and collection programs are useful only if used to reinforce the basic agreements already negotiated. If your payment expectations are made clear to the customer during the initial sales process, at the same time pricing and service levels are considered, your organization will be better positioned to collect those balances. Candid discussions with customers regarding the mutually beneficial nature of the relationship can help assure that interest expenses can be minimized and potential liquidity problems avoided. By projecting an image of being firm about collections, most companies will be successful at controlling accounts receivable.

Payment terms can be used to make earlier customer payment beneficial to your customer. For example, offering customers a 1 percent discount for net payment in 10 days as opposed to 30 days is the equivalent of offering that customer 18 percent (365 divided by 20) on his or her money.

Frequently, companies that offer discounts are dissatisfied with the results because customers continue to pay late but also take the discount. This problem means the customer does not grasp the relationship. It must be understood, during the sales negotiation, that the company intends to enforce the ten-day maximum and that the payment must be in your office by the tenth day to be eligible for discount.

Collection programs must also be used to reinforce terms agreed to in the original negotiation. While some discount terms are dictated by industry practice, other discounts can be established on a case-by-case basis, often to mutual advantage. For example, a company borrowing at 12 percent would find it advantageous to offer terms of 1 percent 10/net 60 (effective annual rate of 7.3 percent = 1 percent x (365/[60−10]), while a customer investing at 6 percent would find it advantageous to take the discount.

Collection programs that represent "hounding" will typically have the effect of generating animosity and reducing the likelihood of early payment. If, however, the original negotiations explain your collection program and your expectations pertaining to credit, a collection call could simply reiterate the interrelationship between pricing, service, and payments. Frequently, a collection call serves not only to collect bills on time but also to build a better relationship.

Your collection procedures should be designed to alert customers to an escalating concern on your part. Three consecutive telephone calls from your collection manager to the customer's accounts-payable clerk will not be as productive as one call from your collection manager, a second call from your controller to the customer's controller, and finally a call from the president of your company to the president of the customer company. This approach can serve to emphasize that the relationship is becoming strained as invoice payments are delayed and that your entire organization is becoming increasingly concerned about the status of that customer's account.

Credit limits can also be used as a method of creating awareness of credit problems at successively higher management levels in your company at a relatively early point. If a customer purchases goods every 10 days and your payment terms are net 30 days, then credit limits that are equal to 45 days of sales will effectively limit shipments to the customer and help assure that no invoice becomes a collection problem in your company because accounts reached "critical" levels.

Another critical element in a sound accounts-receivable collection program is invoicing. If invoices are prepared in a timely manner and forwarded to the customer at the earliest possible date, then customer complaints that invoices were too late to take the discount or to process through its accounts-payable system can be minimized. In situations involving large volumes of invoices, improvements to the invoicing process may require automated systems to speed the processing. The invoicing process should be evaluated to ensure that invoices are properly prepared, with all terms and conditions, and that necessary documentation is forwarded with the invoice. In evaluating information required for invoice preparation, data requirements may include information typically associated with your accounts-payable system. For example, professional service companies that invoice based on time and expense may need accounts-payable detail to properly bill their expenses. Construction companies that bill on cost-plus basis also require a significant amount of accounts-payable data on which to base invoice. A complete range of financial and operational information required for invoice preparation should be considered in determining the enhancements to your company's information system that may be required for improved invoicing.

One final note on payment terms for those companies that work on large contracts or that have a few very major customers: negotiating specific terms and methods of payment can be critical. If large amounts are to be received from a limited number of customers, it may be advantageous to negotiate with those customers for wire-transfer payments and possibly trade-offs in price to gain earlier availability of those funds. Again, a candid relationship with the customer regarding the full range of issues for a mutually beneficial relationship is critical to maintaining sound control of accounts receivable.

Accounts Payable

Since working liabilities are not always equal to working assets, accounts payable can be used to bring them more into balance. In a practical sense, you can take certain actions that have the effect of giving you noninterest-bearing loans from your suppliers.

When you negotiate the terms of your relationship, try to extend your payment period to the maximum. This is simply a matter of keeping your money as long as possible before paying it out. This will cut down on the amount you might have to borrow and pay interest on to keep faith with your suppliers. Negotiated payment terms with your vendors should include the exploration of benefits that can be accrued from cash discounts, convenient timing of payments to coincide with your cash-flow cycle, or even more specialized arrangements such as lines of credit, bartering, and equity investments. Any saving could be important in reaching your goals of profit and growth. Most suppliers and vendors would appreciate your spelling out these goals, knowing that they will benefit in the long run as you prosper and become a bigger customer. This is another example of how a close, candid relationship can benefit both customer and supplier.

BANK CASH MANAGEMENT SERVICES

What They Are and How to Use Them

While the greatest opportunities for effective cash management are internal to the company, banks offer a variety of services that can be used to further improve cash flow and asset utilization.

Once a customer has mailed a check to the company, there are several techniques that can be used to accelerate the conversion of the check into available funds. Perhaps the most commonly used technique is the lockbox, a service provided by most major banks. Under the lockbox system, the bank, operating under contract to the company, maintains a post office box to which the company's customers send their checks. The bank (1) collects the contents of the box several times daily and often on weekends and holidays; (2) processes the contents in accordance with the company's instructions; (3) credits the incoming checks to the company's account; and (4) forwards various information and documents (such as empty envelopes, check stubs, invoices, and photocopies of checks) to the company. The company can also establish lockboxes in cities other than the one in which the company's main office is located.

The lockbox system improves cash flow because (1) incoming mail time is reduced (the bank receives the mail at a central post office and picks it up more frequently than would the company); (2) the checks received are entered directly into the bank's check-processing system, (eliminating as much as one day of the processing lag that would occur if the company processed the incoming checks itself); and (3) the bank can clear the checks more rapidly because it receives them at a central location earlier in the day than would be the case if the checks were deposited in the afternoon. In addition to accelerating the incoming cash flow by as much as one or two days, a lockbox system transfers a certain work load from the company to the bank and provides improved controls as a result of the separation of the billing and receivables functions.

Two primary types of lockbox services are available from most larger banks: (1) the wholesale lockbox and (2) the retail lockbox.

The wholesale lockbox is generally a customized service designed for companies dealing with business customers. Generally, transactions flowing through a wholesale lockbox are relatively few in number but large in dollar amount. "All in" charges for this service generally approximate $1 per transaction, with a minimum monthly charge often exceeding $100. Care must be taken to assure that a wholesale lockbox is cost-effective. For example, if a 90-cent transaction charge is assessed and one-day float reduction results from the lockbox, then, based on a 12 percent cost of funds, the break-even transaction size is approximately $1,350.

If smaller transactions are routed through the lockbox, the bank service charges will exceed the resulting benefits. (This might, however, be offset by savings resulting from the transfer of the company's work load to the banks.) For this reason, wholesale lockboxes are often inappropriate for companies dealing primarily with consumers.

A retail lockbox is characterized by a high volume of relatively low dollar-amount transactions. Unlike their customized wholesale lockbox service, banks handle retail transactions on a "production-line" basis. If a company's transactions meet the bank's specifications for this automated processing, substantial cost savings can be achieved. The specifications might include a standard envelope size and a standardized payment coupon readable by the bank's automated machinery.

In addition to the cost savings, a retail lockbox service can provide the company with a daily magnetic tape (or similar medium) detailing each transaction processed, including account number and payment amount. The company can then use this tape to update its files. The charges for a retail lockbox are generally less than half those for the wholesale lockbox—perhaps 15 cents per transaction, but with a high monthly minimum. While a retail lockbox does result in some float reduction, this advantage is generally small compared with the advantage of transferring a substantial work load from the company to the bank. Often it is possible for a bank to process retail transactions more efficiently than the company can because the bank can invest in and support a sophisticated remittance-processing system.

Even if a company uses a lockbox system, some transactions will be sent directly to the company. In such cases, the company should establish procedures designed to ensure that such incoming funds are deposited at the bank on a timely basis. Unless the funds are of nominal amounts, they should not be mailed to the bank since this impairs cash flow. Rather, they should be hand-delivered daily in time to receive same-day credit from the bank.

Electronic Data Interchange

Electronic data interchange (EDI) is the exchange of information between a company and its trading partners either directly or through third-party value-added networks (VAN). Electronic data interchange has evolved over the last few years from a few exchanges addressing the needs of specific industries to a wide array of transactions crossing industry boundaries. The perceived benefits of EDI are increased timeliness of information exchange between trading partners; decreased manual processing, paper, and mailing costs; and, perhaps most importantly, reduced data-entry errors by clerical staff.

The natural evolution of EDI is to financial EDI. Financial EDI involves the transmission not only of remittance data but also of electronic payment instructions. Thus, financial EDI requires the banking system to participate in the exchange of electronic information, and indeed many banks actively promote financial EDI. Financial EDI is used for the transmission of a variety of data, including lockbox information reports, daily bank-balance and transaction reports, and monthly account-analysis reports.

Although financial EDI has these uses and benefits, many perceive electronic invoicing and payment as providing the most benefit to financial EDI users. Electronic invoicing enhances the accounts-payable process of electronically matching the invoice with the purchase order and receiving documents, reducing the clerical staff required to manually perform this matching process. In addition, receiving electronic payments enhances the automated cash-application process. Companies need not wait for checks to clear. Finally, receiving remittance information in electronic form virtually eliminates the need for manual data entry of customer identification and invoice payment information.

Before implementing EDI, a company should develop a strategy to help determine the company's overall goals and capabilities. Implementing financial EDI requires each company to compare the benefits of financial EDI to the barriers associated with incorporating EDI capability into the company's data processing and accounting systems, including obtaining and implementing EDI software and hardware. Companies need to identify what EDI software and hardware should be used for the EDI transactions, and determine whether existing systems can be modified or enhanced to accommodate the requirements of financial EDI.

Check Clearing

While certain checks, particularly those deposited through a lockbox, may clear on a same-day basis, other checks, particularly those drawn on Federal Reserve "country" points, may take up to two days to clear. Thus, while the date that a bank gives the company credit for a deposit is important, the date on which the funds become available is even more important.

Funds availability is governed by the bank's own check-clearing system and is generally spelled out in the "funds-availability" schedule published by most banks. This schedule specifies the clearing time (in business days) and deposit deadline for checks drawn on various locations. The funds-availability schedule should be an important consideration in selecting a bank.

Utilizing the Funds

The two basic ways of obtaining full utilization of funds are (1) concentrating the funds and (2) managing the bank balances.

Funds Concentration

A major cash management function for a company with multiple bank accounts is to concentrate its funds. For example, in the case of a retail chain, each store in a branch-banking state would make a daily deposit at a local branch of a bank with which the chain had established a "concentration account." These funds would automatically be concentrated into a single account and, if necessary, transferred to the company's main bank in another state. The use of a concentration account usually results in lower bank service charges because the bank maintains only one account rather than numerous accounts.

Outgoing Funds

As previously discussed, a variety of factors should be considered in determining when to mail checks to vendors. On the one hand, borrowing expense can be minimized by delaying the mailing of the check. On the other hand, it is important to maintain good vendor relationships and discounts can be worthwhile in many cases. Considering mail, processing, and check-clearing times, a week or more will often elapse from the date a check is mailed to the date it clears. An effective cash-management system will utilize funds during this period, perhaps by using an interest-bearing account, estimating check clearings, or using a controlled-disbursement account, which slightly extends clearing time and provides daily reports of checks clearing.

Other Bank Services

A variety of other bank services can be used by various companies to improve cash flow, concentrate funds, and manage bank balances.

Not all services are appropriate for all companies, and the cost of some can exceed their value to a smaller company. Nevertheless, it is important for the cash manager of a company to understand available services such as the following so that appropriate and cost-effective services can be used.

Account Analysis. Compares the value of balances with the bank's charges for services provided. If balances for a given month are inadequate to support services provided, a service charge may be assessed.

Deposit-Reporting Systems. Daily reports of account balances and activity in the account.

Wire Transfers. Instantaneous transfer of funds, often used for intracompany and investments transactions. Occasionally used for larger customer and vendor transactions, often as a special sales term.

Zero-Balance Accounts. A "master" account serves as a depository account, and "subsidiary" accounts serve as disbursement accounts. As checks clear against the subsidiary accounts, the bank automatically transfers funds from the master account to cover the checks.

CASH-POSITION MANAGEMENT

The best possible system of accounts receivable and payable will achieve only a portion of its potential value if not used in conjunction with an effective system of managing cash on hand. Specific activities include cash forecasting; management of bank balances, and investments or borrowings.

Cash Forecasting and Daily Cash Positioning

1. *For Planning.* The management of cash or near-cash balances for most early-stage, high-growth companies can be significantly enhanced by simply forecasting receivable collections in relation to accounts payable and payroll disbursements. Automated accounts payable and receivable systems can provide very timely information for use in generating at least weekly

projections of required cash outlays in relation to anticipated cash collections. This information, considered with scheduled cash transactions such as debt-service payments and short-term investment maturities, can alert management to critical cash balance shortages or cash balance excesses. Early knowledge of these circumstances will provide greater flexibility in planning alternate courses of action.

2. *For Investment or Payment of Borrowings.* In addition to forecasting cash for planning purposes, business managers often utilize information from banks in conjunction with internal systems and procedures daily to convert cash in the bank into an earning asset. These information systems and procedures are collectively referred to as daily cash positioning or daily cash worksheet preparation. Cash-positioning procedures are performed daily because the actual cash balance in the bank will vary considerably from day to day, even though cash transactions on the company books may occur at less frequent intervals. The timing of these procedures is usually in the morning so that investment decisions can be made prior to daily financial institution transaction deadlines.

The key to successful management of bank balances is timely and accurate information. This begins with the opening bank balance according to the bank's books. This information must be obtained from the bank, perhaps via a phone call, or through the use of a balance reporting system. There is often a wide discrepancy between the bank balance and the balance on the company's books. This is due primarily to checks that have been issued but not yet cleared. The estimated amount of checks clearing that day should then be subtracted. (If controlled disbursement is used, the bank will be able to provide an exact amount of that day's clearings.) Then, any transactions (such as wire, investments, or borrowings) that result in same-day settlement should be added or subtracted. Deposits being made that day generally should not be considered, because they will not result in available funds that day. Finally, a target balance, or "cushion," should be subtracted. Note, however, that it is often preferable to compensate a bank with direct fees rather than balances because the effective earnings credit on the balances is generally less than investment or borrowing rates. This cushion is to allow for unexpected transactions or variances in estimates and to leave a balance that helps compensate the bank for services provided, as shown in the account analysis. The net result of all of these computations is the projected ending net balance. If negative, additional funds will need to be deposited, perhaps by borrowing. If positive, funds can be withdrawn and invested, or used to pay down borrowings.

Electronic Funds Transfers

Over the past few years many companies have started utilizing electronic funds transfers (EFTs), rather than checks, for disbursements. This increase in the use of EFT transactions caused the addition of Article 4A (Funds Transfers) to the Uniform Commercial Code (UCC). Essentially, UCC 4A establishes the liability for fraudulent wholesale wire transfer and nonconsumer automated clearinghouse (ACH) transactions to the originating corporation or bank based on the application of "commercially reasonable security procedures." While ACH transactions are usually completed on a next-day basis, the typical wholesale wire transfer involves a larger amount of money and most are completed on a same-day basis. Thus, companies may be able to minimize their liability for a fraudulent EFT transaction by placing greater emphasis on EFT procedures and controls. In particular, corporations that fail to utilize wire-transfer control procedures offered by banks may have a high level of exposure.

These controls can be as simple as restricting access to the hardware and software used for EFT transactions. For example, many EFT transactions are now processed through personal computers (PCs) rather than mainframe computers. While mainframe computers are usually located in secured areas, PCs are often located on desks or in other open areas accessible to unauthorized personnel. To help prevent the possibility of a fraudulent EFT transaction, the hardware and software for processing EFT transactions should be located in an area that has restricted access. In addition, no one authorized person should have control of the entire EFT system. For example, one employee should input wire-transfer information into an automated bank wire system and a separate employee should release the transmission.

Another control might be the establishment of a security administrator to be responsible for changes in existing user identification, receiving of test-key material, assigning new users and functions, and assigning transaction limits on accounts. However, the security administrator should have no transaction authority on any EFT system.

Other controls are often internal to the EFT software and hardware, and typically involve the use of passwords to control access to the EFT system and encryption or authentication to protect the EFT transmission. A password, by definition, is a secret word that enables a particular user to be admitted to the system. However, passwords are good only if they are kept confidential. Having passwords on display on computer monitors, cubicle walls, or desks for all to observe defeats the purpose of the password. Furthermore, passwords should be a minimum of six characters and changed every 30 days. Likewise, persons attempting to gain access to the system by password should not be permitted more than three tries to find the right password before they are logged off the system. Additionally, EFT systems should be designed to minimize or eliminate the possibility of unauthorized access via telephone.

In encryption, the EFT transmission is scrambled with the use of an algorithm and secret key. Authentication is similar to encryption in that it also uses an algorithm and secret key, but rather than scrambling the data, a code is generated that is specific to the combination of EFT data, secret key, and algorithm. For both encryption and authentication, only the intended receiver of the EFT transmission has the secret key and algorithm to decipher the data.

Companies should also include EFT procedures and controls in any disaster contingency plan. Disasters include storms that cause telephone or power outages, bank failures, fires, or other problems that lead to a failure of financial systems at the company or the banks used for EFT transmissions. Disasters increase the potential for a fraudulent disbursement by the loss of controls provided by the financial systems. For example, a systems failure could result in the loss of separation of controls provided by automated bank wire systems related to the entry and release of EFT information.

Short-Term Investments

Beyond the controls discussed in the previous section, short-term investments raise an additional set of issues:

- Only certain types of investments with low-risk, high-liquidity characteristics should be authorized. These types of investments should be identified in official company documents filed with the bank. Usually, these investments include U.S. Treasury securities, major bank certificates of deposit, high-grade commercial paper, major bank acceptances, and securities of government agencies.

- Each investment should be entered in the company records, and the internal documents supporting the transactions should be matched to investment purchase confirmations—received from the financial institution—on a timely basis.

Note that a viable alternative to procedures of estimating a net cash position, and then adjusting investments and borrowings, is to have the bank do most of the work. Many banks offer a "sweep" arrangement, where excess funds can be automatically invested in repurchase agreements or similar instruments, and any deficit positions can be automatically funded by accessing a preapproved line of credit. While banks may assess fees for this service, and while interest rates may not be as good as if the company managed its own, such bank services can be invaluable if they enable the entrepreneur to focus on more important areas.

PHASES OF CASH MANAGEMENT DEVELOPMENT

Sales versus Availability and Cost of Capital

Typically, a growth company's financial strength will improve dramatically over time. The availability of alternative sources of financing increases because banks and other financial institutions will more readily advance cash based on strong financial positions and performance. (Actually, a highly successful growth company will frequently find that working capital can be financed from internal sources after some period of time.) In addition, the cost of capital will decline dramatically with increased financial strength (see Exhibit 12–4). Because financial institutions will finance working capital for the successful growth company, raising capital through costly venture placements will be avoided and bank credit lines at prime or slightly higher interest rates will be available.

Timing Cash Management Improvements

The typical growth company will move through three distinct phases of cash management development as cash flows grow from zero to approximately $40 to $50 million per year. The transition from one

EXHIBIT 12–4.   Phases of Cash Management Development

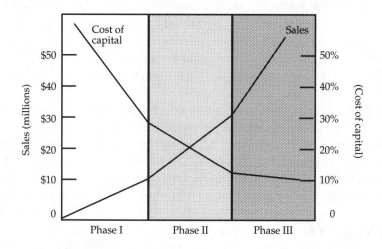

phase to the next will vary by industry and company, but the transition points will occur based on the cost/availability of working capital and on the total-dollar cash flow through the company.

Phase 1 can be characterized by a company with sales between $1 million and $10 million per year. This company is experiencing high growth, high costs of capital, and frequently unavailable sources of working capital. During this phase, management should focus heavily on short-term cash planning procedures/systems, vendor and customer relations and policies, and improved planning and control of purchases and inventory. The desired effect is to minimize the net working-capital requirements of the business and thereby reduce both the cost of working capital and the pressures for additional external financing.

As the company's sales grow to around $10 million per year, profitability and financial strength typically will improve to the point that working capital is more available and the cost of capital is dramatically reduced. These are characteristics of a company entering Phase 2 of cash management development. Phase 2 will often continue until the company's sales reach approximately $30 million per year. In this $10 million to $30 million range of sales, cash flows will run from $40,000 to $120,000 per business day. In addition to enhancing management information systems to control and plan receivables, payables, and inventory (to minimize net working capital), the company should begin to focus on the management of banking relations and cash-investment balances. Bank relations should be redefined to include more favorable terms on credit and the expansion of bank services to assist in managing cash at these greater levels. Bank services that may be of assistance include balance reporting of "current day" collected and uncollected balances, and controlled disbursing to enhance management's ability to plan daily cash and investment (or loan reduction) activities.

As the company's sales reach approximately $30 million per year, important working-capital financing alternatives are usually available and the cost of such financing declines. These are characteristics of the company entering Phase 3 of cash management development. Above this level of sales, due to the magnitude of cash that flows through the company on a daily basis, even small improvements in the number of days required in working capital (the flow of cash) can have a dramatic effect on the benefits derived.

You may find that cash management "studies" will prove beneficial in identifying bottlenecks in the cash-flow cycle that result from interdepartmental differences in priorities, policies, or procedures. These interdepartmental conflicts frequently can be resolved when the differing priorities are compared with the priority for sound working-capital management. At this level of development you may also find that evaluations of alternative short-term investments may be useful in improving your investment yield. Often, significant enhancements to management information systems, or increased sophistication of banking and cash-processing relations, will result from evaluations of the company's total working capital, planning, and control systems.

═══ 13 ═══

MANAGEMENT BUYOUTS

Dialogue of a conversation between the president of a parent company and the president of one of its subsidiaries:

President (sub): We, our management group and I, would like to buy our company.

President (parent): So you want to buy your sub! Do you have enough money to do that? You know with your earnings the last few years and our investment in the company, it will be a tough deal to finance. Plus, I'm not sure we want to sell. You guys may just now be turning the company around. You know, I'm not even sure we can negotiate with you since you work for the company. Maybe we should just wait awhile!

President (sub): . . .

You may have already experienced a tense and unresolved discussion like the one above. In addition to failing to get the management buyout process started, the discussion will undoubtedly affect the relationship of these two presidents from this point forward. You may still have the opportunity to join the ranks of management groups who have initiated discussions regarding purchasing their operations. The president of the subsidiary in this example should have been better prepared.

WHAT ARE MANAGEMENT BUYOUTS?

Management buyouts (MBOs) are leveraged buyouts (LBOs) in which managers of a company, subsidiary, or division acquire the operations from the company's parent or owner. The motivations for MBOs are generally tied to management's desire to avoid sale of the division or company to unknown and perhaps unfriendly new owners, as well as the opportunity to control the company's destiny and fortune.

The problems common to the great majority of management groups that desire to own their company encompass the range of transaction issues, plus issues specific to the MBO, such as independence and fiduciary responsibility.

HOW TO DO AN MBO

Understanding Strategic and Financial Positioning

Management should know three things before beginning the MBO process.

The first is the strategic and financial position of the parent or owners. A parent company in search of cash or of diversification out of a subsidiary's market will be more flexible and approachable than one that is cash-rich and plans to use the subsidiary as its cornerstone for entering new markets. Knowledge of the parent's or owners' current positioning is critical to both the timing and nature of management's initial approach to the parent or owners regarding a potential MBO.

The second is the subsidiary's strategic and financial position. What niches can it serve? What are its competitive strengths and what resources are needed to either gain or maintain its competitive advantage? This information is important not only for discussions and negotiations with the parent company but for proving to investors and lenders the viability of the MBO.

The final item is a valuation of the subsidiary. Many management groups make the critical mistake of taking shortcut methods to arrive at a valuation, such as using the price/earnings multiples of similar companies without considering differences in capital structure and other factors. It is difficult to achieve success in an MBO without a solid understanding of the valuation of the operation to be acquired.

Since this also will be a critical factor in determining both purchase price and management's stake in the equity of the post-MBO company, the importance of this information cannot be overestimated.

The Acquisition

Many of the components of an MBO follow the same process the business combination follows (see Chapter 10). The process, however, is complicated by the position of the management group.

The managers of the company know more about the company than anyone else. They are insiders. Management could control the outcome of the price negotiations for the company by managing profits down for a period of time and could profit by buying the company just prior to a turn upward in operations.

The managers of one company were attempting to put together an offer for their subsidiary. The president of the company was not in favor of an MBO because of the inherent conflicts of interest and told his management group "No." However, management persisted and was subsequently fired by the company president. Obviously, management in this situation took the wrong approach. The right approach is one that recognizes such conflicts, promotes open communication, shares respective strategies, builds confidence, and develops the MBO as a viable alternative. The difference in approaches can be demonstrated by the following examples:

- A parent company was interested in diversifying out of certain operations. The parent had established a certain price and, when it was unsuccessful in its attempts to sell these operations to others, approached the subsidiary's management. The subsidiary was able, with some financial support from the parent, to consummate the transaction. To accomplish this, management of the subsidiary had performed a sound assessment of the strategic and financial position of these operations and convinced both the parent company and outside lenders that the MBO transaction was viable.

- A privately owned company is not up for sale. The company is being managed by family members who have lost touch with the market and are unwilling to approve the capital outlays required to grow the business. Nonfamily management should be in a position of honoring their fiduciary duty and absolving themselves of conflict if the analysis for requesting capital outlays is the same analysis used by the management group to value, acquire, and finance the purchase of the company.

Many other situations exist for acquisition-minded management teams. The inherent conflict of management as insiders is not as significant a problem today because MBOs have proliferated and have become accepted as a diversification strategy. However, elimination of the inherent obstacles to a management (insider) offer, if present, must be first on the list for accomplishing the MBO.

The next step in the MBO process is to prepare a letter of intent. Initial structuring decisions and proposals should be included as part of the letter of intent. A well-designed letter of intent is an excellent vehicle to use as a starting point in discussing an MBO with the owners' or parent's management. Final structure and preparation of the definitive agreement will come during the financing phase after the letter of intent is accepted.

Structuring

Structuring of the MBO is generally driven by five considerations:

- Cash flow
- Ownership expectations by management
- Tax issues
- Accounting issues
- Financing requirements by lenders and investors

Cash Flow

No factor in an MBO is as critical as cash flow. Historical and projected operating cash flow before interest, taxes, and depreciation are the most common measures of value and continued growth for the company undergoing an MBO. The historical cash-flow measure is important to establish the creditability and quality of the company, as well as its products, market, facilities, and management. The projected cash-flow measure is important for communicating management/ business strategy and demonstrating the continued viability of the business. Cash flow is also the determinant of debt capacity and equity returns.

Ownership Expectations by Management

Management needs to honestly evaluate its contribution to the MBO in establishing its expectations for ownership. The ability to "get to the goal line" and complete the MBO, as well as to manage the post-MBO company, must be weighed against the needs of financing sources and their desired rates of return. Managers who use a realistic approach to this assessment and who have done some homework usually arrive at the appropriate modification of their expectation of ownership and accomplish the deal. Part of this realization is the fact that a certain amount of the ownership will be earned in the post-MBO period. The pre-MBO period is also the right time to think about written agreements among shareholders—particularly management who become shareholders—which include appropriate exit clauses for situations where things just don't work out.

Tax Issues

Tax issues are important to structuring only to the extent that taxes reduce cash flow and, in turn, net realizable value of the company. Probably the most critical element of tax structuring for the MBO is the deductibility of interest expense. Recent tax legislation has sought to limit but has not eliminated the deductability of interest expense in the case of high-yield debt instruments. Other tax structuring techniques to minimize tax costs, such as asset acquisitions and non-competition agreements, can be applied to MBO transactions. Recent tax legislation has again created a gap between capital gains and corporate tax rates. This will serve to reduce the flexibility of the buyer and seller in agreeing to alternative structures and require assistance from professional advisors to reconcile respective positions. Tax structuring must be balanced with the other structuring considerations.

Accounting Issues

Accounting issues ultimately affect the post-MBO company's balance sheet and income statement. Accounting for the MBO generally will not affect the company's operating cash flow. The only situation when accounting for the MBO would affect cash flow would be when book income (GAAP) is substantially higher than taxable income. In these situations, the company could incur an alternative minimum tax liability.

Probably the most important accounting issue in today's environment for the MBO is the new set of rules, developed by the Emerging Issues Task Force of the Financial Accounting Standards Board, for accounting for "Basis in Leveraged Buyout Transactions" (EITF Consensus No. 88-16). This set of rules, if applicable to the MBO (which is likely), can yield surprising results on the balance sheet of the post-MBO entity. These rules could reduce the write-up value of assets acquired from the predecessor entity, and reduce the stockholders' equity contributed by old-company managers to the new company.

How the parent or owners will account for the transaction must also be considered. As part of the positioning of these parties, especially in situations where owners provide some financing, it is important to understand how the parent will have to record a sale and if it will be able to recognize a gain in accordance with SEC Staff Accounting Bulletin Topic #5, entitled Gain Recognition on the Sale of a Business or Operating Assets to a Highly Leveraged Entity.

A final accounting consideration is the allocation of purchase price. The requirement to revalue inventory to selling price, less cost of disposal, can result in a deterioration in margin in the period or periods following the closing of the MBO. Understanding this situation and communicating it to all parties on a timely basis can prevent panic at a critical time in the transaction.

Financing Requirements

Structuring for financing is the process of matching the company's operating cash flow to an appropriate debt and equity mix under current financial market conditions. Typically, the financing structure will include senior debt, mezzanine debt, and equity (see Chapter 1). The terms and conditions required for each capital layer are dependent on the quality of the historical and projected operating cash flows, the quality of the company's assets, and the level of financial support, if any, from the parent or former owners. Since the 1980s, the level of equity required in MBOs has increased. Since most of this requirement is usually met by former parent companies, the importance of the positioning described previously has become a more significant factor in consummating an MBO.

WHAT TO EXPECT

Price of the Deal

Deals are priced in many ways. A rule-of-thumb measure used by many deal makers is a multiple of "earnings before interest and taxes" (known as EBIT) for similar companies with comparable capital structures. The multiple for the deal is dependent upon the availability of cash capital in the market, the quality of earnings, the strategic position, and the prospects for growth. A price based upon a multiple in the range of five to eight times EBIT, less outstanding debt, is not unusual. Discounted cash-flow techniques are also used. Ultimately, the price of the deal will depend on the company's assets and future earnings potential. Comparable price/earnings multiples and current cash-flow analyses will need to be evaluated to determine the ultimate value range.

Advisory Services and Transaction Fees

The management group attempting the MBO generally is unprepared for the difficult and challenging obstacles to be encountered. Because the management group has expertise in running the business, not in doing a corporate-finance deal, it will need advisors to guide it through the transaction. When managers select their overall transaction advisor, they should ensure that the advisor is experienced in MBO transactions and ascertain the fee for the service. Many merchant bankers and investment bankers advise and assist management groups with MBOs, and their fees can include both cash and substantial equity in the company. Careful selection of the overall transaction advisor will increase the likelihood of a successful transaction and maximum ownership retention by the management group.

Transaction and financing fees for the MBO can be quite high. Total fees in the range of 4 to 7 percent of the total transaction are common, and smaller deals (below $10 million in debt and equity) can cost a higher percentage.

Raising Debt and Equity

The management business and cash-flow forecasts, participation by former owners, the underlying business (and assets) and management quality will determine the ease of raising and the cost of debt and equity for the MBO. Senior debt will generally carry an interest rate of prime plus 1.5 percent to 2.5 percent, with a five- to seven-year amortization schedule. Mezzanine debt is generally a five- to eight-year fixed-rate note without amortization prior to the repayment of the senior debt. The notes are usually priced at 3 to 6 percent above the ten-year Treasury rate or similar interest-rate measures, and usually have equity "kickers" in the form of warrants to bring the total internal rate of return to the provider up to a range of 20 to 30 percent. Underwriting requirements and debt covenants will vary by lender and by company. Investors will generally expect a rate of return on equity of 40 percent or more depending on the company.

Finding debt and equity partners for today's MBO is difficult but posssible. If the industry and company are stable and growing, if the price negotiated is reasonable, and if the management team is qualified, the deal can be financed. Management should interview and select debt and equity partners carefully. If a mistake in selection is made, correction may be painful and take years.

The Management Stake

Management's ownership position is affected by all of the deal factors, including the contribution of management to the execution. If the management group has already negotiated and obtained a letter of intent for the MBO acquisition, it will retain more equity than if a merchant banker performs that service. Likewise, if managers have equity capital to invest, they will retain more ownership. In most cases, management does not have the capital or the experience to negotiate the letter of intent for acquisition.

If management has no capital and does not manage negotiations, ownership retention of 5 to 15 percent should be expected. When management has the deal but no capital, ownership retention can range between 30 and 50 percent. In MBOs, management should not expect the higher range unless the deal is very strong or managers contribute some capital. As a general rule, ownership greater than 50 percent can be accomplished only through significant management capital contributions. Structuring of management's ownership should be carefully evaluated to minimize or eliminate exposure to taxation of the stock ownership obtained by management.

Managers will also be expected to enter into long-term employment and noncompetitive agreements. These contracts and stockholders' agreements will serve to protect the ownership of each debt and equity stakeholder.

Operations (Post-MBO)

The management of the post-MBO company will be different. Lenders and equity partners will expect management's operations forecast to be attained. If it is not attained, management's position may be in jeopardy. Perhaps the most difficult adjustments for management are the primary focus on cash flow (versus earnings) and the need to ensure the execution of various administrative tasks (such as personnel and insurance) previously handled by corporate departments that usually do not exist in the post-MBO environment.

One of the most critical post-MBO mistakes management makes is proclaiming that everything will remain status quo. In fact, few if any MBOs are completed without significant change—be it in employment levels, reduced employee benefits, or similar changes. Sound judgment suggests that any such changes be made quickly and fairly. The risk of delay can place the entire transaction in jeopardy shortly after it is consummated. In addition, the complexity of recording the transaction and monthly reporting for lenders will challenge the ability of the company's financial staff and management.

IS IT ALL WORTH IT?

This should be the first question asked by the management group instead of the last. The allure of guiding your own destiny and the opportunity for wealth must outweigh the tension and time. With a solid self-assessment of strategic and financial positioning and some assistance from experienced professional advisors, the odds of successfully completing an MBO will increase greatly. The intangible rewards of being your own boss are not quantifiable. However, the potential financial rewards can be demonstrated. Consider the following example:

XYZ Company is a manufacturer of nondurable consumer goods. The company's sales have grown at 12 percent per year for the past five years to a current level of $25 million. Net operating cash flow has grown steadily and currently is $6 million annually. Management expects that the company will continue its steady growth and that industry consolidation will offer opportunity for acquisition of similar companies.

Management offers to buy the company for $30 million and is successful in the acquisition. Since management negotiated the acquisition agreement, it is able to retain 20 percent ownership and can earn an additional 15 percent through stock options if its forecast is met.

In year four, no acquisition has been made and management has not met its forecast. Management's financial partner and lender asks management to sell the company. Sales and operating cash flow have grown, but only at a rate of 7.5 percent per year. Net operating cash flow in year four is $8 million. Economic factors and the economic outlook in year four are the same as when management bought the company. The company is sold at a multiple of six times operating cash flow ($48 million). Management's share of the net proceeds (after debt retirement of $26 million) is $4.4 million.

The final question: Is the risk of failure worth the chance of success?

14

EMPLOYEE STOCK OWNERSHIP PLANS

An employee stock ownership plan (ESOP) enables you to raise capital from inside, rather than outside, your company. Through an ESOP your employees can become investors in your company.

An ESOP is a qualified retirement benefit plan designed to invest primarily in the securities of its sponsor or other affiliated corporations. ESOPs are defined contribution plans, meaning that annual contributions are determined by the plan sponsor within certain limits prescribed by law. Unlike other qualified plans, ESOPs have the unique ability to borrow funds for the purpose of purchasing employer securities. Consequently, a variety of corporate financial transactions may be facilitated through the use of a carefully structured ESOP. The financing of mergers, acquisitions, and divestitures with pre-tax dollars and the ability to "cash out" existing shareholders on a tax-advantaged basis are examples of current ESOP financial strategies.

UNLEVERAGED ESOPS

The simplest form of ESOP is known as an unleveraged ESOP, in which the company makes an annual contribution of cash to the ESOP. The ESOP then returns the cash to the company by purchasing stock.

Alternatively, the company can simply contribute its stock to the ESOP. These shares are immediately allocated to employee accounts. Exhibit 14–1 illustrates.

Because it can be used to improve cash flow, an unleveraged ESOP is an attractive alternative to a cash profit-sharing plan. For instance, suppose a company makes an annual contribution to its profit-sharing plan equal to 10 percent of its $1 million payroll. While the full $100,000 contribution is tax-deductible, the productive use of that cash is lost to the business, locked up in a trust account. If the company instead contributed those funds to an ESOP, it would get the tax deduction and retain the $100,000 in the business.

LEVERAGED ESOPS

The remainder of this chapter will focus on leveraged ESOPs, so named because they are able to borrow money to purchase employer stock.

Because they can borrow to fund their purchase of stock, leveraged ESOPs can make large purchases of stock at one time, even to purchase an entire company.

Exhibit 14–2 illustrates how a leveraged ESOP might work. The company establishes an ESOP and guarantees payment of the ESOP loan. The ESOP borrows money from a third-party lender, then uses the loan proceeds to purchase stock from the company. The company makes an annual cash contribution to the ESOP sufficient to retire the principal and pay interest on the debt. The shares are allocated to participants' accounts each year as the debt is amortized.

Tax Benefits

The leveraged ESOP is an attractive corporate finance tool because it enables the sponsoring company to borrow at a significantly lower

EXHIBIT 14–1.   Unleveraged ESOP

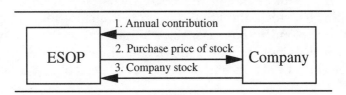

EXHIBIT 14–2.   Leveraged ESOP

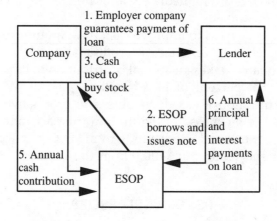

effective cost, a result of tax treatment that allows a tax deduction for ESOP principal repayments and dividends paid on ESOP stock, and in certain cases enables the company to obtain favorable borrowing rates. Annual contributions to an ESOP used to repay ESOP loan principal are tax-deductible up to a limit of 25 percent of payroll. This means the company can repay the loan out of pre-tax, rather than after-tax, earnings. There is no limit on the tax deductibility of ESOP contributions used to pay interest on an ESOP loan.

In addition, dividends paid on ESOP stock are generally deductible if they are either used to retire the ESOP loan or allocated to participant accounts. Most common stocks do not have a high enough yield for this feature to have much impact. However, this feature can make selling convertible preferred stock to an ESOP attractive, particularly when principal repayments on the loan are expected to exceed 25 percent of payroll.

The higher preferred dividend yield provides an extra source of tax-deductible funds for ESOP loan repayments. Convertible preferred shares are also less risky for participants, but still permit upside participation. The conversion premium means that fewer dilutive shares are issued. Finally, if the ESOP owns 50 percent or more of the employer's stock, the ESOP lender will qualify for a 50 percent interest exclusion. In that case, since 50 percent of the interest paid by the ESOP is not taxable to the lender, interest rates charged by the lender may be significantly less, about 80 percent of a comparable non-ESOP loan.

Accounting

Leveraged ESOPs require special accounting treatment. The company must book the ESOP debt on its balance sheet because its obligation to make contributions to the ESOP to repay the debt is considered a guarantee. The ESOP's payment to the company for the stock increases cash. Under current treatment, the number of shares outstanding increases by the amount sold to the ESOP, and these shares are considered outstanding for purposes of computing earnings per share (EPS).

The sale of new shares increases stockholders' equity, but this increase is exactly offset by a "contra-equity" account called unearned compensation. The unearned compensation account reflects the commitment to distribute future benefits to employees. The unearned compensation will be amortized as the shares are allocated to the participant accounts in the plan. Over time, the debt will be repaid and the unearned compensation account will be amortized, in essence converting a debt financing to an equity financing. Compensation is charged to operations based on the cost basis of the shares allocated to plan participants.

If your company's ESOP is currently leveraged or will be in the future, the accounting treatment for annual contributions and dividends paid on ESOP shares may be changed pursuant to a recently issued AICPA Exposure Draft of a proposed Statement of Position (SOP) on Accounting for ESOPs.

Under the proposal, compensation expense attributable to shares committed to be released from an ESOP suspense account would be determined based on the average fair market value of the shares over the period being reported, not the cost basis as reflected in current practice. As a result, a company with a leveraged ESOP and a rising share price would expect to accrue higher compensation expense under the proposed new treatment.

In addition, current accounting guidelines for ESOPs allow dividends paid on ESOP shares to be debited directly to retained earnings. Under the SOP, dividends paid on *unallocated shares* held by the ESOP would not be charged to retained earnings, but instead would be reported as a reduction of debt or accrued interest or as compensation expense, depending on whether the dividends were used for debt service or paid to participants.

Finally, in contrast to current treatment that requires all shares held by an ESOP to be outstanding for EPS purposes, the proposed SOP would require only shares allocated or committed for allocation to be treated as outstanding. Unlike the first two changes discussed, this provision would be favorable to most companies maintaining leveraged ESOPs because of the reduced EPS dilution.

The proposed SOP would require changes in accounting for new leveraged ESOPs formed after September 23, 1992 (or for shares acquired with the proceeds of an exempt loan after this date), and would be effective for fiscal years ending after December 15, 1993.

Companies would be permitted to apply the proposed SOP to shares held by an ESOP prior to September 23, 1992. However, if a public company elects to retain its current accounting for shares held by an ESOP on September 23, 1992, disclosure of pro forma income before extraordinary items, net income, and EPS, computed as if the employer had adopted the proposed SOP, would be required.

THE ESOP AS AN EMPLOYEE-BENEFIT PLAN

In considering the various uses for ESOPs, keep in mind that the basis of ESOP tax incentives is to enable employees to obtain stock. Employees become beneficial stockholders as the ESOP debt is repaid. As the company repays the ESOP debt, shares are allocated to the individual accounts of ESOP participants. Employees obtain ownership benefits without cost through the ESOP. This dual purpose of providing tax-advantaged financing in exchange for transferring stock to employees is the key element of ESOP legislation.

Aside from its value as a corporate-financing tool, an ESOP is attractive in ways that a traditional pension plan is not. Unlike a cash-based pension plan, an ESOP can substantially boost employee morale. By extending ownership to a broad group of employees, the ESOP links the financial future of the employees to that of the company, thus aligning the goals of the employees with those of the company. Studies indicate that stock ownership results in improved employee performance. Companies with ESOPs often enjoy improvements in employee productivity, quality of work, and longevity with the company. Improved performance is most evident in companies where an ESOP owns a significant amount of stock, such as companies that have gone private in an ESOP leveraged buyout.

ESOPs also have the potential to provide employees with financial rewards significantly greater than those provided by other benefit plans. This is partly because of the higher contribution limits permitted for ESOPs as compared with other defined contribution plans. But because they are primarily invested in only one security (common or convertible preferred stock of the employer), leveraged ESOPs are subject to greater volatility than other employee benefit plans, which are required to make diversified investments.

USING A LEVERAGED ESOP TO RAISE CAPITAL

The basic financing use of a leveraged ESOP is as an alternative to a traditional straight debt financing. An ESOP is an attractive alternative because it will reduce the cash requirements for debt servicing. Exhibits 14.3–14.6 illustrate the cash-flow benefits of an ESOP financing.

For the company in this example, the use of convertible preferred securities would result in additional cash-flow savings of $78,000, bringing the total difference in cash flow between a conventional loan and the ESOP loan in this example to $480,000.

By using the convertible preferred, the company can repay the loan more rapidly. The 25 percent of payroll-contribution limit for principal payments on ESOP loans may prevent some companies from obtaining the full level of financing needed to complete a desired transaction. In these cases, the ability to apply ESOP dividends to debt repayment can be a crucial factor in making ESOP financing a viable

EXHIBIT 14–3. Conventional Loan

Assume that a company with a 35 percent effective tax rate wants to borrow $1,000,000. The company is able to obtain conventional financing at a 10 percent interest rate payable in seven equal annual principal payments.

Year	Principal	Interest	Tax Savings	After-Tax Cash Cost
1	$ 142,857	$100,000	$ 35,000	$ 207,857
2	142,857	85,714	30,000	198,571
3	142,857	71,429	25,000	189,286
4	142,857	57,143	20,000	180,000
5	142,857	42,857	15,000	170,714
6	142,857	28,572	10,000	161,429
7	142,858	14,285	5,000	152,143
	$1,000,000	$400,000	$140,000	$1,260,000

EXHIBIT 14-4. Basic ESOP Loan—Ten Percent Interest

Now suppose the same company borrows $1,000,000 with an ESOP loan with the same terms. The company has a payroll base of $600,000, so it may deduct ESOP principal contributions of up to $150,000 per year.

Year	Principal	Interest	Tax Savings	After-Tax Cash Cost
1	$ 142,857	$100,000	$ 85,000	$157,857
2	142,857	85,714	80,000	148,571
3	142,857	71,429	75,000	139,286
4	142,857	57,143	70,000	130,000
5	142,857	42,857	65,000	120,714
6	142,857	28,572	60,000	111,429
7	142,858	14,285	55,000	102,143
	$1,000,000	$400,000	$490,000	$900,000

The cash-flow savings from the deductibility of principal amounts to $350,000 over the term of the loan.

EXHIBIT 14-5. ESOP Loan with Reduced Interest

Now further assume that the ESOP will own 50 percent or more of the employer's stock. In that case, the company will be able to obtain an interest rate of about 80 percent of what it would pay for comparable non-ESOP credit. Thus, returning to the previous example, the company would be able to borrow at 8 percent instead of 10 percent.

Year	Principal	Interest	Tax Savings	After-Tax Cash Cost
1	$ 142,857	$ 80,000	$ 78,000	$144,857
2	142,857	68,571	74,000	137,428
3	142,857	57,143	70,000	130,000
4	142,857	45,714	66,000	122,571
5	142,857	34,286	62,000	115,143
6	142,857	22,857	58,000	107,714
7	142,858	11,429	54,000	100,287
	$1,000,000	$320,000	$462,000	$858,000

In this example, the reduced interest rate would produce additional cash savings of $52,000, making the total after-tax cash cost of the ESOP loan $402,000 less than a conventional loan.

option, since it allows companies to exceed the 25 percent of payroll-contribution limit. Of course, the attractive cost of ESOP debt compared with traditional debt is only half the story. The ESOP financing involves a commitment to distribute $1 million of stock to your employees, where a traditional debt financing does not. If traditional

EXHIBIT 14–6.   ESOP Loan with Dividend Payments

If the company were to sell the ESOP a convertible preferred stock with an annual dividend of 10 percent, the preferred dividend payments could be used to retire principal. Dividend payments used to retire principal are also tax-deductible (beyond the 25 percent of payroll limit, or $150,000 in this example), allowing for quicker debt repayment and further cash-flow benefits.

| | Principal | | | | |
Year	Annual Contribution	Preferred Dividend	Interest	Tax Savings	After-Tax Cash Cost
1	$150,000	$100,000	$ 80,000	$115,500	$214,500
2	150,000	100,000	60,000	108,500	201,500
3	150,000	100,000	40,000	101,500	188,500
4	150,000	100,000	20,000	94,500	175,500
	$600,000	$400,000	$200,000	$420,000	$780,000

debt financing is combined with a tax-deductible distribution of stock to employees, similar tax benefits may be achieved.

THE LEVERAGED ESOP AS A FINANCING ALTERNATIVE

Before you consider a leveraged ESOP as a financing alternative, ask yourself this question: "How do I feel about my employees owning stock in my company?"

If you have strong concerns about sharing ownership with your employees, you should not even consider an ESOP. The ESOP will not be successful unless you adopt it with the intention of acting as if you were in partnership with your employees.

Look again at the comparison of a traditional debt financing with an ESOP financing. Assuming that the company borrows $1 million at 10 percent, the present value of its after-tax payments in a traditional debt financing is $1 million. In an ESOP financing, assuming that the lender qualifies for the interest exclusion, the present value of after-tax debt payments is roughly $680,000. In terms of the present value of the cash flows in the debt financing, the company will save $320,000 by using the ESOP. However, you also must consider the $1 million in stock the company will have issued in addition to the debt. In terms of the total financing costs of the debt and the equity, the company is $680,000 worse off with the ESOP financing ($320,000 benefit from debt financing less $1 million value of stock).

For the ESOP financing to be attractive as opposed to the traditional debt financing, the ESOP will have to bring the company $680,000 in nonfinancing benefits that the debt financing does not offer. There are, of course, quantifiable benefits an ESOP may provide:

- As a result of installing the ESOP, the company may be able to restructure another retirement plan to reduce or eliminate its cash cost. The present value of future contributions to this plan could be substantial. Or perhaps the company was planning to implement a retirement plan in any case.
- In exchange for participation in the ESOP, employees may be willing to accept a reduction in their pay or forgo future pay increases.
- If the ESOP is properly communicated, productivity may increase substantially, and the cost of distributing ESOP stock may more than pay for itself through resulting earnings improvements.
- If the owner of a closely held company sells stock to an ESOP and is able to defer the taxes on the rollover, the immediate benefits of the tax deferral and the diversification of his or her portfolio will be substantial. For example, if the owner sells $1 million in stock to the ESOP and is able to structure a "permanent" deferral (deferral until death) of the capital-gains taxes, the immediate benefit may be as high as $350,000 ($1 million gain times 35 percent tax rate). The value of knowing that estate taxes have been provided for and that the company will not be broken up on the owner's death may be of even greater value.
- In a leveraged buyout, ESOP participation and the attendant employee motivation, added to tax and cash-flow benefits, may provide the difference between a successful deal and insolvency.

THE LEVERAGED ESOP AS A MARKET FOR SHARES

A stockholder of a closely held company can sell stock to an ESOP, defer taxes on the gain on the stock indefinitely, and use the proceeds to obtain liquidity and diversity in his or her personal portfolio. But in order to do this, the stockholder must structure the sale to meet the requirements of Internal Revenue Code Section 1042.

The stockholder must have held the stock for at least three years prior to the sale. The seller must invest the proceeds from the sale in "qualified replacement property" within a 15-month period, beginning 3 months before the sale and ending 12 months after the sale. Qualified replacement property is generally securities of an unrelated domestic corporation whose passive-investment income does not exceed 25 percent of revenues. Examples of qualified replacement property include stocks and bonds of U.S. companies. However, mutual funds and securities of the seller's corporation or of any related companies are not considered qualified replacement property.

The most difficult requirement to satisfy is that the ESOP must own, immediately after the sale, at least 30 percent of the total value of all of the company's outstanding stock or at least 30 percent of each class of outstanding stock. While the ESOP is required to hold 30 percent of the stock immediately after the sale, that does not mean that a single individual has to sell the entire 30 percent to the ESOP. As long as the ESOP has a total of 30 percent after the sale, individual sales of any magnitude and over any period of time will qualify for tax-deferred treatment.

The basis in the replacement property will be the same as the original basis in the stock. Income taxes on the replacement property will be deferred until the maturity or sale of the property, at which time the prior unrecognized gain will be recaptured. Some dispositions of replacement property, including disposition because of the seller's death, are exempt from the recapture provisions. In this case, the seller's estate is permitted to step up its basis in the qualified property to its then-current market value. Thus, the replacement property is transferred to the seller's heirs tax-free, permanently deferring taxation on the original gain.

The transaction also benefits the company because the stock is purchased through annual, tax-deductible contributions to the ESOP, and the purchase of the stock does not result in any cash reduction or permanent drain of company equity. As the ESOP debt is repaid and the unearned compensation account is amortized, the company's book value returns to its original, pre-ESOP level.

Contrast this with a traditional share repurchase without an ESOP. Consider as an example a company with $10 million in equity and $10 million in debt. This company buys out a 30 percent shareholder at a time when the company's stock is valued at two times book value. The company borrows the $6 million purchase price. After the transaction, the company's debt would increase to $16 million, and its equity would decrease to $4 million. Its debt-to-equity ratio would increase from 1 : 1 to 4 : 1, from ideal leverage to leveraged buyout.

The existence of an ESOP can be highly beneficial to a closely held company even if the ESOP does not own 30 percent of the shares. The ESOP may still serve as a market for shares and provide liquidity for untraded or thinly traded stocks. Although the advantages of a tax-deferred sale will not be available to the seller, the ESOP offers the same advantages to the company when a minority shareholder sells out.

An ESOP sale is generally less expensive than a sale to a third party, since there is no due diligence required. The existence of the ESOP and its presence as a willing buyer may eliminate the need for the company to maintain insurance policies on the lives of founding shareholders. Finally, the annual ESOP valuation provides information on the company's financial progress.

THE ESOP LEVERAGED BUYOUT

ESOPs have participated in LBOs about as long as there have been LBOs, at least since 1956, when Louis Kelso led the ESOP LBO of Peninsula Newspapers. In the last few years, ESOPs have become an important financing alternative in corporate acquisitions, particularly in leveraged buyouts where a substantial amount of debt must be raised. The tax-deductibility of ESOP debt repayments and the lower ESOP interest rates (if the ESOP owns more than 50 percent of the company) translate into increased cash flow for the leveraged company. This increased cash flow often means that an LBO with significant ESOP financing has a margin for error that a traditional LBO may not have. Companies that will find ESOP leveraged buyouts attractive include the following:

- Companies that expect to have positive pre-tax income (after interest expense) shortly after the buyout
- Companies with a substantial total payroll—30 to 40 percent of the estimated total acquisition cost is ideal
- Companies that, in exchange for the implementation of the ESOP, may restructure another retirement plan in order to reduce or eliminate its cash cost

- Companies that may obtain other labor-cost concessions in exchange for participation in the ESOP

While the financing advantages make the ESOP leveraged buyout attractive, there are several disadvantages.

First, if the ESOP is not already in existence, implementing one can be costly and time-consuming. If the timing of the transaction is important, implementing an ESOP may not be feasible. A major issue with any ESOP LBO is that management and outside investors will eventually yield a significant ownership interest in the company to employees, potentially losing voting control. Several companies have overcome this disadvantage by creative uses of multiple classes of stock and management stock compensation plans, designed to act together to gradually return voting control to the management group.

Charter Medical Corporation used this strategy in its 1988 management buyout. Immediately after the LBO, Charter's ESOP had 83 percent voting control of the company, with the management group controlling the remaining 17 percent. According to Charter's merger proxy, the management group could increase its voting control in Charter from 17 percent to 54 percent in five years. This is based on the assumption that all dilutive securities convert into common stock and that Charter performs well enough for all restricted stock to be earned (24.5 percent of initial shares outstanding).

SIZE OF A LEVERAGED ESOP FINANCING

There are no regulations that directly limit how much stock an ESOP may purchase. However, there are several factors, both statutory and other, that indirectly set such limits. The law establishes a limit of 25 percent of payroll for deductions for employer contributions to a leveraged ESOP to repay principal. There is no limit for contributions to pay loan interest only. The statutory limit for the loan term is 15 years; however, most banks will not offer ESOP loans with terms longer than 10 years.

The combination of these factors means that a rule-of-thumb guideline for the maximum size of an ESOP financing for your company is 250 percent of your payroll (payroll times 25 percent times ten years). This figure may work out to be smaller or larger, depending on such factors as the anticipated growth of your payroll, your credit rating, and the importance of receiving the full tax deduction.

The number of shares released each year for allocation to participants is a function of the loan amortization schedule (i.e., once the loan is paid off all shares will be held in participant accounts). Shorter duration loans will cause shares to be allocated more quickly. Greater flexibility is achieved through the use of a "mirror loan" structure in which the company obtains a loan from a third party (external loan) and then loans the cash to the ESOP (internal loan). The internal loan dictates the number of shares allocated to participants and may be structured with a term significantly longer than an outside lender is willing to provide.

A FINAL NOTE: ESOP TAX LEGISLATION

The ESOP had been around since Congress passed the Employee Retirement Income Security Act of 1974 (ERISA). Shortly thereafter approximality 300 ESOPs came into existence. Since that time, Congress has substantially broadened the tax advantages of ESOPs, which is reflected in the growth in the number of ESOPs to approximately 11,000 today.

From the passage of ERISA in 1974 through the Tax Reform Act of 1986, Congress passed legislation that was consistently favorable to ESOPs, with each new piece of ESOP legislation expanding the ESOP's tax advantages. The Omnibus Budget Reconciliation Act of 1989 was the first time Congress rolled back ESOP tax benefits. The policy reason for these changes was to correct perceived abuses of the ESOP as a takeover deterrent. Underlying that goal is the ongoing need to raise revenue.

When all the smoke had cleared, the actual changes to the ESOP laws were much less detrimental than had been feared by ESOP proponents. The main change was the requirement that an ESOP own 50 percent or more of the stock for the lender to qualify for the interest exclusion. While the changes did not harm ESOPs, they did not do much to accomplish Congress's goals in enacting them. As Congress continues its quixotic quest to raise revenues without raising taxes, ESOP incentives will remain a tempting target.

This discussion has been based on tax laws in effect as of February 1993. These laws can be expected to change from time to time. If you are interested in ESOPs after reading this chapter, consult your tax advisor regarding the then-current tax treatment of ESOPs.

Exhibit 14–7 is an illustration of a typical ESOP leveraged buyout transaction. The Dan River Inc. investor group used this type of structure when it took the company private in 1983. The investor group, consisting of Dan River's management and the investment banking firm Kelso & Company, established a new holding company and an ESOP. The total purchase price for Dan River was $154 million. The investor group put up $5 million, and the remaining $149 million was a holding company bank loan. The holding company then issued $110 million of stock to the ESOP, principally for notes. The holding company used the $154 million to buy all the outstanding Dan River stock. Subsequently, Dan River became a subsidiary of the holding company. After the transaction, ownership of the company was split among Kelso (5 percent), Dan River management (25 percent), and the ESOP (70 percent).

Overview of ESOP Legal Requirements

For an ESOP to have its tax-qualified status, there are several legal requirements it must satisfy. Most of these are beyond the scope of

EXHIBIT 14–7.   ESOP Purchase Structuring Example

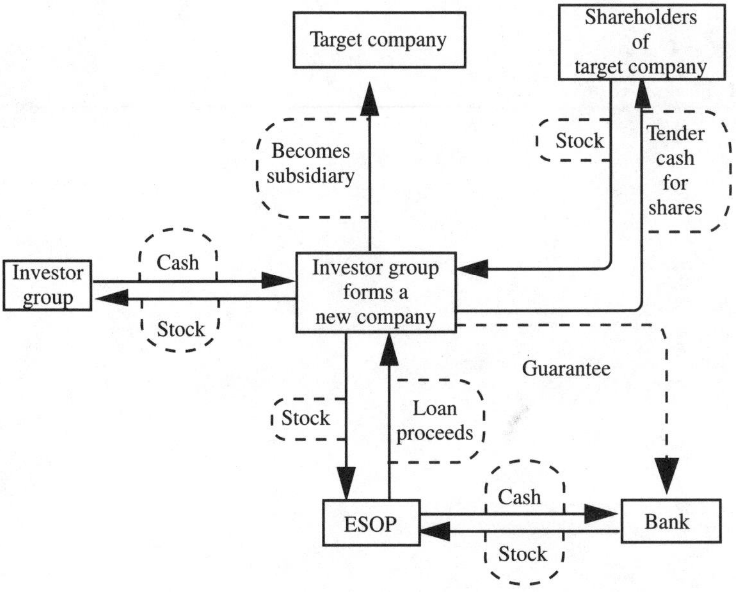

this discussion, but following are a few of the more germane requirements:

- The primary purpose of the ESOP must be to benefit plan participants. In other words, a company should not adopt an ESOP unless it can demonstrate that the ESOP will be a valuable employee benefit (however attractive the ESOP may be to the company as a corporate-finance tool).
- All ESOPs must invest primarily in employer securities. A leveraged ESOP must invest primarily in common stock or non-callable convertible preferred stock of the employer.
- Employees must be given the right to exercise voting rights on certain issues with respect to shares that have been allocated to them.
- Employees must be given the right to receive plan distributions in the form of employer stock. However, in a closely held company, the bylaws may be written to exclude the possibility of terminated employees retaining shares.

15

FRANCHISING

Growing your business as fast as you wish can be risky, time-consuming, and costly. Franchising is an often overlooked method of achieving your objective. Through this style of doing business, you solicit the help of others by sharing both the risk and reward of business expansion. Franchising is an excellent financing concept. Not only do you receive working capital in the form of a franchise fee, you avoid the need to raise capital to finance new locations.

You need to be sure that you have realistic growth goals for your franchising company. We have all heard the stories of franchising companies growing at incredible rates—such as companies selling 50 to 100 new franchises a year. The truth is that most organizations new to franchising do not grow at anything close to that rate in their first five to ten years. Most companies sell between four and ten new franchises a year for the first ten years they are in business. The speed at which your franchise organization grows will depend primarily on four factors: total up-front cost to the franchisee, access to capital to finance the up-front cost, the franchisee's perceived return on the investment, and the success of your existing franchisees.

The more expensive it is for the franchisees to get into the business, the more likely your organization is to experience slower growth. If you can arrange means for your franchisees to finance a part of their up-front cost, you are more likely to attract franchisees. By reducing the up-front cost you make it easier for more people to acquire one of your franchises and improve the rate of return on their investments. Ultimately, *the success of your franchisees* is the determining factor in how fast your company grows.

WHAT IS FRANCHISING?

History doesn't pinpoint exactly when franchising started, but indications can be found that the emperors of early centuries franchised tax collectors to gather the revenues of the empire.

Today's franchising is found in many kinds of businesses, but in only two basic forms: the product/trade format and the business format.

The product/trade format is used extensively by manufacturers to bring their products to the marketplace. Examples include automobiles, gasoline, tires, auto parts, soft drinks, and many other consumer products.

While product/trade-format franchises still represent the majority of franchise operations, the business-format franchise is becoming increasingly popular. In the business-format franchise, a company "packages" its trademark, processes, products, and system of doing business into a business approach, then transfers the right to use the approach for a specific period of time. The purchaser of a business-format franchise may be looking to start a new business from scratch, utilizing another's experience and expertise, or may be an existing business owner in the same line of business looking to capitalize on the marketing clout, synergy, and economies of scale of being part of a large organization.

The process of taking an existing business and changing it to your business format is called "conversion franchising." Century 21 is an example of a company that uses this process, signing on formerly independent real estate agents into its national network.

THE DIFFERENT FRANCHISING METHODS

There are various ways to transfer these rights, but typically the franchisee pays the franchisor a one-time fee up front for the right to conduct business using the format in a defined territory, then an ongoing royalty, usually based upon sales, for the continued right to operate. The franchisee may also participate in local and national advertising and pay a fee based on a percentage of sales. This is referred to as a single-unit license.

The franchisor may wish to sell the rights to more than one franchised territory to the franchisee, in which case a multiple license may be used. In this method, the franchisee signs an agreement and agrees to buy several units at the same time. Usually the front-end fee for the later units, part of which is paid as a deposit, is less than that for the first unit, since the cost to the franchisor to locate and select franchisees and assist in opening these units is less. Ongoing royalty fees are the same as for a single license.

A company may also sell a master license. Using this approach, the franchisor, for an agreed-upon price, transfers the rights to a much larger geographic area, perhaps several states, to the licensee. The franchisor then permits the licensee to sell licenses to others in that defined territory. These "sub-franchisees" enter into the same license agreement as a regular franchisee; however, the master-license holder will receive a portion of the license fee and the future royalty. In return for receiving part of the proceeds, the master licensee undertakes some of the responsibilities typically performed by the franchisor.

Another approach that has become popular in recent years is the area developer. With an area-development agreement, the franchisor sells the exclusive right to an individual for a defined period of time to open numerous locations on a predetermined, agreed-upon schedule. The area developer pays the franchisor a separate fee to purchase these exclusive rights. He also pays a license fee at the opening of each location. The license agreement is usually the same as that provided a single-license holder.

Should franchising be your best alternative to expand, each option needs to be reviewed to determine which best fits the company's business plan. Each has advantages and disadvantages, which need to be carefully weighed.

WHEN TO CONSIDER FRANCHISING

Can you franchise your business? To do so, it is important to have a proven concept, already in operation. It should also be profitable. Your company must be able to duplicate this business for others to operate, and such things as inventory stocking levels, staffing, daily and monthly accounting, advertising, marketing, and dealing with computerized systems must be easily learnable by franchisees. As the franchisor, you must provide the franchisee a base of support that includes sales promotion, marketing, advertising, and real estate site selection. The latter is extremely important in that the real estate must be in a location natural to the business concept. You should also be able to assist franchisees in finding financing for the real estate if this is an important ingredient in the business concept.

In developing the format, it is desirable that some aspect of the business be patentable or difficult to duplicate, in order to create an entry barrier to others and provide a sufficient return for franchisees. In many cases, a well-developed business format and extensive knowledge of the business you are formatting will serve as a temporary entry barrier until your company becomes well known and creates a more permanent block to others through name recognition and a perception of quality. On an ongoing basis, you must be committed to developing new products and services so that franchisees' businesses can continue to grow and your company can increase royalty revenue.

Some characteristics of your business and/or industry that indicate franchising is appropriate are as follows:

- Significant economies of scale are gained in your business by having a large organization.
- A business need exists to capture a large market share on a national, regional, or local level.
- The need exists for daily owner or management involvement in the operations of each location.
- A significant number of "mom and pop" businesses could be enticed to join a franchise organization and create a market leader.

ADVANTAGES AND DISADVANTAGES

Among franchising's advantages are speeding the growth of your business and promoting your market image more quickly than you yourself could. It would be extremely difficult for your company to open locations simultaneously in eight to ten major cities. Franchisees can do this for you. Franchising also helps distribute start-up costs to others and provides front-end cash from the license fee to offset the costs incurred by your personnel helping to open locations.

Studies performed for the International Franchise Association show that if you are careful in selecting franchisees, their failure rate is relatively low and your chances of expanding your business are good. In effect, local entrepreneurs are building a customer base and are like partners representing you at the local level.

Another important advantage is that your capital requirements for expansion are generally less than they would be if you tried the expansion alone. While investments by a company of $250,000 to $500,000 to get into franchising are not uncommon, these sums can be considered rather limited when considering the number of locations and amount of growth experienced by a good franchisor. Also, there is no equity dilution to your company, since the franchisee functions more like a business partner than a shareholder.

Some of the disadvantages of franchising are that it relies on a proven concept that can be duplicated and easily performed by others. This requires extensive testing of the business ideas and operations so that no surprises arise as the franchisees begin to operate. In line with this, your business takes on an added dimension. You need to be prepared to help others operate their businesses; this changes how you spend your time.

In making the decision to finance your company's growth through franchising, you and your management team should focus on the fact that you are moving into a new line of business. In building the company to its current status, you have been operators of the business and in total control of all decisions made with regard to each location. In franchising, you are becoming consultants to other business owners who have paid you for the right to utilize your business format, and you cannot exercise total control over how they operate their businesses. Many companies experience a decrease in the performance of their core business during the transition to a franchising organization.

OTHER IMPORTANT CONSIDERATIONS

One of the initial decisions you will have to make once you have decided to use franchising to finance growth is establishing the initial franchise fee and the ongoing royalty fees. Initially, the bulk of your profits and cash flow from your franchising activities will depend on franchise sales and the initial franchise fees. Somewhere in the three- to five-year period, your profitability and cash flow should become determined primarily by the level of your ongoing royalty stream. In setting these fees, you need to remember that the initial and ongoing fees must be adequate to generate a profit for your company but not so burdensome to franchisees that they cannot make a reasonable return on their investments for the risk they are taking. In calculating the return on investment for the franchisees, one must not consider the salary the franchisee gets for working in the business. The franchisee could earn a salary at a job and invest his or her money in some other investment opportunity.

Franchising can also require a front-end investment by your company of largely intangible costs that need to be monitored closely. Adequate capitalization of your existing business is important before you undertake this challenge.

There are a lot of legal complexities in offering franchises. A uniform offering circular under the Federal Trade Commission guidelines must be prepared and provided to each prospective franchisee. Many states consider franchise sales the same way they consider securities sales, and require registration by the franchisor before the company is permitted to sell franchises. Attorneys who specialize in franchising need to be consulted to avoid difficulties in the selling process. In addition, your company must develop training programs and detailed manuals on how to operate the business on a day-to-day basis. Such things as store layout, equipment requirements, leasing requirements, inventory levels, business forms, and marketing and advertising techniques need to be clearly defined in these operating manuals. This, too, can require a substantial amount of time and money.

As your business continues to grow, you will probably need to own and operate a reasonable percentage of the existing locations if you wish to take your business public. Underwriters frequently see a weakness in a franchisor if there is an overdependence on royalties and license fees from noncontrolled entities. This situation may require your company to buy back the more successful franchisees at premium prices at a time when the company has other goals and objectives. You may also find that the company no longer needs to grow through franchising, since you have met your objectives and have developed a strong reputation. As with any business, the franchisor must have a strategy that anticipates the future and is flexible enough to meet changing needs.

16

TAX PLANNING

The very idea that a company's tax program can be an important contributor in raising capital for growth is probably a pleasant surprise for many entrepreneurs. Nobody likes taxes. But there is a bright side to this inescapable drain on cash. A tax program that takes advantage of every possibility the law allows can save substantial sums, and money thus saved can significantly reduce dependence on outside financing.

The logic is disarmingly simple:

- Pay only the minimum amount of taxes due.
- Pay them on the latest date permissible.

Simple as the strategy is, carrying it out is one of the most complex challenges in the life of a company, starting even before the company comes into existence. It begins with deciding what kind of organization to create in the first place in order to realize the best tax position for the owners. From that moment on, tax considerations enter into virtually every major decision. Tax laws are very complicated and are constantly changing. The application and impact of tax laws can vary widely depending upon the specific facts involved. Professional advisors should be consulted before you make any decisions.

MINIMIZING THE EFFECT OF INCOME TAXES
ON CASH FLOW

For a growing business, income taxes can represent one of the most significant continuing obligations. Managing this obligation requires

advance planning and a properly maintained tax-management system, which can significantly reduce the adverse effect of taxes on cash
flow. The start-up phase of a business is not too early to begin planning.

The major elements of an effective tax-management system are as
follows:

- A comprehensive tax calendar
- Tax-minimization strategies and related implementation plans
- A competent compliance function
- Good accounting records

Each business should maintain a complete tax calendar to plan for
all required tax filings and payments. By doing so, management can
anticipate filing requirements and payments, identify tax-planning
opportunities, minimize the tax burden and its effect on cash flow,
and avoid penalties. Often, the penalties associated with not filing or
late filing are much higher than the cost of borrowing funds.

A tax advisor can generally help set up a comprehensive tax calendar. If you construct your own, small-business guides published
by the Internal Revenue Service can help by providing information
on federal taxes and requirements for compliance. Information about
state or local taxes may be available by calling the appropriate agency
(generally the secretary of state's office or the state's department of
revenue).

Tax planning involves studying the tax law to develop strategies
to minimize tax liabilities. Very rarely do the federal income tax laws
permit business income to be excluded from taxation. Therefore, almost all tax strategies relate to three areas:

1. The timing of income and deductions
2. The character of income or loss (e.g., ordinary losses versus
   passive-activity losses; ordinary losses are generally deductible
   in full while passive-activity losses are subject to the limitations
   discussed later in this chapter)
3. The avoidance of double taxation of income

The results of tax planning must be seen not only in terms of
advantages and tax savings, but also in terms of possible disadvantages and costs. Hence, tax strategies should take into account how

decisions made primarily for tax purposes might affect future opportunities. For example, use of the last-in, first-out (LIFO) inventory method may save tax dollars, but the reduction in earnings for financial-reporting purposes may have an adverse effect on a company's ability to raise capital. In addition, effective tax planning requires the integration of planning for the business and planning for its owners. For example, the owner's decision whether to purchase an asset and lease it to the business or to have the business purchase the asset directly should be made only after fully considering the tax ramifications to both the owner and the business.

Good tax planning involves reviewing all proposed transactions for their potential tax impact, both federal and state. Planning before the fact is important because there are generally few, if any, options available after the transaction has taken place. Remember, it is easier to prevent a problem than to correct one.

Planning for taxes at the state and local levels is often overlooked. Generally, state and local taxes are not carefully examined because they are erroneously considered insignificant when compared to federal taxes. However, state and local taxes can be quite costly in certain situations. It is usually beneficial to examine how they would be affected by any major or unusual transaction. For example, whether a new business segment operates as a division or a branch, or as a separate corporation in a particular state may have a significant impact on how much state tax is paid. Restructuring such a transaction may be an appropriate strategy if state or local tax savings result in an overall benefit.

Proper tax planning requires the use of professionals. Your tax advisor or qualified tax personnel should possess the skills necessary to map out your business-tax strategies and to inform you of any potential tax developments that may affect your tax planning. Your tax advisor or tax personnel should be identifying tax-planning needs and volunteering ideas instead of merely reacting to your inquiries. Your obligation is to keep your advisor informed of changes in the business and of proposed transactions so that he or she may evaluate any tax ramifications and planning opportunities. If you are not pleased with your outside tax advisor, change and do not be discouraged. Sometimes it takes a succession of tax advisors before you find one who is right for your needs.

Note: Tax compliance (filings and payments) can be delegated to your outside tax advisor. Just be sure that you discuss in advance how your in-house personnel can be used to the maximum extent to perform routine tasks and provide assistance to the advisor. In this manner, you can use your advisor for the more important aspects of proper tax compliance and pay only for the skill level required.

The need for good accounting records in the tax-planning process should be obvious. Accounting records are the basis upon which many tax-planning strategies are conceived and evaluated; for example, selection of tax-accounting methods, selection of a tax year-end, and the estimated tax payment required. Accounting records are also used as supporting documentation in the event of a tax audit. Maintain good accounting records and you are certain to reduce the chance of making poor decisions based on insufficient or incorrect information.

SELECTION OF LEGAL BUSINESS FORM

Each business must have a legal form. Although the tax aspects are important, the selection of legal form should not be based on tax considerations alone. Some of the concerns that affect this selection include limitation on liability, ability to finance expansion, management form, and ability to transfer ownership or control. The choice of legal form may depend on the compatibility of the form with the stage of development your business or a segment of your business is in. (See Exhibits 16–1 and 16–2.)

The most common business forms are sole proprietorship, partnership, regular corporation (C corporation), and S corporation. Each of these forms has advantages and disadvantages. It is important to understand the differences because the manner in which they are taxed and the circumstances in which a particular form should be used can have a significant effect on your business's cash flow.

Sole Proprietorship

A sole proprietorship is the easiest business form to begin and operate. In general, all items of business income, deduction, loss, and credit are reported directly on an individual's tax returns and taxed at personal rates. An owner's liability for debts of the business is not limited to the assets of the business, because the owner and the business are considered to be one and the same. Since the owner generally can

EXHIBIT 16–1. Comparison of Legal Business Forms—Tax Considerations

Item	Sole Proprietorship	Partnership	S Corporation	Corporation
Ease and effort of transfer of ownership interest.	Transfer causes termination.	Transfer of more than 50% of interests may cause the termination of the old partnership and creation of a new one. Depending on the partnership agreement, a transfer may have to be approved by the other partners.	Generally, stock is easily and readily transferable and transfer has no effect on the corporate entity. Consideration must be given to the effect of the transfer on the S election to be sure it does not result in an unintended termination.	Generally, stock is easily and readily transferable and transfer has no effect on corporate entity.
Who is the taxpayer?	Owner is taxed on income of business on his or her personal return.	The partners are taxed on the taxable income of the partnership, whether or not cash is distributed to them.	The stockholders are taxed on the taxable income of the corporation, whether or not cash is distributed to them. Certain gain from disposition of assets may trigger a tax, though, and some S corporations may be subject to tax on passive income.	The corporation is taxed on its taxable income, whether or not it is distributed to the stockholders.

(continued)

EXHIBIT 16-1. Continued

Item	Sole Proprietorship	Partnership	S Corporation	Corporation
Selection of taxable year.	Must be the same as owner's individual return year.	Must conform to that of partners owning a majority interest or that of the principal partners, generally the calendar year, unless consent of the commissioner is obtained for a valid business purpose. Special rules also allow other year-ends, provided an estimated tax payment is made for any deferred income.	Must be on calendar year unless the company can show existence of a business purpose. Special rules allow alternate year-ends, provided an estimated tax payment is made for any deferred income.	No restriction unless a personal-service corporation, in which case a calendar year generally must be used.
Distribution of earnings— impact on owner.	No additional tax to owner.	No tax effect on partner unless a cash distribution exceeds a partner's tax basis in his or her partnership interest.	Similar to partnerships unless corporation has earnings and profits from a period when it was a regular C corporation.	Taxable to stockholders as ordinary dividends to the extent of earnings and profits.
Distribution of earnings— impact on entity	No impact on proprietorship.	No impact on partnership.	Gain must be recognized by S corporation on distribution of appreciated property.	Gain must be recognized by C corporation on distribution of appreciated property.
Limitations on earnings accumulation.	No limit; no impact.	No limit since all income is taxed to partners, whether it is distributed or not.	No limit since all income is taxed to the stockholders, whether it is distributed or not.	May be subject to penalty tax if accumulation is unreasonable.

Net operating loss.	Fully deductible to extent proprietor is at risk in the activity.	Deductible by partners subject to basis, at-risk, and passive-loss limitations.	Deductible by stockholders subject to basis, at-risk, and passive-loss limitations.	Deductible by the corporation only within prescribed carryback and carryover periods.
Salaries paid to owners.	Owner is not an employee; salary is not a deduction for the business.	Payment for services is treated as a payment to an unrelated party unless the payment amount is based on partnership income. However, partner is not treated as an employee for withholding purposes.	Same as regular corporation. The salary level may also be important if salaries may be a device for shifting income among stockholders within the same family group.	Owners are employees and their salaries are taxable to them and deductible by the corporation. Salaries must be reasonable in relation to services rendered.
Capital gains and losses.	Taxed to owner as such.	Taxed to the partners as such, regardless of the amount of ordinary net taxable income or loss of partnership.	Generally, taxed to the stockholders as such, but may also be taxed to the corporation in certain cases.	Taxed to the corporation.
Allocation of net income or loss or different types of income and deductions among owners by agreement.	Not applicable.	Can be done, as long as special allocations have substantial economic effect.	Not possible.	Not possible.
Passive-investment income.	No effect.	No effect.	May cause tax at corporate level for some S corporations.	May create a personal holding company taxed at penalty rates.

(continued)

EXHIBIT 16-1. Continued

Item	Sole Proprietorship	Partnership	S Corporation	Corporation
Charitable contributions.	Deductible subject to normal limitation on individuals.	Not deductible by the partnership on its return, but by the partners on their individual returns subject to the limitations applicable to individuals.	Same as partnership.	Deductible by the corporation limited to 10% of taxable income. Excess may be carried over.
Alternative minimum tax preferences.	Tax preferences appear on individual return.	Tax preferences pass through to the partners.	Same as partnership.	Corporation may be subject to the alternative minimum tax in addition to tax on taxable income.
Sale of ownership interest.	May be part capital gain and part ordinary income.	May be part capital gain and part ordinary income.	Normally, all capital gain; may be ordinary income if corporation is collapsible.	Normally, all capital gain; may be ordinary income if corporation is collapsible.
Tax on transfer of assets to business entity.	Not applicable.	Generally none.	None, if transfer qualifies under Section 351.	None, if transfer qualifies under Section 351.
Liquidation of the business—impact on owner.	There is no formal liquidation.	Normally, no tax unless cash or equivalent exceeds basis in partnership interest. Excess is then taxed as capital gain. Loss may arise and be deductible in limited circumstances.	Amount received in excess of basis in stock is taxable as capital gain, or ordinary income if the corporation is collapsible.	Amount received in excess of basis in stock is taxable as capital gain, or ordianry income if the corporation is collapsible.

Liquidation of the business—impact on entity.	There is no formal liquidation.	No gain or loss at partnership level.	Corporation may be taxed on distribution or disposition of appreciated assets in certain cases.	After 1986, corporation must recognize gain on sale of assets or on distribution of appreciated assets to stockholders.
Effect of owner's death or sale of interest on basis of assets in business.	None.	Election may be filed to adjust basis of partnership assets applicable to transferee partner's interest.	S corporation basis in assets does not change. Stockholder's basis in S corporation stock will likely differ from owner's share of net corporate assets (tax basis).	Same as for S corporation.
Life.	Unspecified. Terminable at discretion or death of owner.	Usually set up for a specific agreed-upon term; generally will be terminated by death, withdrawal, insolvency, or legal disability of a general partner.	Unlimited or perpetual unless limited by state law or terms of its charter. Election may be revoked or terminated without affecting continuity of life.	Unlimited or perpetual unless limited by state law or terms of its charter.
Liability of owners.	Owner fully liable for all debts.	Each general partner is fully liable for all debts. A limited partner's liability is usually limited to the amount of his or her capital contribution.	Stockholders are generally sheltered from any liabilities of the corporation.	Stockholders are generally sheltered from any liabilities of the corporation.

(continued)

EXHIBIT 16-1. Continued

Item	Sole Proprietorship	Partnership	S Corporation	Corporation
Management of business operations.	Owner responsible for all management functions.	Usually, all general partners will be active participants in management. However, other partners may grant management control to one or more partners by agreement. Limited partners may not participate in management.	Control can be exercised by a small number of officers without having to consult other owners. Generally, a large portion of owners are active since the number of stockholders cannot exceed 35.	Regardless of the number of stockholders, control can be exercised by small number of officers and directors without having to consult other owners.
Availability of outside capital or financing.	Limited to personal borrowing capital of owner, including both business and personal assets.	Although public financing is available, more typically limited to borrowing from partners or outsiders, or to admitting new partners who contribute additional capital.	Limited in that there can be only one class of stock outstanding, but the corporation may sell bonds so long as they are not considered to be a second class of stock.	May sell stocks to public.

EXHIBIT 16-2. Comparison of Legal Business Forms—Nontax Considerations

Item	Sole Proprietorship	Partnership	S Corporation	Corporation
Entity.	Inseparable from individual owner.	Usually recognized as separate by the business community but not for all purposes.	Completely separate from owners and recognized as such.	Completely separate from owners and recognized as such.
Life.	Unspecified. Terminable at discretion or death of owner.	Usually set up for a specific agreed-upon term; generally will be terminated by death, withdrawal, insolvency, or legal disability of a general partner.	Unlimited or perpetual unless limited by state law or terms of its charter. Election may be revoked or terminated without affecting continuity of life.	Unlimited or perpetual unless limited by state law or terms of its charter.
Liability of owners.	Owner fully liable for all debts.	Each general partner is fully liable for all debts. A limited partner's liability is usually limited to the amount of his or her capital contribution.	Stockholders are generally sheltered from any liabilities of the corporation.	Stockholders are generally sheltered from any liabilities of the corporation.

(continued)

267

EXHIBIT 16–2. Continued

Item	Sole Proprietorship	Partnership	S Corporation	Corporation
Management of business operations.	Owner responsible for all management functions.	Usually, all general partners will be active participants in management. However, other partners may grant management control to one or more partners by agreement.	Control can be exercised by a small number of officers without having to consult other owners. Generally, a large portion of owners are active since the total number of stockholders cannot exceed 35.	Regardless of the total number of stockholders, control can be exercised by small number of officers and directors without having to consult other owners.
Availability of outside capital or financing.	Limited to personal borrowing capital of owner, including both business and personal assets.	Although public financing is available, more typically limited to borrowing from partners or outsiders, or to admitting new partners who contribute additional capital.	Limited in that there can be only one class of stock outstanding, but the corporation may sell bonds so long as they are not considered to be a second class of stock.	May sell stocks or bonds to public.

be held liable for all debts of the business, a creditor will evaluate all of the owner's personal assets and liabilities and earnings potential before lending funds. Other factors important to sole proprietorships include, on the minus side, the nonavailability of lower-cost employee benefit plans and fewer alternatives for raising capital. On the plus side is the avoidance of legal and other professional fees commonly incurred in establishing a separate legal entity and fewer tax-return filing responsibilities.

Partnership

The partnership form of business is often used to bring together people who have different talents and financial resources. A partnership may be either a general or limited partnership. A partnership is not subject to federal income tax. Rather, the items of business income, gain, deduction, loss, and credit flow through the partnership to each of the partners and are reported on the partners' income tax returns. The earnings of a partnership can generally be distributed to its partners tax-free.

A general partnership is easily formed; a formal written agreement is not required. In contrast, a limited partnership requires a written partnership agreement. In addition, a certificate of limited partnership must be filed in the state in which the partnership is formed. The dissolution of a partnership or the transfer of a partnership interest can be difficult. Transferring ownership may be easier, however, if a well-drafted buy-sell agreement is executed. To prevent misunderstandings and spell out the rights of individual partners, a detailed partnership agreement should be prepared at the beginning regardless of whether a general or limited partnership is being used.

As with the sole proprietorship, the liability of a general partner is not limited to the partnership's assets, so the general partners' individual assets can be at risk. In a limited partnership, a limited partner is generally subject to the claims of the business's creditors only to the extent of the capital he or she has contributed to the partnership (or is obligated to contribute in the future under the partnership agreement). However, to be considered a limited partner rather than a general partner (whose liability is not limited), the partner must not actively participate in the management of the partnership. Furthermore, the statutory formalities for creating a limited partnership must be complied with, or else the organization may be treated as a general partnership. A limited partnership must have at least one general partner whose assets are subject to the claims of the creditors of the business. The general partner's liability can be limited, however, by having a corporation serve as the general partner.

Additional partnership factors are estate-planning difficulties, technical tax laws regarding contributions of property, complex tax laws regarding the allocation of income and losses to partners, and various limitations on the deductibility of tax losses by partners.

Regular Corporation (C Corporation)

Each state has certain requirements for forming a corporation. After it is formed, there are further requirements for its operation that must be followed to maintain corporate existence. The corporation is taxed as an entity; its income or loss does not flow through to its shareholders. Accordingly, losses of a C corporation generate a current tax benefit only to the extent they can be carried forward or back to offset income of the corporation in other years. The income of a corporation is generally taxed using a graduated rate structure, with an effective rate of 34 percent applying to taxable income from $75,000 to $10,000,000. The current maximum effective rate of 35 percent applies to income over $10,000,000. However, a corporation with taxable income between $335,000 and $10,000,000, or a corporation that is a personal-service corporation (a corporation whose principal activity is the performance of personal services where such services are substantially performed by employee-owners) does not benefit from the graduated rate structure and is effectively taxed at a flat 34 percent rate up to $10,000,000 of income. A 3 percent surtax applies to income between $15,000,000 and $18,333,333, phasing out the benefits of the 34 percent rate and effectively taxing entities with income above this amount at a flat 35 percent rate. In addition, regular corporations are subject to the alternative minimum tax (AMT) provisions. The AMT's goal is to prevent corporations with substantial economic income from using preferential deductions, exclusions, and credits to eliminate their tax liability. To achieve this goal, the AMT is structured as a separate tax system with its own allowable deductions and credit limitations. The tax is imposed on corporations at a rate of 20 percent. It is an alternative tax because after computing both the regular tax and AMT liabilities, the corporation pays the higher of the two. An additional environmental tax is imposed equal to .12 percent of the amount by which a corporation's alternative minimum taxable income exceeds $2 million. It is imposed even if the corporation is not subject to AMT.

A corporation is a "double tax" entity. Its income is first taxed at the corporate level and a second time when it is distributed to its shareholders.

The corporation generally provides the protection of limited liability (avoidance of personal liability) to all of its shareholders. Thus, only amounts actually invested in the corporation are at risk; a shareholder's personal assets are not subject to claims of business creditors. The limited liability feature of corporations is often cited as the most important reason for operating in corporate form. However, creditors often require a shareholder to personally guarantee the debts of the corporation, thus reducing the benefit of operating as a corporation. Other factors to consider when contemplating corporate formation include possible additional taxation on any accumulated, undistributed corporate income; the corporate alternative minimum tax; and the costs of administering the many legal and accounting requirements.

If corporate form is selected, consideration should be given to qualifying the corporation's stock as small-business stock (Section 1244 stock). If the stock of the corporation qualifies as small-business stock, it may be possible to recognize an ordinary (rather than capital) loss of up to $50,000 ($100,000 on a joint return) upon disposition. This can be important because ordinary-loss treatment is generally preferable. Capital losses must first be used to offset capital gains, and any excess capital loss is limited to a maximum offset against ordinary income of $3,000 per year. Ordinary losses are usually deductible in full. Generally, absent some cogent business reason, care should be taken to ensure that the stock of any qualified corporation qualifies as small-business stock.

Certain investment provisions were enacted as part of the Omnibus Budget Reconciliation Act of 1993 in order to induce investors to invest in small businesses and start-up ventures. Noncorporate taxpayers may exclude up to 50 percent of the gain they realize on the disposition of qualified small-business stock issued after August 10, 1993, and held for more than five years. Generally, in order to qualify as small-business stock, the stock must be issued by a C corporation that actively conducts a qualified trade or business, and whose aggregate gross assets do not exceed $50 million. The excludable gain is limited to the greater of a cumulative limit of $10 million or ten times the adjusted basis of all qualified stock of the issuing corporation that the taxpayer disposed of during the tax year.

Additionally, an investor is allowed to defer recognition of capital gain realized on the sale of publicly held securities to the extent the proceeds are invested in the stock of a specialized small-business investment company (SSBIC) within 60 days of the sale. The amount of gain that can be excluded is limited to an annual amount of $50,000 with a lifetime cap of $500,000 for individuals and an annual amount of $250,000 with a lifetime cap of $1 million for corporations. An SSBIC is any corporation or partnership licensed by the Small Business Administration under Section 301(d) of the Small Business Investment Act of 1958 (in general, a minority-owned business). The above two provisions are additional inducements to individual and/or corporate investors to invest in small business and therefore increase the amount of funds available to small businesses.

S Corporation

An S corporation is a corporation for legal purposes (it retains the limited liability feature of a regular corporation), but it is taxed much like a partnership. Income, deductions, gains, credits, and losses are reported directly by the shareholders on their income tax returns. The S corporation's earnings can generally be distributed to its shareholders tax-free.

To be taxed as an S corporation, the corporation must make an affirmative election, with the consent of all shareholders, on or before the 15th day of the 3rd month of the tax year for which the S election is to be effective. An S election is made on Form 2553. To be eligible for S corporation status, the corporation must satisfy certain eligibility requirements, including the following:

- No more than 35 shareholders are permitted (a husband and wife are treated as one shareholder).
- Only individuals (other than nonresident aliens), estates, and certain trusts can own stock in an S corporation.
- Only one class of stock is permitted, but voting rights within the class can differ, and the stock may include shares with no voting rights.
- No active subsidiaries may be owned by the S corporation.

Since a corporation that operates as a regular corporation before converting to S status may be subject to corporate-level taxes, the decision of whether to elect S status effective for the corporation's first year should be carefully considered.

Once an S election is made, it applies for all succeeding years, unless the election is terminated. An S election may be terminated by revocation with the consent of shareholders holding more than one-half of the corporation's stock on the day the revocation is made. An S election may also terminate automatically if the corporation fails to meet any of the eligibility requirements previously discussed or fails a passive-investment income test. Once the corporation's S election is terminated or revoked, it will be taxed as a C corporation, and generally must wait five years to reelect S status.

When to Use What Entity

Nontax issues aside, each business form will have certain tax advantages and disadvantages in relation to the stage of development of your company or a segment of your company that you may wish to spin off for tax advantage or other purposes.

Start-Up Phase. The start-up phase of a business generally requires capital and produces tax losses. These tax losses can often be best utilized if they are passed directly to the investors or owners who provided the initial funding for the business and used to offset tax liability on their income tax returns. Both partnerships and S corporations are "pass-through" entities that permit investors to utilize the tax losses on their income tax returns. Losses may be limited, however, to the amount of the investor's basis and amount at risk, or under the passive-activity loss rules.

In the case of a partnership, basis is generally equal to the investor's contribution, plus undistributed earnings and allocable portions of debt. The amount at risk is similar to basis, but generally includes only loans for which the partner remains personally liable (recourse loans). An investor's basis in an S corporation is equal to the investor's capital contribution, plus undistributed earnings and the S corporation's indebtedness to the investor. Basis and amounts at risk do not include the investor's share of corporate liabilities; only direct loans from the investor to the S corporation are included. If losses go unutilized because an investor has insufficient basis or amounts at risk, they may be carried forward and utilized in years when the investor's basis or amount at risk increases (through additional capital contributions, loans, or an increase due to profit in excess of distributions to the investor).

If an investor's interest in a partnership or S corporation is considered a passive activity, the deductibility of losses may be further limited. A passive activity generally includes a trade or business activity in which the investor does not materially participate and any rental activity. To materially participate, an individual must generally be involved in the activity on a regular, continuous, and substantial basis. As a general rule, a limited partner in a partnership will automatically fail the material participation standard.

The passive-activity rules deny a deduction for the net losses from passive business activities. That is, an investor (other than certain closely held C corporations that are allowed to utilize passive-activity losses to offset net active income) may use passive losses only to reduce or eliminate income from passive activities. If a net loss remains, it generally may not be used to offset other income. However, the loss may be carried forward as a passive-activity loss and used to offset passive income in future years. Further, any disallowed losses generally may be claimed in full in the year the activity is disposed of in a taxable transaction.

A drawback posed by both partnerships and S corporations is that these forms may restrict certain ways of raising additional capital—issuing stock to additional investors is limited by the maximum number (35) of investors allowed in an S corporation, and there may be little market for partnership investors (other than limited partners) due to potential liabilities.

Growth Phase. The growth phase of a business is associated with expansion and the need for more capital. In this period, the regular corporate form may best meet the business objectives of investor-owners. Operating in regular corporate form during the growth phase makes sense for a number of reasons, including the following:

• Fewer restrictions on the types of allowable investors. Generally there are no restrictions on allowable investors for regular corporations. S corporations, on the other hand, cannot have as shareholders corporations or most trusts.

- Ease of transferability of ownership interests to investors. A regular corporation can issue additional shares without undue burden. However, adding a new partner may require the consent of all existing partners.
- Limitations on allowable classes of stock may be avoided. A regular corporation may issue preferred stock to attract investors. S corporations are limited to a single class of stock.
- Complex allocations of income, deductions, and credits as a result of ownership changes are not required. Changes in ownership during a tax year can result in burdensome calculations for partnerships and S corporations; a regular corporation is a separate taxable entity and therefore allocations are unnecessary. (If the corporation has unused credits and net operating losses, these credits and losses may be limited when a substantial change in ownership occurs.)
- Limited personal liability. As a business grows, its exposure grows as well. In the start-up phase of a business, potential liability may be small and investors are usually willing to assume risk. As the business grows, the level of personal risk may become unacceptable and a change of form (from partnership to corporate) is warranted.

These advantages of operating as a regular corporation during the growth phase of a business, however, must be carefully weighed against the disadvantages, principally the "double tax" on corporate earnings distributed to shareholders. Furthermore, an S corporation that terminates its S election and becomes a regular corporation generally must wait five years before it can reelect S status and will be subject to corporate-level taxes if it does reelect S status.

Beyond the Growth Phase. Once past the growth stage, a corporation generating consistent taxable income and cash flow should consider adopting (or reelecting) S corporation status if it meets the qualifications. Higher profits make double taxation a more critical problem if owners desire regular dividend distributions. The S corporation eliminates the double tax problem, since earnings are taxed only at the shareholder level.

For years beginning before January 1, 1993, individual shareholders of S corporations received an added boost because the corporate income was taxed at individual rates, which were lower than the regular corporate rates. Under current law, the top marginal rate for a corporation is 35 percent versus 39.6 percent for an individual. Additionally, the highest marginal rate for an individual, 39.6 percent, is effective at much lower levels of income, beginning at $250,000. The highest marginal rate for a corporation is 35 percent and applies to income greater than $10,000,000. Although individual rates are no longer lower than corporate rates, there can still be a significant advantage to operating as an S corporation because the most significant tax benefit is retained—the avoidance of double taxation. Moreover, the tax basis of an S corporation shareholder's stock is increased by the taxable income generated by the S corporation.

By electing S corporation status, a business can avoid certain other taxes that apply to regular corporations (the environmental tax and the accumulated earnings tax) and can also avoid the complex corporate alternative minimum tax rules.

Although operating as an S corporation is usually desirable, there are some drawbacks. One is the taxation of certain fringe benefits to more-than 2-percent owner-employees. For example, benefits such as group medical and life insurance that may be provided tax-free to shareholder-employees of regular corporations are taxable to most shareholder-employees of S corporations. At the time this publication went to press, current law allowed a deduction for 25 percent of shareholder-employee health insurance. Proposed legislation would change this to 100 percent.

You should also be aware of certain consequences of converting an existing corporation to an S corporation. A 34 percent corporate tax may apply to the S corporation's recognition of built-in gains (appreciation that accumulated on the corporation's assets before the corporation converted to S status) when the assets owned on the day the corporation became an S corporation are later sold, distributed to shareholders, or otherwise disposed of. An S corporation with accumulated earnings and profits remaining from years in which it operated as a regular corporation may also be subject to a tax of 34 percent on its net passive-investment income in excess of 25 percent of its gross receipts. (S corporations with undistributed earnings and

---

* Recent proposals have been made to increase the top marginal rate to 36% for individuals and to 36% for corporations with taxable income of more than $10 million.

profits from years as a regular corporation will lose their S status if their passive-investment income exceeds the 25 percent threshold for three consecutive years.)

Further, as discussed later in this chapter, a special tax is imposed on corporations that have been using the LIFO method of valuing their inventories and convert to S status. In addition, unused loss carryovers of a regular corporation may be suspended (not available for utilization against S corporation income).

Finally, the state tax implications of electing S corporation status should be carefully reviewed to avoid unpleasant surprises. For example, the combined shareholder and corporate state taxes associated with operating as an S corporation may be significantly higher than a regular corporation's state tax burden. In addition, compliance may be more complex because more returns may need to be filed even though the company may not do business in that state.

In summary, it should be remembered that it is possible to change the business form as the business matures. A sole proprietorship could be incorporated or changed into a partnership. A partnership could be incorporated. Since tax rules covering the conversion of entities can be complex and restrictive, consultation with a tax advisor is recommended whenever a change is being contemplated.

SELECTION OF ACCOUNTING METHODS

The accounting method selected by your company can significantly affect its tax liability. The election of an overall accounting method generally occurs with the first tax-return filing. Thus, your initial return takes on great importance.

Most individuals and many owners of professional-service businesses use the cash method of accounting; however, most other businesses must use the accrual method of accounting. For tax purposes, use of the cash method of accounting is restricted to farming businesses, certain PSCs, S corporations, partnerships (unless the partnership has a regular corporation as a partner), and small businesses (corporations or partnerships with average gross receipts for each of the preceding three years of not more than $5 million). All other corporations, partnerships with corporate partners, and businesses that are considered "tax shelters" must use the accrual method of accounting.

Cash Method

The cash method is used primarily due to its simplicity and flexibility. It also can help you defer recognition of taxable income by accelerating expense payments or deferring collections at year-end. In general, under this method, items that constitute income are recognized when actually received. Expenditures are deducted for the tax year in which actually paid. As you can see, this permits great flexibility in monitoring taxable income.

However, if an expenditure results in the creation of an asset that has a useful life that extends substantially beyond the close of the tax year, the expenditure must be capitalized and the asset depreciated over its useful life. If inventories are material to the business, a taxpayer must use the accrual method to measure sales and cost of goods sold.

Accrual Method

Under the accrual method of accounting, income is included in gross income when it is earned, whether or not the cash has actually been received. Income is considered to be earned when all the events have occurred that fix the right to receive such income, and the amount of such income, can be determined with reasonable accuracy.

Accrual-basis taxpayers may deduct an expense in the year the liability becomes fixed and the amount can be reasonably determined. In addition, economic performance must have occurred for an expense to be deductible. The point at which economic performance occurs depends upon the underlying transaction as follows:

1. For liabilities arising from receipt or use of property and services—when the property or service is received or used
2. For liabilities requiring the taxpayer to provide property or services—when the taxpayer provides the property or performs the service
3. For liabilities requiring a payment to another person resulting under a workers' compensation act or arising out of any tort—as the payments are made to the person

An exception to the economic-performance rule is provided for certain recurring items. To qualify, the exception must occur within a reasonable period after year-end, but no later than eight and one-half months following the end of the taxable year.

Deferring Taxes

It is possible to defer taxes and thereby maximize cash flow by choosing the appropriate method of accounting. The cash method of accounting offers the advantage of being able to time receipts and expenditures. For example, a cash-basis taxpayer can control the inclusion of income by accelerating or slowing up its collections from customers or can control deductions to some extent by accelerating or deferring payments for such items as repairs, supplies, or taxes.

The accrual method of accounting provides less control over income recognition and deductions and makes planning more difficult. Income is generally recognized when earned, which is usually before receipt of payment. Deductions may be permitted before payments are made, but this has been modified to some extent by the economic-performance requirement. An accrual-basis taxpayer may be able to defer income by reducing shipping and invoicing near year-end, or making sales on consignment or approval. Deductions can be accelerated by requesting the delivery and billing of supplies or repairs before the end of the year. Consideration should also be given to making the maximum deductible charitable contributions (up to 10 percent of taxable income for corporations) and contributing the maximum deductible amount to tax-qualified retirement plans.

Changing Accounting Method

In general, you officially choose your overall method of accounting by the method used on your first income tax return. A taxpayer is allowed to use different methods of accounting for each trade or business. However, at a minimum, a complete and separate set of books and records must be kept for each trade or business. Thereafter, you must use the same methods unless you obtain permission from the IRS to change by filing an application on Form 3115 within the first 180 days of the tax year in which the change is desired. A request for a change will usually be approved if the taxpayer agrees to make certain adjustments to income, beginning with the year of change, over a one- to six-year period. These adjustments are required to prevent items of income and expense from being duplicated or omitted as a result of the change in accounting method.

TAX ACCOUNTING FOR INVENTORIES

Taxpayers are required to maintain inventory records to clearly reflect income. (Inventories must include all finished goods, work in process, and raw materials that will become part of the product or will be offered for sale.) Tax accounting for inventories involves the method of inventorying goods (quantities) and the method of inventory costing. Since inventories significantly affect the amount of taxable income, inventory planning can create large tax savings.

Valuation of Inventory

Inventory may be valued at either cost or the lower of cost or market. The cost of merchandise purchased during the year is usually the invoice price less trade or other discounts, plus freight and other handling charges. The cost of goods produced or manufactured during the year usually includes the following:

1. Cost of raw materials and supplies used
2. Cost of direct labor
3. Indirect production costs for the item

For tax purposes, uniform capitalization rules generally require producers of tangible property to capitalize all direct and indirect costs incident to and necessary for production. Generally, retailers and wholesalers must also capitalize indirect costs associated with inventories, such as storage and warehousing costs, and purchasing costs. However, an exception to the uniform capitalization rules may be available for retailers and wholesalers if their average annual gross receipts for the three preceding years did not exceed $10 million.

Most taxpayers will adopt the lower of cost or market method of valuation. Under this method, each item in the inventory is valued at both cost and market value, and the value at which it is included in inventory is the lower of the two calculations. This method allows for the tax deduction of an unrealized loss (when market value of inventory is lower than cost). As a result, this method will effectively defer taxes until the market value is higher than cost, at which time the deduction is reversed.

Determining Inventory/Cost Flow

There are three available methods for determining inventory:

1. Specific identification
2. FIFO
3. LIFO

In the specific-identification method, a cost-flow assumption is not used. Instead, each unit is priced at its cost. This method is generally used by jewelry retailers or custom-equipment manufacturers.

Under the FIFO (first-in, first-out) method, the cost-flow assumption used is that the first goods purchased or produced are the first goods sold. This method will generally be used by a taxpayer that cannot identify its goods with specific invoices and wants to be able to use the lower of cost or market method of valuation.

Last-in, first-out (LIFO) is a method of sequencing the flow of costs through the inventory so that the most recent costs incurred to acquire or produce inventory are charged to the cost of sales. Consequently, current costs are matched against current revenue. This is particularly effective in reducing the impact of inflation on profits. The single most important reason taxpayers adopt LIFO is the tax savings and increased cash flow that result.

Theoretically, the use of the LIFO method results only in deferring taxes and can be considered as an interest-free loan from the government. The LIFO reserve on the balance sheet, after applying the taxpayer's effective tax rate, provides an estimate of the magnitude of this interest-free loan. As long as inflation continues and a taxpayer's LIFO inventories remain relatively constant or increase in size, the tax deferral tends to become permanent.

There are several factors you should consider in determining the potential tax savings to be generated by LIFO. For example, if anticipated future purchase or production costs of inventory are expected to decline, LIFO would not be beneficial. If inventory levels are expected to decline significantly in the near future, the tax deferral will be decreased or eliminated. The LIFO method could increase your taxes in future years if the market value of your company's inventory were below its LIFO cost, since a taxpayer on LIFO is not allowed to write-down its inventories to market when market is lower than cost. Also, LIFO may cause a company's taxes to increase initially, since the opening inventory in the year LIFO is adopted must be at cost. If the previous year's closing inventory were stated at a lower amount because of a write-down to market, the write-down must be restored to income over a three-year period that begins in the tax year when LIFO is elected. Other considerations are the taxpayer's effective tax rate and the interest rate.

If a corporation uses the LIFO method and subsequently elects S corporation status, the corporation must include its LIFO reserve in its taxable income for its last year as a regular corporation. The resulting increase in income taxes (if any) is payable over a four-year period.

There are also financial and administrative aspects to adopting LIFO. Once the LIFO election is made for tax purposes, the LIFO method must also be used for credit purposes and for the purpose of reports to shareholders, partners, proprietors, and beneficiaries. A corporate taxpayer should consider the impact LIFO will have on its creditors, financing agreements, profit-sharing plans, and shareholder agreements. In addition, there is generally a cost burden in calculating the LIFO costs. The LIFO election is made by filing Form 970 with the tax return for the year of adoption. Once a company adopts its inventory methods, it may not change without IRS consent.

MINIMIZING TAX LIABILITIES

There are various strategies or elections, in addition to inventory methods, a company can use to minimize its tax liability. It is important that a taxpayer get help from qualified tax personnel since, in some cases, if these strategies are not properly implemented or elections not properly made, the benefits may be permanently lost. In many cases, these techniques may produce results different from those obtained for financial-accounting purposes. These differences between tax accounting and financial accounting are usually represented by the lower current—but higher deferred—tax liabilities on a taxpayer's balance sheet.

Research and Development

Research and development (R&D) expenditures are the costs of developing an experimental or pilot model, a plant process, a product, a formula, an invention, or similar property improvements. Research and development expenditures do not include the cost of ordinary testing or inspection of materials or products for quality control, efficiency surveys, management studies, consumer surveys, advertising, or promotions. A taxpayer has three alternatives for the treatment of R&D expenses. The expenditures may be expensed in the year paid or incurred, or they may be deferred and amortized. If neither of these two methods is used, the expenditures must be capitalized and a deduction will not be allowed until the project is abandoned or deemed worthless. It is generally preferable to expense the R&D expenditures. There are also tax credits for increased R&D expenses (see "Tax Credits" section following). Chapter 11 has a more detailed discussion of the tax breaks accorded research and development expenditures.

Tax Credits

The Internal Revenue Code provides for various nonrefundable tax credits that reduce tax liability on a dollar-for-dollar basis, including general business credit which includes a credit, for increasing research activities; a rehabilitation investment credit; and a targeted jobs credit. A limitation applies to the use of the general business credit; thus, a taxpayer usually will not be able to totally eliminate its federal income taxes through the use of credits. However, amounts in excess of the limitation may be carried back 3 years and forward 15 years.

Credit for Increasing Research Activities. A tax credit is allowed for increased research and development expenses equal to 20 percent of the excess of qualified research expenses for the taxable year over a base amount. The term "qualified research" refers to research and development conducted in the experimental or laboratory sense. The base amount is generally computed using historical R&D expenses and gross receipts, and serves to limit the costs eligible for the credit to those representing an increase over prior years' expenditures. The base amount cannot be less than 50 percent of the expenses for the current year. The amount of R&D expenditures a taxpayer can deduct or capitalize must be reduced by the R&D credit unless a reduced credit election is made. This is desirable in certain circumstances when AMT may be involved or tax rate increases are expected. The R&D credit is currently scheduled to expire for costs paid or incurred after June 30, 1992, but it may be extended.

Rehabilitation Investment Credit. Expenditures to rehabilitate certified historic structures and other qualified buildings that are to be used for nonresidential purposes qualify for the investment tax credit. There must be substantial rehabilitation, which generally means that the rehabilitation expenditures incurred during any 24-month period that ends with or within the year for which the credit is claimed must exceed the greater of the adjusted basis of the property or $5,000.

Rehabilitation includes renovation, restoration, or reconstruction of a building, but does not include an enlargement or new construction. For buildings other than certified historic structures, a rehabilitation project must meet certain structural tests based on the area of the external walls and internal structural framework that is retained in place compared with the total area of each before the rehabilitation. For qualified buildings placed in service after 1986, the credit is equal to 10 percent of qualified expenditures for nonresidential buildings first placed in service prior to 1936, and 20 percent for certified historic structures. Both residential and nonresidential buildings may qualify as certified historic structures. The basis of the rehabilitated property must be reduced by the amount of rehabilitation investment credit allowed. In addition, once the building is placed in service, the modified accelerated cost recovery system (MACRS) straight-line method of depreciation must be used for the basis of the property attributable to expenditures for which the credit was taken.

Targeted Jobs Credit. The targeted jobs tax credit (TJTC) is part of a federal incentive program designed to encourage taxpayers to hire individuals from several targeted groups (e.g., economically disadvantaged youths and ex-convicts). The credit equals 40 percent of the first $6,000 of the eligible employee's wages for the first year of employment. The TJTC is available to qualified employees who began work on or before July 1, 1992, but this date may be extended. Generally, if the TJTC is claimed, the deduction for salaries and wages paid during the year must be reduced by the amount of the credit.

Stock and Other Compensation Techniques

A concern common to many growing businesses is the attraction and retention of highly qualified key personnel. The resulting challenge is to identify and implement cost-effective compensation programs that employees perceive to be valuable while accomplishing business goals. Various noncash compensation techniques are frequently used by businesses to successfully attract key personnel while avoiding an excessive drain on cash flow, in many cases generating cash flow through tax savings. Some of the more common stock-based compensation techniques used by businesses include restricted stock plans, nonqualified stock options, incentive stock options, phantom stock plans, and stock appreciation rights. Various types of qualified retirement and deferred compensation plans are also commonly used. Before implementing one of these plans, however, its effects on your financial statements should be reviewed with your accountant.

Restricted Stock. The first type of noncash compensation plan frequently used by corporations to compensate key employees involves the transfer of "restricted" stock to the employee in exchange for services. When property is transferred in connection with the performance of services, the employee must recognize the excess of the fair market value of the property over the amount he or she pays for such property as income. However, when the property is subject to restrictions that place substantial limitations on the employee's right to enjoy the property, income is not recognized until the first taxable year in which the restrictions lapse. The corporation is generally allowed a deduction for the amount of income that must be recognized by the employee in the year in which the employee recognizes the income. As the income and corresponding deduction can be sizable for key employees, care must be taken to structure the agreement so it does not fall within the categories of executive compensation that are subject to an annual deduction limitation of $1 million, effective for years beginning on or after January 1, 1994.

By making the stock subject to substantial restrictions (e.g., vesting in the stock would be contingent upon completion of a number of years of service), the employer can encourage an employee to stay, while providing the employee with an often very desirable form of noncash compensation, an equity interest. While the employer's deduction for any resulting compensation is deferred until the stock becomes substantially vested, the employee's taxable income is similarly deferred. In addition, the employer receives a compensation deduction (in an amount equal to the income reportable by the employee) without having an actual cash outlay. Restricted stock plans are often used with start-up and closely held companies where a meaningful equity interest can be given to an employee.

Employees have the option of electing to include the value of the stock in income when it is received rather than when the restrictions lapse. An employee might want to make this election if the value of the stock is relatively low when it is first received but the stock is expected to appreciate substantially before it becomes vested. By making the election, the employee limits the amount of income he or she must report (the employer's deduction is also reduced). The election must be made no later than 30 days after receipt of the stock. Also note that the tax ramifications of the issuance of restricted stock by an S corporation are not entirely clear.

Nonqualified Stock Options. A stock option typically allows an employee to purchase employer stock at a set price. A nonqualified stock option (NQSO) is a compensatory option that is not an incentive stock option (ISO), discussed in the following section. Typically, an NQSO is granted to an employee at no cost. Generally, the employee has no income on the date the option is granted. However, the employee has compensation income in the amount of the excess of the stock's value over its exercise price on the date the option is exercised. The corporation that grants the option is generally entitled to a compensation deduction of an identical amount at the same time the employee recognizes the income.

Incentive Stock Options. Incentive stock options are issued under a stock-option plan that meets certain requirements specified in the Internal Revenue Code, including one that the option price be no less than the value of the stock at the time the option is granted. As with a nonqualified stock option, the employee has no income on the date the option is granted. An ISO differs from a NQSO, however, in that no income results to the employee on the exercise of an ISO (although the excess of the value of the stock over the exercise price generally must be included in income for purposes of the alternative minimum tax) provided that certain holding-period requirements are met. If the employee meets the holding-period requirements and recognizes no income on the exercise of the option, the corporation is not entitled to a compensation deduction. (From a corporation's standpoint, a very significant advantage of a NQSO over an ISO is that the employer corporation receives a deduction for the amount of income reported by the employee upon the exercise of the option. In addition, NQSOs do not have to meet the statutory requirements for ISOs, and thus are more flexible than ISOs.)

Phantom Stock Plans. Under a phantom stock plan, employees are awarded hypothetical shares of the company's stock in the form of "units" that are assigned a value based on the fair market value of the stock that date. The employee is compensated through the increase in value of the stock of the company from the date it was awarded to the time specified in the plan. In some plans, the employee may be entitled to the original value of the unit in addition to the subsequent appreciation. The plan may also provide for additional compensation payments to the employee granted the units in the amount of dividends paid on the corporation's outstanding stock. Upon the initial award of the phantom stock, the company takes no deduction and the employee recognizes no income. When the deferral period ends, the employee receives cash and recognizes income in the amount of cash received. Any "dividends" paid on the phantom stock are included in the employee's income as compensation and are deductible by the corporation when paid.

Stock Appreciation Rights. A stock appreciation right (SAR) is a right given to an employee to receive cash or stock or both equal to the appreciation in the price of stock from the date of the SAR grant to the date of its exercise. SARs are often issued in conjunction with NQSOs and ISOs. Under this type of plan, the employee has the choice of receiving cash by exercising the SAR or getting stock by exercising the option. The employee generally does not recognize income from an SAR until the exercise date. At the time the employee receives either stock or cash and recognizes income, the corporation is allowed an equal deduction.

Qualified Retirement and Deferred Compensation Plans. Generally, a qualified retirement plan is a plan established or maintained by an employer for the benefit of employees and their beneficiaries that meets specific qualification requirements and either provides retirement income to employees or defers recognition of income by employees for a fixed number of years, until the occurrence of a stated event or the attainment of a stated age. The employer contributes funds that are accumulated in trust and held for distribution to the employees or their beneficiaries in accordance with the terms of the plan. To achieve "qualified" status, a plan must meet the following general requirements: (1) contributions must be made to a trust established for the exclusive benefit of employees and their beneficiaries; (2) the plan must meet certain minimum eligibility and participation standards; (3) the plan must not discriminate in favor of officers or shareholders or highly compensated employees; (4) employee benefits may be forfeitable only under certain conditions; and (5) annual contributions and benefits under the plan are limited. There are other requirements that must be met as well.

The principal tax benefits of a qualified retirement plan are the current deductibility of employer contributions, the deferral of income recognition by the participating employees until the distribution of benefits, favorable tax treatment of distributions to employees, and exemption of the trust from income tax (other than the tax on unrelated business income). Examples of qualified plans include pension plans, profit-sharing plans, stock-bonus plans, ESOPs (see Chapter 14), and cash or deferred arrangements [§401(k) plans].

Debt versus Equity Considerations

Tax considerations can play an important role in determining how owners should capitalize a business, particularly in determining the appropriate mix of debt and equity. A number of tax advantages weigh heavily in favor of issuing at least some debt to the owners of a corporation (rather than just stock), particularly if the business is operated as a C corporation. The principal advantage is that payments of interest on debt obligations are deductible, whereas dividend payments by a C corporation are not. Debt is also more attractive than equity because the payment of principal on maturity of a debt obligation is generally tax-free to the recipient, whereas distributions in redemption of a shareholder's interest in stock may be taxable as dividends. For a more detailed discussion of debt versus equity, see Chapter 5. Because of the tax advantages of using debt rather than equity, the IRS often seeks to reclassify debt as stock for tax purposes. If a corporation issues debt instruments in an unrealistically high proportion to its stock, the corporation is considered to be "thinly capitalized" and the IRS may succeed in treating the debt issued to owners as stock for tax purposes.

Depreciation

Use of Modified Accelerated Cost Recovery System (MACRS) is generally mandatory for all types of eligible property placed in service after 1986, unless a business owner makes a special election to use another method. Eligible property includes all types of tangible property (both real and personal). Under MACRS, you must recover the cost of qualifying property over a specified number of years.

The date new property is placed in service can significantly affect the amount of your depreciation deduction. Generally, personal property is treated as having been placed in service at the midpoint of a tax year (July 1 for calendar-year taxpayers) no matter when it was actually purchased and placed in service. However, if more than 40 percent of the property purchased during the tax year is placed in service during the last three months of the year, all property purchased and placed in service throughout the year will be treated as being placed in service in the middle of the quarter in which it was purchased (which generally will provide a smaller depreciation deduction). Planning on an annual basis may be required to avoid reducing depreciation deductions on property already placed in service during the year. This involves placing assets in service earlier in the year or in the following year to avoid the 40 percent rule.

The annual depreciation deduction corporations can take for company-owned automobiles is significantly limited. You may want to consider leasing rather than purchasing automobiles because, while leased automobiles are subject to similar limitations, the adjustment required for lease expenses is generally much lower than the depreciation adjustment. Lease payments are also not a preference for the alternative minimum tax, whereas depreciation must be adjusted for AMT.

Under certain circumstances, you can elect to deduct up to $17,500, for years beginning after December 31, 1992, of an asset's cost for the year it is purchased and placed in service, rather than depreciating it. To qualify for expensing, the asset must generally be tangible personal property purchased for use in the active conduct of a trade or business. The $17,500 expensing limitation is reduced dollar for dollar by the cost of property (otherwise qualifying for the deduction) in excess of $200,000 that you place in service during a year. Other restrictions also apply.

Start-Up and Organizational Expenditures

A taxpayer that pays or incurs start-up or investigatory expenditures for a trade or business that subsequently begins operations can elect to amortize the expenditures over a period of not less than 60 months commencing with the month the business begins. Business start-up costs are incurred after the decision to start the business but before operations begin. Investigatory costs are incurred in reviewing a potential business in order to reach a decision to acquire or enter the business.

Corporations and partnerships may also elect to amortize organizational expenditures over a period of not less than 60 months. Organizational expenditures are costs incident to the creation of a corporation or partnership, including the cost of legal and accounting services and filing fees. Costs associated with issuing shares, the admission of partners, and the transferring of assets are examples of costs not considered organizational expenditures.

To amortize start-up or organizational expenditures, the taxpayer must attach a statement to a timely filed tax return. The statement must contain a description and amounts of the expenditures, the dates they were incurred, the month the business began or was acquired, and the number of months in the amortization period. If the election to amortize is not made, the expenditures are capitalized and a deduction is not allowed for such expenditures until the business is sold or liquidated.

State and Local Taxes

It is important that consideration be given to the substantial role state and local taxes play in a business's overall tax liability. The first step in state tax planning involves identifying those states in which the business has sufficient presence ("nexus") to create a responsibility for paying tax and filing returns. Once it has been determined where a company has nexus, proper controls can be established to ensure that filing responsibilities and tax-return requirements are met on a timely basis.

There are several strategies a business may want to consider to minimize its state and local tax burden, including the following:

- Establishing a holding company in a selected state to defer or eliminate taxation of income attributable to stocks, bonds, licenses, or other intangibles. (This has come under close scrutiny by local tax authorities.)

- Merging, transferring, or otherwise reorganizing corporate operations or structures to offset profits and losses of related entities and attribute earnings to lower-taxing states.
- Establishing valid management-fee arrangements and other intercompany transactions to maximize tax benefits of current expenses.
- Selecting the best tax-return filing options to minimize the group's tax liabilities.

Because laws vary broadly from state to state, you may want to consult with a professional experienced in state tax matters before implementing any tax-planning strategies.

Planning for state and local taxes other than income taxes should also be considered. For example, through proper planning, it may be possible to reduce capital-stock taxes or unemployment taxes. It may also be possible to minimize your property tax burden. A company's annual property tax expense will frequently amount to more than 2 percent of its asset value—a significant expense, particularly in tough economic times. Managing this expense and achieving fair adjustments within compliance guidelines often requires planning and control by property tax specialists.

MINIMIZING ESTIMATED TAX PAYMENTS

The strategy in making any kind of estimated tax payment is to pay the minimum required amount and no more on the required due date. Because the amount paid is an estimate of the tax liability, keeping the payment to the absolute minimum requires maintaining accurate accounting records and knowing the filing requirements and exceptions.

Estimated Tax Requirements

Generally, a corporation must make quarterly estimated tax payments, which are due on the 15th day of the 4th, 6th, 9th, and 12th months of the corporation's taxable year.

Corporations may be penalized for not paying enough tax for an installment period. In general, for years beginning before December 31, 1993, the required quarterly installment is one-fourth of 97 percent of the tax shown on the return for the year. For years beginning after December 31, 1993, this is increased to 100 percent of the current year liability. An exception to the penalty is available for corporations, other than "large" corporations, that pay, each quarter, at least 25 percent of the tax shown on their return for the preceding year. An exception based on annualized (or seasonal) income is also available. An S corporation is required to make estimated tax payments for any corporate-level tax it is liable for.

Quick Refund of Overpaid Estimated Tax

If a corporation overpays its total tax liability by making estimated tax payments higher than necessary, it may make an application on Form 4466 for a quick refund. The refund request must be made within two and one-half months after the close of the corporation's taxable year and before the date on which the corporation files its tax return. However, the overpayment must be equal to at least 10 percent of its expected tax liability and not less than $500.

Refund Claims

A refund related to a carryback of benefits (such as a net operating loss or certain tax credits) may be claimed using Form 1139 and generally must be acted upon within 90 days by the IRS. The corporation must file Form 1139 within one year after the year in which the loss or credit arises; after then only an amended return Form 1120X may be filed to claim the refund. The IRS has no requirement to respond within a certain period on an 1120X, so the 1139 should be filed whenever possible. If you incur a net operating loss in the current year but reported taxable income in the preceding year, the taxes payable on the income of the preceding year may be postponed by filing Form 1138, which allows you to extend the time for payment of taxes upon expectation of a net operating loss that can be carried back. Although you will be charged interest on the postponed tax payment, the payment of taxes followed by a refund resulting from a net operating loss is avoided.

USE OF FOREIGN ENTITIES

When U.S. taxpayers decide to conduct business outside the United States, tax planning is essential. The form in which the foreign business is structured will influence its tax consequences. Likewise, the tax rules of the foreign countries in which the business will operate are a critical consideration.

Foreign operations can be conducted as a branch of a U.S. company, as a partnership, as a foreign corporate subsidiary, as a special entity called a Foreign Sales Corporation (FSC), or as a hybrid entity with different corporate or other characteristics depending on the law of the country involved. For example, in certain countries, an entity can be a corporation under the foreign country's law, but can be treated as a partnership for U.S. purposes. The entity chosen can affect the foreign taxes as well as the U.S. taxes on your foreign earnings.

The issues involved are complex from the standpoint of both the U.S. federal tax laws and the numerous foreign tax jurisdictions. Generally, using a branch of a U.S. company in a foreign country can be beneficial if losses are incurred but may be detrimental when the branch becomes profitable. The same is generally true of partnerships, although there are exceptions in both cases.

The use of a foreign corporation to conduct business abroad will usually provide the most opportunity to maximize tax deferral and plan for the repatriation of profits. While a thorough discussion of the tax ramifications of doing business in foreign countries is beyond the scope of this book, the following section touches on the rules and regulations for the Foreign Sales Corporation, a special-purpose entity that provides a tax incentive to U.S. exporters.

Foreign Sales Corporation

For a number of years, the U.S. government has used tax law to encourage exporting, in an attempt to lower the U.S. trade deficit. Currently, the primary tax vehicle to stimulate exports is called the Foreign Sales Corporation.

Qualification Requirements of a Foreign Sales Corporation. To qualify as an FSC, a corporation must

1. Be organized under the laws of a foreign country or a United States possession. The foreign country must be a party to an exchange-of-information agreement with the United States or be an income-tax-treaty partner the Treasury certifies as having an acceptable exchange-of-information program under the

treaty. (The U.S. Virgin Islands and Barbados are two currently used jurisdictions.)

2. Not have more than 25 shareholders.
3. Not have preferred stock.
4. Maintain an office outside the United States and maintain a set of permanent books and records at that office.
5. Have at least one director who is not a U.S. resident.
6. Not be a member of a controlled group of which an Interest Charge Domestic International Sales Corporation (IC—DISC) is a member.
7. Elect to be an FSC.
8. Have a tax year that conforms to the taxable year of its majority shareholder.

Foreign Sales Corporation Tax Exemption Rules. An FSC will be exempt from U.S. tax on a portion of its income attributable to foreign-trading gross receipts, which include gross receipts from the following:

1. Sales or leases of export property or use outside the United States
2. Services related and subsidiary to the sale or lease of export property
3. Certain engineering or architectural services for projects located outside the United States
4. Export-management services provided for an unrelated IC—DISC or FSC if at least 50 percent of the FSC's gross receipts are from Nos. 1 and 2 in this list.

Export property is property manufactured, produced, grown, or extracted in the United States by a non-FSC and held primarily for sale, lease, or rental in the ordinary course of business by or to an FSC for direct use, consumption, or disposition outside the United States. For property to qualify as export property, not more than 50 percent of the fair market value may be attributable to products imported into the United States. In addition, certain property, such as oil and gas, is specifically excluded from the definition of export property.

For export sales to qualify as foreign-trading gross receipts, the FSC must satisfy the "foreign-management" and "foreign-economic-process" requirements.

The FSC will meet the foreign-management test if

1. All directors' and all shareholders' meetings are held outside the United States.
2. Its principal bank account is maintained outside the United States.
3. All dividends, legal and accounting fees, and officers' and directors' salaries are disbursed from foreign bank accounts.

To satisfy the foreign-economic-process requirement, certain export-selling activities must be conducted outside the United States. Specifically, the FSC or an agent of the FSC must participate in the solicitation, negotiation, or making of the export transaction contract outside the United States.

Finally, and equally important, the FSC or its agent must incur outside the United States either 50 percent of the direct costs of all, or 85 percent of the direct costs of two, of the five following types of activities: advertising and sales promotion, processing of customer orders, transportation, billing and collections, and the assumption of credit risk.

Income may be allocated to the FSC based upon arm's-length pricing. Alternatively, most taxpayers use the greater of two administrative-pricing rules for allocating income to the FSC:

1. 23 percent of the combined taxable income earned by the FSC and its related supplier attributable to foreign trade gross receipts
2. 1.83 percent of the FSC's foreign-trading gross receipts, but not more than 46 percent of combined taxable income

The amount of the FSC exemption depends on the transfer-pricing rules used to allocate income between the FSC and its related supplier. If the shareholder is a U.S. corporation and the arm's-length pricing method is used, the exemption will be 30 percent of the FSC's foreign-trade income. The exemption for a U.S. corporate shareholder under the administrative-pricing rules is 15/23 of the amount determined under the administrative-pricing rule used.

There is no exemption allowed for nonexport profits, investment income (such as dividends, interest, royalties, rents, and certain other passive income), or carrying charges (unstated interest and amounts in excess of the sale price for an immediate cash sale).

Foreign Sales Corporation Taxation. An FSC will file a U.S. income tax return and be liable for U.S. tax on its nonexempt income under the normal U.S. tax rules.

Shareholder Taxation. A domestic corporation will generally be allowed a 100 percent dividends-received deduction for amounts distributed from an FSC out of earnings and profits attributable to export income. Thus, a U.S. corporate exporter selling through an FSC subsidiary that uses the administrative-pricing rule can, in effect, obtain a U.S. tax exclusion equal to 15 percent of the taxable profit generated from export sales.

Small Exporters. Because of the administrative costs inherent in the foreign-management and foreign-economic-process requirements, two alternatives are provided for small export business: (1) the small FSC and (2) the IC-DISC.

1. A small FSC is a foreign corporation that meets the requirements to be an FSC, but need not satisfy the foreign-management and foreign-economic-process tests. Foreign Sales Corporation benefits are available for export income on up to $5 million of export gross receipts. An FSC may not elect to be a small FSC if it is a member of a controlled group that includes an FSC other than a small FSC.
2. An interest-charge IC-DISC is a special-purpose entity similar to an FSC, which in general is entitled to a 94 percent deferral of DISC taxable income. However, the shareholder of the IC-DISC must pay interest yearly on tax-deferred, post-1984-accumulated DISC income. The interest will be pegged to the Treasury bill rate and will be deductible by the shareholder. (If the shareholder is an individual, the deduction for the interest expense will be subject to the general rules applicable to the deductibility of interest.) The interest-charge DISC deferral is limited to the income on $10 million of gross receipts. Taxable income attributable to gross receipts in excess of $10 million will be taxed currently to the shareholder.

For small exporters who find the foreign-economic-process requirements too burdensome, a small FSC or IC-DISC may be more desirable.

Tax Havens and Foreign Holding Companies

Some taxpayers may find it useful to set up a base or holding company in a tax-haven country or in a country with an extensive treaty network. The base company will direct business activities in other countries through foreign subsidiaries, branches, or agents.

A third-country base or holding company may be used because it imposes low tax or no tax on income earned locally or from operations in other countries.

In addition, an intermediary third-country tax haven or holding company can be used to lower foreign withholding taxes on profits repatriated to the United States or to shift income from subsidiaries in high-tax countries, in an effort to lower the enterprise's worldwide effective tax rate.

It should be noted that U.S. taxation of foreign earnings is governed by an extensive body of tax law, including multiple regimes intended to limit deferral of U.S. tax and complex rules restricting the use of foreign tax credits. A technical discussion of these issues is beyond the scope of this chapter; however, a thorough understanding of their impact and effect is critical when structuring foreign operations.

17

INTERNATIONAL EXPANSION

It is no longer the case that only large companies are involved in exporting. Companies are increasingly becoming involved internationally at an early state of development. Young businesses are recognizing that revenues from overseas markets are an integral part of their growth strategy. This is especially true of high-technology companies, whose innovative products, services, and technologies must become quickly known throughout the world.

Companies first entering the international arena are often overwhelmed by the special and seemingly complex financial transactions inherent in international business. Financing arrangements are particularly important in international transactions for a number of reasons:

- *Cost.* Exporting requires relatively significant investments of both time and money. A small to mid-sized company may have difficulty tying up its own capital for an extended period.
- *Competitiveness.* Often, favorable financing terms will "make or break" a sale. Financing terms are a competitive factor weighed by buyers when making a purchase decision.
- *Risk.* Risk is a factor in all business transactions—it becomes magnified when business is transacted internationally. However, there are methods of financing, as well as insurance options, that can reduce the risk.

Financing international business can be daunting; however, there are many resources, both private sector and governmental, that can help the new-to-export company face the challenge of financing an overseas sale.

The ability to monetize international receivables can give a company the opportunity to deploy its capital more effectively. Debt instruments that are standard in international trade can be an inexpensive source of liquidity compared with a company's normal sources of funds.

BANK EXPORT FINANCING

A company new to exporting may ask why it would want to trade internationally on any other terms than cash in advance. Although these terms may seem reasonable and justified, they may be unrealistic in light of the extremely competitive global-trading environment. Sophisticated importers have been demanding—and receiving—terms that include financing as an integral part of the sale. In making a decision on which bid to accept, the importer is not just looking at the cost of the merchandise itself but also at the credit terms available.

Thus you, the exporter, might well be compelled to provide a "package" that includes credit if you are to be successful in winning international business. Additionally, these terms may or may not be tied to what is considered the useful life of the product. The main motive for the terms is the importer's need to obtain financing and place this cost back to the exporter. To further complicate matters, companies all over the world often have access to government export-assistance programs to help give their customers better terms, which may mean that the playing field for U.S. competitors is not always level.

These realities mean that exporters will generally have to deal with international credit instruments and will have international trade receivables on their balance sheets. If the exporter obtains bank financing based on receivables, he or she will find that most banks will not accept international trade debt as part of their borrowing formula. These facts make knowledge of international trade instruments and techniques for monetizing them especially important.

Confirmed Irrevocable Letter of Credit

Except for cash in advance, the most secure form of international trade terms is a confirmed irrevocable letter of credit, an instrument that dates back to the Middle Ages. Letters of credit were invented in the Italian city-states to assist traders and wealthy individuals who traveled to places where their names and reputations were unknown to obtain credit and other courtesies. This was done by one bank writing a "letter" to another, vouching for the individuals' worth and ability to honor their debts.

Basically, the purpose of a letter of credit today is the same as it was then: a bank promises to support its importing customer, which induces exporters to sell and ship products to this customer with full expectation of prompt payment.

Confirmed Letters of Credit

In the previous scenario, the exporter's bank does not vouch for the creditworthiness of the importer or the importer's bank. It simply receives the letter from its fellow bank and passes it on to its customer. In modern terms, the exporter's bank receives a letter of credit from another bank, which is its correspondent, and "advises" the letter of credit to its customer, the beneficiary. The importer's bank, called the opening or issuing bank, promises to pay the exporter if all the terms and conditions of the letter of credit are met.

However, there are times when this bank guarantee is not enough; for example, when the bank is in a foreign country and unknown to the exporter. Even more importantly, the country where the importer and its bank are located may be one with foreign-exchange problems or other "country-risk" factors. In these circumstances, the exporter wants more assurance of payment. Confirmed letters of credit provide this additional assurance. Instead of simply advising the credit, the domestic bank will add its confirmation, which means that if all conditions are met they will pay the exporter/beneficiary, regardless of the ability of the importer's bank to do so. The domestic bank effectively tells the exporter that the foreign bank's credit is as good as its own and that they can proceed with confidence.

Typically, the letter of credit is deemed irrevocable, which means it cannot be revoked or changed until its expiry without the agreement of all parties.

A letter of credit should also state that it is subject to the Uniform Customs and Practices (UCP) for Commercial Documentary Credits. The UCP is a set of written rules and regulations prepared by an international body and periodically revised. A letter of credit that is subject to UCP assures all parties that there is a clear, concise code in place that is transnational in scope, and that all parties agree to submit themselves to this code.

Today's letters of credit have many required components, including shipment and expiry dates, product description, required documents, and names of importer and exporter. Most frequently, a draft is drawn on the bank that will be examining all the documents and ascertaining whether all the terms and conditions have been met. This bank is called the negotiating bank because it takes documents, examines them, and pays if all is in order. In confirmed letters of credit, the confirming bank and negotiating bank are often the same financial institution.

Acceptance Letter of Credit

Terms of letters of credit can call for payment at sight or may call for an acceptance of the draft that is part of the letter of credit documentation. If at sight, the negotiating bank simply pays the beneficiary immediately if there are no discrepancies in the documents presented, that is, all the terms and conditions of the letter of credit have been strictly met. If an exporter wants to give its customers credit terms, it may do so with an acceptance of a letter of credit. If the letter of credit calls for acceptance terms, the negotiating bank accepts the draft associated with the letter of credit and assigns a specific maturity date, then pays the exporter on maturity.

This accepted draft is a negotiable instrument that carries the credit of the negotiating bank. The exporter can remove this receivable from its books and get funds before draft maturity by discounting the accepted draft with the negotiating bank. Normally, the discount rate for these accepted drafts correlates with the negotiating bank's borrowing rate, a rate typically much lower than an importer can get with its own credit. Thus, the discounted draft provides an inexpensive source of funds to the exporter.

Back-to-Back Letters of Credit

Instruments that warrant special mention are back-to-back letters of credit. These arise when an exporter, often an agent or other entity with limited financial resources, approaches its bank requesting a letter of credit to be opened on the exporter's or its supplier's behalf based on another letter of credit opened by a foreign bank that calls for typical letter of credit terms, that is, payment after shipment and presentation of the specified documents. Essentially, the agent is asking its bank to base the issuance of its letter of credit on the fact that an order has been accepted by a customer and a letter of credit has been opened by a reputable financial institution and the bank not relying on the exporter's financial resources alone. In this case, the exporter is able to get preexport financing.

Although this scenario may appear logical and reasonable, the reality is that the exporter/agent's bank could find itself in a situation where it is forced to pay under its letter of credit while the lack of fulfillment of the initial letter of credit terms means that the first letter of credit may never be negotiated. The result is that the first letter of credit may not be such an absolute assurance of payment after all. Most banks avoid getting involved with back-to-back letters of credit, because they can hinge on contract performance and not simple documentary performance. It is important for the exporter to realize that banks deal in documents for letters of credit and do not want to get involved with contractual performance, disputes, or other issues between the exporter and the importer. Banks are in the business of opening and confirming letters of credit based on the credit of the appropriate parties and then negotiating and paying on the letter of credit based on the satisfactory fulfillment of all the terms.

Exporters should tap the expertise of their banks to gain information and guidance about their own particular credit needs and the intricacies of letters of credit.

Documentary Collection

Documentary collection is a less costly though riskier method of arranging international sales. With a collection, the exporter draws a draft on the importer, instructing him or her to pay either on presentation (sight draft) or at an agreed-upon future date (time draft). The draft may name the exporter as the party to be paid, but more commonly, it specifies payment to the order of a bank handling the collection for the seller (collecting bank). Technically, a sight draft may be presented for payment as soon as the foreign bank receives the documents. In practice however, the importer will frequently "sight" the draft only when the goods arrive in the country.

There are risks to this method of exporting: there is no guarantee that the importer will "sight" or accept the draft; the importer may decide not to buy the goods after shipment has been made; the importer's financial position may have changed before the draft is presented for payment or matures; or the importing country may make policy changes affecting the importer's ability to pay. The exporter thus has a risk until payment is received. The collecting bank is simply the entity that receives and presents the importer with the relevant documents. It has no obligation to pay or back the credit in any way. Drafts that are accepted under this method may be negotiable and may be discounted and sold to other entities. However, this task may be difficult unless the draft is drawn on a major, well-known company in a developed nation with few, if any, perceived country-risk factors.

Letters of credit are but one vehicle an exporter can use to facilitate international trade. Confirmed letters of credit are secure and liquid but are more expensive than other trade documentation for the importer. The advantages they bring to a transaction might not be needed if, for example, the opening bank is a major Western European financial institution that a U.S. bank can discount. Conversely, an exporter might deem it vital to get a U.S. bank confirmation for a letter of credit issued by a bank in a lesser-developed country, yet find its bank is reluctant to oblige due to cross-border risks. Banks still vividly remember the 1980s, when huge write-downs of international loans were necessary due to foreign-debt crises. At the same time, tough international competition is allowing more sophisticated importers in those very countries to demand—and get—financing terms.

OTHER EXPORT PROGRAMS

To compete, exporters need to have knowledge of programs and financing techniques to help them win sales at a reasonable risk and cost. Here are the most common and useful programs available.

Private Insurance

Private insurance is available to cover international commercial and political risks. Private insurance can generally offer more flexible terms and, unlike programs of the Export-Inport Bank of the U.S. (the Eximbank) discussed in detail later in this chapter, is not restricted to the coverage of U.S. goods. To a great extent, the private insurance programs parallel those offered by the Eximbank. However, they cannot offer the ability to shift the risk to the U.S. government, as can the Eximbank. This may prove problematic from a bank's viewpoint because it must analyze the risk associated with the insurance company as well as the intrinsic risk of the underlying trade transaction.

Forfaiting

Like letters of credit, forfaiting is a centuries-old method of monetizing trade receivables. A trade transaction takes place with a draft being drawn by the exporter and guaranteed by a bank in the importer's country. This draft is a negotiable instrument. There is an international market for discounting these drafts, with pricing depending on bank and country-risk factors. Historically, forfaiting has been an especially popular technique for Eastern European trade. Forfaiting can also occur with drafts drawn on large companies with no additional bank guarantee. Then the pricing for forfaiting the draft is dependent solely on the perceived creditworthiness of the drawee company.

Development Banks

Exporters that have partners in other countries may be able to apply for funds not available to a U.S. firm from other development banks. Some of these banks are listed here. Of course, each has both loan guidelines and targeted regional or industrial sectors which are served.

African Development Bank Group
Asian Development Bank
Caribbean Development Bank
East African Development Bank
European Bank for Reconstruction and Development (EBRD)
European Investment Bank (EIB)
Inter-American Development Bank
World Bank Group

To compete internationally demands knowledge and expertise of the different risk factors. By familiarizing yourself with the details of the techniques outlined briefly here, and by turning your bank export specialist into a cooperative partner, you, will be in a position to keep financing problems from interfering with your international sales successes.

GOVERNMENT EXPORT-FINANCE PROGRAMS

There are several government sources of finance for international business activities. The federal government provides a variety of financing programs through a number of different agencies. State agencies also provide export-finance programs to companies located in their state. Finally, governments throughout the world offer incentives to companies to invest in their countries. These incentives often include direct grants and low-interest loans. (See Exhibit 17–1.)

Federal Assistance

The federal government offers international financial assistance to companies primarily through five agencies: The Small Business Administration (SBA), the Eximbank, the Overseas Private Investment Corporation (OPIC), the Department of Agriculture's Foreign Agricultural Service, and the U.S. Trade and Development Agency (TDA). In addition, the U.S. Department of Commerce can provide potential exporters with advisory and counseling services to help the new-to-export company succeed in the international marketplace.

The U.S. Agency for International Development's (USAID) Center for Trade and Investment Services (CTIS) also promotes increased business activity between the private sectors in the United States and the USAID-assisted developing countries. The Center for Trade and Investment Services is the agency's new central information and referral service for U.S. businesses interested in opportunities abroad. It provides detailed information on general trade and investment trends, business opportunities, and USAID's private-sector programs overseas. In addition, CTIS identifies and facilitates firm-neutral marketing of business opportunities in USAID-assisted countries and sponsors industry-specific transaction conferences.

These agencies and their export assistance programs are outlined in the sections that follow.

Small Business Administration*

The Small Business Administration has a number of programs to assist companies with their international financing needs.

---

* *Your Business and the SBA—1989 Edition Revised*, U.S. Small Business Administration.

EXHIBIT 17–1. Export Assistance Available Through Federal Agencies

	Direct Loans	Guaranteed/ Insured Loans	Insurance	Direct Payments	Equity Participation
Export-Import Bank Telephone: (202) 566-8990	Offers direct loans for large projects and equipment sales that require long-term financing.	Guarantees loans made by cooperating commercial banks to U.S. exporters and foreign buyers. Programs include Working Capital Guarantee Program, Commercial Bank Guarantees, and Small Business Credit Program.	Credit insurance is available for up to 100% of losses for political reasons and 90–100% for commercial losses.		
Overseas Private Investment Corporation Telephone: (202) 336-8799	Offers direct loans for projects in developing countries sponsored by or significantly involving U.S. small businesses or cooperatives.	Guarantees loans and other investments made by eligible U.S. investors in friendly developing countries and areas against loss.	Finances insurance programs for investors in overseas projects; offers insurance and financing services for U.S. service contractors and exporters operating in developing countries.	Offers direct payments for reimbursement of eligible cost items under OPIC's Project Development Program. In general, total contribution is limited to $150,000 per project.	Under certain circumstances, OPIC may purchase equity in the project, including convertible notes and other debt instruments with equity participating features.
Small Business Adminstration Telephone: (202) 205-6720	The 7(a) loan program can be used by exporters for fixed asset acquisition.	Export revolving line of credit guarantees can be used to finance materials and labor used to produce goods for export, or			Through the Small Business Investment Company, SBA provides equity or working capital for exporters.

Department of Agriculture, Foreign Agricultural Service Telephone: (202) 720-4327

to penetrate or develop foreign markets. Eximbank and SBA offer co-guarantees for small business exporters and trading companies. Export Credit Guarantee Program (GSM-102) and Intermediate Export Credit Guarantee Program (GSM-103) can be used to provide export credit guarantees to increase exports of U.S. agricultural commodities.

Offers direct payments for reimbursement of eligible promotional expenses of a U.S. agricultural commodity adversely affected by unfair foreign practice.

U.S. Agency for International Development Telephone: (202) 663-2323
U.S. Trade and Development Agency Telephone: (703) 875-4357

Offers guarantees and limited loan assistance under the Private Sector Investment Program.

Provides grant funding of feasibility studies, consultancies, and other project planning services for major projects in developing countries, provided the host government lends its endorsement.

Small businesses may be eligible for the SBA's regular 7(a) business-loan guarantee program, which provides loan guarantees for fixed assets and working capital. Through this program, the SBA can guarantee up to 90 percent of a bank loan up to $155,000. For larger loans, the maximum guarantee is the lesser of 85 percent or $750,000. To be eligible, the applicant's business generally must be operated for profit and fall within size standards set by the SBA. Export trading companies (ETCs) and export management companies (EMCs) also may qualify for the SBA's business-loan guarantee program.

The Export Revolving Line of Credit (ERLC) guarantees provide short-term financing for exporting companies in existence for a year or more to fund the development or penetration of foreign markets, or to finance labor and materials needed for manufacturing or wholesaling for export. Proceeds of the ERLC can also be used to finance professional export marketing advice or services, foreign business travel, or participation in trade shows. However, ERLC proceeds may not be used to acquire fixed assets or capital goods for the use in the applicant's business or to liquidate existing debt. Applicants for an ERLC must meet the eligibility criteria applicable for 7(a) loans. Export trading companies, export management companies, and other trading entities are also eligible under the program. Applicants who produce, manufacture, or sell products for export but who do not themselves directly export their products are eligible under ERLC, provided entry of the products into international commerce is clearly documented. Lenders may twice renew guarantees with a maturity of 12 months or less; thus, the ERLC program has a maximum maturity of 36 months. The SBA can guarantee up to 90 percent of loan amounts up to $155,000, and up to 85 percent for larger loans. Small businesses can have SBA guarantees in addition to an ERLC, as long as SBA's total guarantee does not exceed $750,000, or $1.25 million if combined with an International Trade Loan. Any number of withdrawals and repayments can be made as long as they do not exceed the dollar limit of the credit line and the disbursements are made within the stated maturity period.

Coverage by the ERLC is not available for receivables from countries that are not open to Eximbank coverage at the date the goods are shipped or at the date of execution of services. In addition, proceeds from a loan must be used only to finance goods and services that contain at least 50 percent U.S. content. Products or services that are not shipped from the United States or its territories or possessions are ineligible under the credit line, notwithstanding the fact that the seller may be a resident of the United States or that profits are repatriated to the United States.

The International Trade Loan Program provides long-term financing for the acquisition, construction, renovation, modernization, improvement, or expansion of productive facilities or equipment in the United States for production of goods and services destined for international trade. Loan maturities cannot exceed 25 years, excluding the working capital portion of the financing, which could be in the form of either ERLC or a portion of the term loan. The SBA's guarantee cannot exceed 85 percent of the loan amount, thus precluding loans of $155,000 or less. The agency's maximum share for facilities or equipment loans is $1 million, plus $250,000 for working capital. To meet eligibility requirements, applicants must establish that loan proceeds will significantly expand existing export markets or develop new ones, or that the applicant's business is adversely affected by import competition.

Exporting companies that need equity capital financing in excess of the SBA's $750,000 statutory maximum may be able to apply for the necessary financing from a Small Business Investment Company (SBIC). An SBIC is approved and licensed by the SBA. However, unlike the SBA , it can invest in export-trading companies in which banks have equity participation as long as other SBIC requirements are met.

The SBA Office of International Trade offers a range of counseling and advisory services to encourage small businesses to consider the global marketplace. This office also provides information on the SBA loan programs available to assist exporters. Export support is available through

- One-on-one counseling by Service Corps of Retired Executives (SCORE) volunteers with international trade experience;
- Initial consultation with an international trade attorney;
- Export Information System, which provides an initial screening of world markets to determine the export potential of a commodity or manufactured product;
- Export marketing publications and resource guides;
- Matchmaker Trade Missions, cosponsored by the U.S. Department of Commerce, which arranges direct contacts for American companies with potential partners in new international markets;

- Training on various aspects of the export process through conferences and seminars nationwide;
- Counseling through some collegiate Small Business Development Centers (SBDCs) and Small Business Institutes that have international trade centers.

Both the financial programs and the counseling are available through the SBA's network of field offices.

The Eximbank of the United States and the SBA have created a co-guarantee program that provides co-guarantees to small business exporters and trading companies. The co-guarantees are available for loans ranging from $200,000 to $1 million and cover 90 percent of the principal amount. The SBA and the Eximbank each cover 50 percent of the guarantee, unless a different percentage is approved. Other requirements are determined by SBA rules and export revolving line of credit regulations. The guaranteed loans should be used for the purchase of goods for export; materials or component parts; or goods, services, or labor to be used in producing goods or services for a future or existing export sale or foreign business development such as marketing, travel expenses, trade fair participation, or other promotional activities. The SBA services of all co-guaranteed loans, and all applications for co-guarantees of loans should be processed through the applicant's local SBA office.

Export-Import Bank of the United States

The Eximbank was created in 1934 and established as an independent U.S. government agency in 1945 to assist American businesses in exporting. Located in Washington, D.C., the Eximbank is designed to enhance the competitive position of U.S. exporters of all sizes by offering financing competitive with financing provided by foreign export credit agencies to assist sales by their nation's exporters.

The Eximbank assists U.S. exporters in obtaining preexport financing by guaranteeing their repayment of export-related working capital loans from commercial lenders. It helps exporters extend credit to their foreign customers by covering the political and commercial risks of nonpayment. It encourages commercial financing of U.S. exports by guaranteeing repayment of loans made to foreign buyers of U.S. exports and encourages foreign buyers to purchase U.S. exports by offering competitive, fixed-rate loans.

To qualify for support, the product or service must have at least 50 percent U.S. content and cannot be military-related. Transactions must have a reasonable assurance of repayment and must not adversely impact the U.S. economy. While the Eximbank is not a foreign aid or development agency, it has co-financed projects with the U.S. Agency for International Development, the World Bank, and regional development banks. The Eximbank provides financing for export businesses in several different ways.

Loans. Loans to provide foreign buyers with competitive, fixed-interest-rate financing for U.S. export sales include direct loans to foreign buyers of U.S. exports and intermediary loans to fund responsible parties that extend loans to the foreign buyers. The foreign buyer is required to make a minimum cash down payment of 15 percent. The Eximbank's loans cover the remaining 85 percent of the contract price (100 percent of the financed portion). United States capital equipment and services are eligible for medium-term or long-term financing. For U.S. export items containing foreign-made components, the Eximbank will cover up to 100 percent of the U.S. content, provided the total amount covered does not exceed 85 percent of the contract price of the item and the total U.S. content is not less than 50 percent of the contract price of the item.

The Eximbank's lending rates are based on average U.S. Treasury rates for the preceding month plus 1 percent, and conform to Organization for Economic Cooperation and Development (OECD) Commercial Interest Reference Rates (CIRR). Fees charged are based on the nature of the product or service being exported, the risk assessment of the foreign buyer or guarantor, and the amount and term of the credit. The Eximbank applies a risk-related exposure fee schedule that is designed to be as competitive as possible with fees charged by official export credit agencies of other countries.

Guarantees. Guarantees provide repayment protection for private-sector loans to creditworthy buyers of U.S. goods and services exports, and are available alone or in combination with intermediary loans. Most guarantees provide comprehensive coverage of both political and commercial risks, although guarantees covering only political risk are also available. The Eximbank's interest coverage on new medium-term and long-term guarantee authorizations is 100 percent. Therefore, guarantees of commercial loans to foreign buyers of U.S. goods or services cover 100 percent of principal and interest against both political and commercial risks of nonpayment. Medium-term guarantees cover the sale of capital items or project-related services. Long-term guarantees are available for major projects, large capital goods, and project-related services.

Working Capital Guarantees. These help U.S. companies meet the cash-flow needs that arise from exporting and include a Working Capital Loan Guarantee program to meet the need for working capital. This program encourages commercial lenders to make loans to U.S. businesses for various export-related activities. This program is especially beneficial to small or medium-sized businesses and to minority-owned enterprises that are unable to secure credit from a commercial lender. The exporter may use the guaranteed financing to purchase finished products or materials, products, services, and labor to produce goods or services for export, or to cover stand-by letters of credit and bid and performance bonds. In addition, the borrower can use the guaranteed financing to fund marketing activities provided sufficient collateral and cash flow exist.

The Eximbank's working capital guarantee covers 100 percent of the guaranteed loan's principal and interest. Although the lender must apply directly for the final commitment, exporters may apply for a preliminary commitment, which is valid for six months, and then search for lenders. The guarantee may be for a single export-related loan or a revolving line of credit. There is no minimum or maximum loan amount. Since the purpose of the loan guarantee is to cover the potential risk of a commercial lender in making funds available to an exporter, the loan requires full collateral at all times. The repayment period is generally 12 months; however, working capital guarantees may be renewed.

Export Credit Insurance Policies. These are available for single and repetitive export sales and for leases. Generally, export credit insurance policies cover 100 percent of the principal for political risk and 90 to 100 percent for commercial risk, plus a specified amount of interest. Short-term policies, including short-term single-buyer and short-term multibuyer insurance policies, are used to support the sale of consumer goods, raw materials, and spare parts with repayment terms up to 180 days. Medium-term single-buyer policies are issued on a case-by-case basis for credit terms ranging from 181 days to 5 years (exceptionally, 7 years), depending on the contract value. These policies are issued to insure medium-term export credit sales of primarily new and used capital equipment and services, as well as planning and feasibility studies. The policies cover 100 percent of the principal for political risk and 90 percent for commercial risk. A 15 percent cash down payment is required from the buyer.

The Eximbank has undertaken a major effort to assist small businesses involved in export activities. In fiscal year 1992, the Eximbank established a new Small Business Group and implemented a number of insurance program enhancements to facilitate exports by small business. New-to-export policies are available to companies that are just beginning to export or that have average annual export credit sales of less than $2 million over the most recent two-year period and meet the SBA's definition of small business. New-to-export policies are blanket policies insuring multibuyer short-term export credit sales. These policies offer enhanced commercial risk protection, including 95 percent commercial coverage and 100 percent political coverage with no deductible. The maximum repayment period ranges from 180 to 360 days. These coverage and eligibility requirements are also valid for an umbrella policy, which allows commercial lenders, state agencies, finance companies, export-trading and management companies, insurance brokers, and similar agencies to act as intermediaries (administrators) between the Eximbank and their clients in assisting their clients in obtaining export credit insurance. In 1992, commercial risk coverage under the umbrella policy was increased from 90 to 95 percent. Other types of policies are also available, among which are lease insurance policies, financial institution buyer credit insurance policies, and bank letter of credit insurance policies.

Overseas Private Investment Corporation*

The Overseas Private Investment Corporation (OPIC) is a self-sustaining U.S. government agency that serves to promote economic growth in developing countries by encouraging U.S. private investment in those nations. OPIC supports U.S. investors with a variety of financial instruments such as direct loans, loan guarantees, and equity investment, and with a political-risk insurance program.

---

* *Investment Finance Handbook*, OPIC.

OPIC provides a broad range of investor services, which consist of five principal components: Advisory Services, Investment Missions, the Opportunity Bank, the Investor Information Service, and Outreach. These services are designed to assist small and medium-sized businesses in successfully planning and implementing overseas investment projects. Through OPIC's Advisory Services, companies obtain professional guidance and assistance with business-plan development, prospective joint venture partner identification, field reconnaissance and prefeasibility evaluation, and project finance sourcing.

Investment Missions are conducted periodically to selected countries in which OPIC operates. Each mission, lead by a senior OPIC official, provides U.S. companies with a unique and valuable opportunity to become familiar with investment opportunities available in the country of interest. Investment interests of American companies can be matched with investment opportunities offered by project sponsors in host countries through OPIC's Opportunity Bank, a computerized database available on-line through the LEXIS/NEXIS services of Mead Data Central. The Investor Information Service is a publications clearinghouse that provides general business, economic, political, social, and investment climate information on more than 125 nations and 20 major market regions. In addition to individual country kits, regional packages are also available. OPIC periodically sponsors and cosponsors seminars and conferences throughout the United States and overseas as a means of informing the United States business community of investment opportunities in the developing world.

OPIC's programs are available for new ventures that are commercially and financially sound or for the expansion of existing viable businesses. In all instances, the projects OPIC supports must assist in the social and economic development of the host country and must be consistent with the economic interests of the United States. OPIC currently operates in over 130 countries around the world.

Finance Program. Through loans and loan guarantees, OPIC can provide a significant portion of medium- and long-term funds for financing in countries where other financial institutions cannot or will not lend. OPIC does not offer concessional financing terms usually associated with government-to-government financing, nor does it offer financing of export sales that are not related to long-term investment. In some situations, OPIC will make an equity investment in a project through the purchase of convertible notes and certain other debt instruments.

Eligibility criteria for all OPIC finance programs include commercial and financial stability and demonstrated management competence and success, as well as significant financial interest in the project on the part of the proposed management team. These criteria are more strictly applied in the case of equity participation.

Financing for smaller programs is provided through a direct loan program funded by OPIC's own resources. These loans generally range from $500,000 to $6 million. Direct loans are strictly for projects sponsored by or significantly involving U.S. small businesses or co-operatives.

Larger concerns not eligible for direct loans can qualify for OPIC's loan-guarantee program. Small businesses and cooperatives investing in large projects may also use this program. OPIC loan guarantees typically range from $2 million to $25 million, but can be for amounts up to $50 million. Under the guarantee program, OPIC determines the appropriate terms of borrowing and can assist the borrower in identifying a financial institution to provide the funds. OPIC generally issues guarantees to U.S. insurance companies, pension funds, and commercial banks that are more than 50 percent owned by U.S. citizens or, if foreign, are at least 95 percent U.S.-owned.

OPIC is very selective in its equity-investment program. Only those projects with well-proven management and prior success will qualify. OPIC will not acquire a majority stake in a company, nor will it remain an investor after the first few years of operations. OPIC's equity investments are generally in the $250,000 to $2 million range, but can be higher.

Political-Risk Insurance. OPIC will provide investment insurance covering expropriation, currency inconvertibility, and political violence for certain types of U.S. investment in developing countries. Investors qualify for this insurance whether or not OPIC is a financial participant in the project. OPIC will usually provide coverage for 90 percent of a proposed investment. In the case of very large investments in countries where OPIC has a large number of policies outstanding, or for very sensitive projects, coverage may be limited to less than 90 percent.

OPIC offers special flexible insurance coverage for investment in mineral exploration and development; oil and gas exploration, development, and production; and certain exporters of goods and services. Services qualifying for special coverage include construction engineering, hospital management, and systems management; specified goods include turbines, computers, telecommunications, and drilling equipment.

OPIC is currently offering assistance to U.S. companies interested in pursuing investment opportunities in Central and Eastern Europe and the newly independent states of the former Soviet Union. To help facilitate the transfer of U.S. commercial expertise and capital to the region, OPIC has established the Project Development Program to assist eligible U.S. firms in conducting preinvestment analyses for investments in covered countries. This three-year program (roughly running from 1992 to 1995) is partially offsetting U.S. companies' up-front costs in evaluating investment opportunities by funding a portion of the costs of preinvestment analyses. To maximize the use of limited resources, OPIC's total contribution will, in general, not exceed $150,000 per project, with the U.S. sponsor required to contribute at least 50 percent of the cost of the preinvestment analysis (25 percent for small businesses). The program does not provide for advance funding of any expenditures and is limited to cost reimbursement. This program is administered by Ernst & Young, and participation in the Project Development Program is independent of participation in any other OPIC programs or services.

U.S. Department of Agriculture—Foreign Agricultural Service

The Foreign Agricultural Service (FAS) of the U.S. Department of Agriculture (USDA) was formed to take a leadership role in the development of foreign markets for U.S. farm products. The FAS has become the Secretary of Agriculture's representative abroad, with responsibility for gathering and publishing most of the U.S. government statistics relating to foreign agriculture, for monitoring and developing U.S. trade policy relating to agriculture, and for market-development activities.

The market-development activities of FAS are devised to involve private-sector agricultural interests in export-market development. Thus, FAS instituted a "cooperator program," which requires that the private-sector organizations involved sign contracts, making them cooperators with FAS in market-development activities.

The cooperators are all private, not-for-profit organizations, formed to promote the interests of the specific products or commodities they represent. Examples of cooperator organizations include the Florida Department of Citrus and the National Forest Products Association. The first step for an exporter interested in FAS programs would be to contact the relevant organization for the exporter's product.

There are two basic programs FAS uses to promote the export of U.S. agricultural products: the Foreign Agricultural Development and Promotion Program and the Market Promotion Program.

Foreign Agricultural Development and Promotion Program. The Foreign Agricultural Development and Promotion Program's objective is to create, expand, and maintain markets abroad for U.S. agricultural products. Funds are jointly contributed by FAS and cooperators and may be used for trade servicing, consumer promotion, market research, or the provision of technical assistance to actual or potential foreign buyers. Government funds are limited to use in activities conducted outside the United States.

Market Promotion Program. The Market Promotion Program (MPP) was authorized by the Food, Agriculture, Conservation and Trade Act of 1990 (1990 Act). It replaced the Targeted Export Assistance Program, which existed to counter or offset the effects of foreign-country subsidies on their products or quotas on U.S. agricultural products. The 1990 Act requires that the USDA use funds or surplus stocks of commodities from the Commodity Credit Corporation (CCC) to "encourage the development, maintenance, and expansion of commercial export markets for agricultural commodities through cost-share assistance to eligible trade organizations that implement a foreign market development program." This program is administered by the USDA's Foreign Agricultural Service and promotes a wide range of U.S. commodity groups in almost every region of the world. Trade organizations as well as private firms submit proposals for MPP that include a detailed description of proposed activities, budget, and resources contributed by the recipient. The USDA's deadline for submitting proposals is specified in the program announcement, which is published annually in the *Federal Register.*

The FAS also administers, on behalf of the Commodity Credit Corporation, the Export Credit Guarantee Program (GSM-102) and the Intermediate Export Credit Guarantee Program (GSM-103). The purpose of these programs is to provide export-credit guarantees to increase exports of U.S. agricultural commodities, to compete against foreign agricultural exports, and to assist developing countries in meeting their food and fiber needs. These programs are applicable to cases in which credit is necessary to increase or maintain U.S. exports to a foreign market and where private U.S. financial institutions would be unwilling to provide financing without CCC's guarantee.

In addition to these programs, a number of other export-promotion programs are available through FAS. Among them are the Export Enhancement Program (EEP), Dairy Export Incentive Program (DEIP), Cottonseed Oil Assistance Program (COAP), and Sunflowerseed Oil Assistance Program (SOAP).

U.S. Department of Commerce—International Trade Administration and Bureau of Export Administration

Through the International Trade Administration and Bureau of Export Administration (BEA), the U.S. Department of Commerce provides advice and counseling services to U.S. exporters. To take advantage of these services, exporters should contact their local U.S. Department of Commerce field office.

International Trade Administration. The International Trade Administration (ITA) provides export promotion services, including the following:

1. Export awareness counseling and publications designed to stimulate interest on the part of U.S. businesses in exporting
2. Information on overseas trade opportunities
3. Guidance to U.S. business on how to find and use market identification, assessment, and contact information
4. Nonfinancial assistance in display and sales promotion (trade exhibits and missions, catalog shows, and promotion through magazine listing)
5. Support to state and private-sector organizers of selected trade fairs and missions
6. Information on trade statistics, tariffs, customs regulations and procedures, and market potential in individual countries
7. Advice and counseling on foreign trade and individual overseas markets

The ITA also promotes trade development by serving as the basic governmental source of industry-specific expertise, policy development, industry competitiveness analysis, and trade-promotion assistance for the business community, as well as for other government agencies. In cooperation with state programs, the ITA also oversees the formation of foreign-trade zones in the United States. These zones enhance communities' investment climates and serve to encourage exports and shift employment from abroad to the United States by allowing companies to perform business activities such as manufacturing under special customs and tariff requirements.

Bureau of Export Administration. The BEA provides detailed information, assistance, and training to businesses and individuals on export-licensing requirements, export-control regulations, and other matters pertaining to the export of certain products which may need a special export license. The BEA can also help to expedite the export-license process when speed is necessary to secure a sale.

U.S. Trade and Development Agency

The U.S. Trade and Development agency (TDA) is an independent U.S. Government agency whose mission is to assist the U.S. private sector in exporting goods and services for major capital projects in developing and middle-income countries that are classified as "friendly" by the U.S. Department of State. The Agency provides grants to fund feasibility studies and other planning services for major projects that will be performed by U.S. companies or consortia, creating significant opportunities for exports of U.S. goods and services. Its emphasis on host-country participation ensures that TDA-funded projects contribute to the economic growth and development of recipient countries. Although feasibility studies dominate its activities, TDA has begun to carry other activities such as technical-assistance programs, orientation visits, and training grants. Projects are identified by host governments, TDA staff, U.S. Embassy staff, or U.S. companies themselves. However, an official request from the host government, or its concurrence in the case of a private-sector project, is a prerequisite for the project commencement. Participation by TDA usually ranges from $150,000 to $750,000 for public-sector projects.

In addition, TDA funds activities designed to bring U.S. technical assistance to eligible countries through Technical Assistance Grants, and sponsors a variety of technical symposia geared to the needs of specific export industries of the United States.

State Export Assistance

In addition to the financing programs offered by states already discussed, many states also offer export financing, especially for small and mid-sized businesses.

FOREIGN GOVERNMENT INVESTMENT INCENTIVE PROGRAMS

Foreign governments often offer incentives to companies to promote investment in their countries. Governments offer such incentives primarily to foster their countries' economic development, create employment, and transfer technology. In some cases, these incentives are offered to both foreign and domestic companies, while in others special incentives are available to foreign investors. The range and scope of investment incentives varies considerably across countries. However, they generally fall into one of three categories: tax incentives, government grants, or low-interest loans.

Tax incentives may be offered by national, regional, and local government authorities. They represent special rates, tax holidays, or exemptions that apply to new investment. The counterpart to any given country's package of tax incentives is a package of government grants or low-interest loans to investors. While the application process to obtain these types of government assistance may at times be arduous, funds available to investors can be substantial. The scope of these programs varies according to the priority areas of the government. These incentives are typically offered by national governments. However, in some cases programs are offered by local regions or municipalities.

Corporate Tax Rate. Some governments offer reduced corporate tax rates to foreign investors. Reduced corporate tax rates may apply to all foreign investment, investment in specific regions of the country, or specific industries. These reduced rates usually expire at the end of a given period.

Selected Regions. To promote economic development in specific parts of a country, both national and regional governments may offer tax incentives, grants, or low-interest loans in those regions. Typically, incentives will be available in less-developed regions or regions in economic distress.

Selected Industries. To promote, strengthen, or accelerate the development of specific industries, governments may offer tax incentives, grants, or low-interest loans that apply to investment in those industries. Typically, these industries are important employers in the economy or promote the transfer of technology to the domestic country.

Capital Investment. Tax incentives on capital investment usually provide for reduced tax rates or tax moratoria on investment for fixed-capital expenditures. These rates may apply only to specific capital costs and for only a limited period of time. Governments often offer grants and low-interest loans to cover up to a specified percentage of fixed start-up project costs. Typically, the greatest amount of government financing is available in areas that the government has designated as needing special assistance. Government assistance is usually awarded on the understanding that substantial private investment will accompany the grant or loan.

Research and Development. Foreign governments frequently offer tax incentives to promote research and development in their countries, anticipating that such R&D will promote technology transfer. Government programs in this category usually involve grants and loans that cover up to a specified percentage of ongoing costs associated with product and process development. Government financing may be limited to specific industries.

Plant and Equipment. Tax incentives and government financing of investment in plant and capital equipment are usually part of overall incentive packages that provide incentives for capital investment. Incentives in this category typically allow various depreciation allowances for plant and equipment. The type of fixed assets applicable may be limited.

Local Property Taxes. To encourage investment in particular regions, local authorities may either offer lower local property tax rates or exempt foreign companies from local taxes altogether. Again, these incentives may apply only for a limited time.

Employment Promotion. Incentives that promote employment usually involve grants or tax write-offs for employee training and development programs, tax relief for profit-sharing schemes, or reduced tax rates for investment that creates a substantial number of new jobs.

Export Promotion. Tax incentives to promote exports typically allow reduced rates on, or exemptions from, corporate taxes on a company's export earnings. They may also allow higher capital allowances for investment that will promote exports.

Tax Holidays. Tax holidays refer to specific periods of time during which a company is exempt from various taxes. As always, these tax holidays expire after a given period and may apply only to specific regions and industries.

Example Programs

Depending on their priorities and resources, governments will utilize a combination of the country's incentives to attract foreign investment to their countries. Following is a brief description of the various incentives offered by Spain, Ireland, and Singapore. Note that incentives vary widely between these countries, which illustrates the importance of researching investment incentive programs closely to find those that will be of greatest benefit to your company's priorities and needs.

Spain. Generally, the regional incentives provided to investors by the Spanish government are in line with European Community requirements. The regional-incentives scheme gives support to investment in certain areas. The geographical coverage of regional incentives is very broad; 83 percent of the Spanish territory is eligible. The regional-incentives scheme is based on nonrefundable subsidies expressed as a percentage of eligible investment expenditure. Four classes of areas have been identified, always respecting the ceiling determined by European Community regulations:

• Class I—areas where maximum rate of award can reach up to 50 to 75 percent

- Class II—areas with a 40 percent limit
- Class III—areas with a 30 percent limit
- Class IV—areas with a 20 percent limit

These subsidies are awarded for investment by either domestic or foreign entities in specified geographic areas and in particular industrial sectors with the aim of promoting a more equitable distribution of income throughout the country.

Investment incentives available to investors in Spain are in the form of fiscal incentives and job creation incentives.

1. *Fiscal Incentives.* Spain's present standard corporate income tax rate is 35 percent. Effective investment in new fixed assets qualifies for a tax credit of 5 percent. Investment in R&D programs for new products or industrial processes qualifies for a tax credit of 15 percent of the intangible expenses incurred and 30 percent of fixed assets relating to the previously mentioned programs. These credits can be subtracted from the amount of corporate income tax payable, with a percentage ceiling of such tax amount, which in 1992 was 25 percent.

2. *Job Creation Incentives.* These incentives include employment creation and training incentives. Employment creation incentives are subsidies for companies that hire employees under indefinite and training contracts. The amount of subsidy depends on the employee's characteristics and ranges from about $4,000, for young people under 29 years old, to $7,000 for people with disabilities. Training incentives consist of subsidies for training expenses and assistance to and training of employees. A subsidy of about $5,500 is available when training contracts are converted into indefinite contracts. In addition, the Ministry of Labor provides training subsidies for companies that hire special kinds of workers, such as young people or long-term unemployed.

   The Ministry of Industry, Trade, and Tourism also administers loans and subsidies for research and development. These incentives consist primarily of subsidies for up to 70 percent, with an average of 25 percent, of the cost of the project as well as low-interest or even interest-free loans.

Ireland. Ireland's incentive programs apply broadly to almost all industries and all regions. The central government relies on a combination of tax incentives and capital-grant programs to promote foreign investment.

The most significant incentives are as follows:

- A 10 percent corporate tax rate on manufacturing profits from January 1, 1981, through December 31, 2000.* This rate also applies to various other sectors, such as international financial services, certain computer services, specified shipping activities, and wholesale sales by special trading houses.
- A capital-grant program that awards up to 60 percent of project capital costs. Projects of all sizes and in all regions of the country are eligible for this grant-in-aid.
- Special incentives for "internationally trading financial service companies" in the International Financial Services Centre in Dublin. These special incentives include the 10 percent corporate tax rate, exemption from local taxes for ten years, generous deduction allowances for leased or purchased property, and exemption from capital-gains tax on trading income.

Singapore. The government of Singapore utilizes a combination of tax and grant incentives to attract foreign investment to its shores. The most substantial tax incentives include the following:

- Exemption from income tax for up to ten years for companies that qualify for "pioneer status," including those in industries involving large capital expenditures, sophisticated technology, and manufacturing skills, or those that provide specified services such as engineering services, venture capital fund activity, or financial services.
- Exemption of taxable income of an amount equal to a specified proportion (up to 50 percent) of new fixed investment in eligible activities.
- A 10 percent income tax rate for companies that are approved operational headquarters companies or that export services, or on companies' qualifying offshore income.

---

* This date is likely to be extended through December 31, 2010, according to the Industrial Development Authority of Ireland.

Grants and low-interest loans are widely available through various agencies of the Singaporean government. Some of the most significant financial-assistance programs are as follows:

- Small Industries Finance Scheme
- Small Industries Technical Assistance Scheme
- Business Development Scheme
- Product Development Assistance Scheme
- Robot Leasing Scheme
- Initiatives in New Technology Scheme
- Equity Participation Scheme
- Venture Capital Programme
- Capital Assistance Scheme
- Market Development Assistance Scheme
- Research and Development Assistance Scheme
- Export Bills Rediscounting Scheme

Particularly attractive are the financial-assistance programs that encourage and assist small and mid-sized enterprises, those that promote research and development, and those that include equity participation. In many (but not all) cases, to qualify for assistance the project must have at least 30 percent equity owned by Singapore citizens or permanent residents.

APPENDIX A

SUMMARY OF FINANCING ALTERNATIVES

APPENDIX A. Summary of Financing Alternatives

Alternative	Terms and Uses	Security	Requirements	Advantages	Disadvantages	Sources
Bank lines of credit or revolving credit	1–3 years; borrowings often float as a percentage of receivables and/or inventory. Seasonal working capital use option.	Unsecured or secured by receivables, inventories, property, plant equipment, fixtures, etc.	Have collateral. Have established sales/earnings record. Have predictable cash flow.	No equity dilution. Support services. Interest deductions. Interest predictable. Flexibility to borrow and repay funds as need dictates.	May need collateral. Leverage can be expensive. Can impede additional financing. Restrictive debt covenants.	Commercial banks. Hybrid lenders. Commercial finance companies.
Short-term notes	60–364 days. Seasonal working capital use.	Unsecured or secured.	Have collateral. Have established sales/earnings record. Have predictable cash flow.	No equity dilution. Support services. Interest deductions. Interest predictable. May be fixed-rate interest.	May need collateral. New documentation required for each borrowing. Must meet maturity.	Commercial banks. Individuals.

| Revolver/term | 1–2 year revolver converting to a 2–7 year term loan. Working capital use. Equipment needs. Acquisitions. Expansion. | Unsecured or secured. | Have collateral. Have established sales/earnings record. Have predictable cash flow. | No equity dilution. Support services. Interest deductions. Flexibility to borrow and repay funds. Principal payments at maturity. Provides long-term commitment. Able to package assets purchased over time into a single loan. May be able to renew revolving portion indefinitely, subject to performance. | May need collateral. Hard to obtain in difficult times. Leverage can be expensive. Can impede additional financing. Restrictive debt covenants. Prediction of interest may be difficult with floating loan rates. | Commercial banks. Hybrid lenders. Institutional lenders. |

(continued)

APPENDIX A. Continued

Alternative	Terms and Uses	Security	Requirements	Advantages	Disadvantages	Sources
Term loan	1-7 years. Equipment needs. Acquisitions. Expansion.	Unsecured or secured.	Have collateral. Have established sales/earnings record. Have predictable cash flow.	No equity dilution. Support services. Interest deductions. Interest predictable with interest-rate protection. May be fixed-rate interest. Repayment over time.	May need collateral. Hard to obtain in difficult times. Leverage can be expensive. Can impede additional financing. Restrictive debt convenants. Interest rate may be higher.	Commercial banks. Hybrid lenders. Commercial finance companies. Institutional lenders. Individuals. Government sources.
Mortgage note	7-30+ year amortization. 5-7 year maturity. Equipment needs. Real estate purchase. Expansion.	Real estate. Equipment.	Have collateral. Have established sales/earnings record. Have predictable cash flow.	No equity dilution. Support services. Interest deductions. Interest predictable with interest-rate protection. Likely fixed rate of interest. Lower repayment terms over longer periods.	Need collateral. Prepayment penalty on fixed-rate loans possible.	Commercial banks. Commercial finance companies. Institutional lenders. Individuals. Government sources. Insurance Companies.

	Term/Use	Security	Requirements	Advantages	Disadvantages	Sources
Subordinate debt	5–10 years. Working capital use. Equipment needs. Acquisitions. Expansion.	Unsecured.	Subordinated to other senior lenders. Have established sales/earnings record. Have predictable cash flow.	Interest deductions. Interest predictable with interest-rate protection. May be perceived as additional equity by senior lender. May be fixed-rate interest. Lower repayment terms over longer periods.	Possible equity dilution. Hard to obtain in difficult times. Leverage can be expensive. Restrictive debt covenants. Interest rate may be higher.	Commercial banks. Hybrid lenders. Institutional lenders. Individuals. Public market. Venture capital. Investment firms.
Asset-based lending	1–3 year contract. Working capital use. Semipermanent working capital. Equipment needs.	Secured. Advance rates vary with industry: • 65–90% of receivables. • 10–60% of inventory. • 50–75% of orderly liquidation value of fixed assets, 50–70% of fair market value of real estate.	Have collateral. Have established sales/earnings record. Have predictable cash flow.	No equity dilutions. Support services. Interest deductions. Interest predictable. Flexibility to borrow and repay funds.	Need collateral. Leverage can be expensive. Can impede additional financing. Restrictive debt covenants. Interest rate may be higher. Lender controls cash.	Commercial banks. Commercial finance companies.

(continued)

331

APPENDIX A. Continued

Alternative	Terms and Uses	Security	Requirements	Advantages	Disadvantages	Sources
Leases	Limited to life of asset leased. Equipment needs. Real estate.	Asset leased.	Have collateral. Have predictable cash flow.	No equity dilutions. Support services. Interest deductions. Interest predictable. May be fixed-rate interest. Lower repayment terms over life of the asset. May not be capitalized.	Need collateral. Interest rate may be higher. Payment may be required at end of lease.	Commercial banks. Leasing companies.
Corporate bonds/ debentures	5–30+ years. Permanent working capital use. Equipment needs. Acquisitions. Expansion.	Unsecured.	Established sales/ earnings record. Have predictable cash flow. Bond rating may be required.	Support services. Interest deductions. Interest predictable. Lower repayment terms. May be perceived as additional equity. May be fixed-rate interest.	Possible equity dilution. Hard to obtain in difficult times. Leverage can be expensive. Can impede additional financing. Restrictive debt covenants. Interest rate may be higher. Generally not available to smaller companies.	Institutional lenders. Public market.

Franchising	Long-term. Working capital use. Equipment needs.	N/A	Developed sound product. Recognizable individuality. Rapid growth of concept. Control over growth. Ability to develop good relationship with franchisees.	Immediate cash flow. No need to repay. No equity dilution. Low risk. Limited capital requirements. Ability to expand rapidly. Distributes start-up costs to others. Provides long-term royalty stream.	Costs to franchise. Share profits with franchisee. Requires extensive testing of concept. Legal complexities.	Franchisees.
Venture capital (VC)	5–7 years. Exploiting new products, services, or market niches. Seeking equity capital in LBO. Equipment needs. Acquisitions. Expansion.	Equity in company.	Need start-up seed capital with potential for rapid growth. Need early-stage second- or third-round capital, with potential for rapid growth. Established and growing rapidly.	Management and financial expertise from equity investor. Strength of equity (i.e., greater leverage and cash flow). Enables company to mature enough to make public financing feasible.	Difficult to obtain. Heavy equity dilution. Process is time-consuming and difficult. No assurance of success. VCs have high expectations. VCs require various reports. Management often	Individuals ("Angels"). Private venture capital funds. Investment bankers. Government venture funds. Public venture funds. Institutional venture capital pools.

(continued)

APPENDIX A. Continued

Alternative	Terms and Uses	Security	Requirements	Advantages	Disadvantages	Sources
				No cash drain for debt repayments or interest and liquidity needs.	gives up economic control to VCs.	SBICs and MESBICs
Public stock offerings	Long-term. Working capital use. Equipment needs. Acquisitions. Expansion.	Equity in company.	Proven management. Established sales/earnings trend. High growth potential.	Capital available in large amounts. Provides liquidity for investors and management. Prestige and visibility. Expands equity base. No repayment. Provides vehicle for attractive stock incentives. Improves marketability. Increased value of stock. Easier to value estate.	Expensive. Timing is critical. Regulation—SEC. SEC disclosure obligations. Equity dilution. Pressure to maintain earnings growth. Outside directors. Management subject to "insider" rules. Shares owned before offering are "restricted."	Investment bankers. Public.

Limited partnerships	Long-term.	N/A	Recognizable expertise in specific technology or attractive product with market appeal. Engaged in development of new process or product. Long R&D cycle (biotechnology).	Tax benefits used to minimize risks. Off-balance-sheet financing. Flexible funds become available. Management retains operating control. General partner gets no-risk capital.	Exclusive rights to technology may be lost. Must comply with legal and tax guidelines for R&D. Risk of disallowance of tax benefits. Exposure to tax law changes. Requires extensive long-range planning.	Investment bankers. Syndicators. Corporate partners. Individuals.
Government financing	Working capital use. Equipment needs. Expansion.	Guaranteed portion cannot exceed certain amounts. Government will guarantee up to 90% of loan.	Cannot be dominant in its field. Must be independently owned and operated. Must meet size standards. Use funds only for eligible activities. Sufficient collateral.	No equity dilution. Support services. Interest deductions. Unable to obtain commercial debt. Typically lower interest rates. Lower repayment terms over longer periods.	Smaller amounts. Need collateral. Leverage expensive. Restrictive debt covenants. Can restrict future expansion. No unessential assets/operations. Cannot pay owners with the proceeds.	SBA field offices. Commercial banks. State agencies.

APPENDIX B

GLOSSARY OF COMMONLY USED TERMS

The purpose of this appendix is to provide a reference source for those unfamiliar with the terminology of the registration process. The descriptions of the terms are not intended to provide precise definitions as much as they are intended to describe how the terms apply when a company goes public.

ACCELERATION REQUEST. A request to the SEC to waive the statutory 20-day waiting period and to declare the registration statement effective at an earlier date.

BEST-EFFORTS UNDERWRITING. An underwriting arrangement in which the underwriters commit to use their best efforts to sell the shares, but have no obligation to purchase any shares not purchased by the public. Under certain best-efforts offerings, the offering is cancelled unless a minimum number of shares is sold.

BLUE SKY LAWS. State securities laws. The states and the SEC have concurrent jurisdiction over securities transactions. Some states have the authority under their blue sky laws to prohibit the offering of securities in their states if the offering is not "fair, just and equitable."

COMFORT LETTER (LETTER TO UNDERWRITERS). The letter or letters underwriters require from independent accountants as part of the underwriters' due diligence process. The matters to be covered in these letters are generally specified in the underwriting agreement. Comfort letters generally require the independent accountants to make representations about their independence and the compliance of the financial statements with the requirements of the Securities Act of 1933, and to provide "negative assurance," based on the results of applying certain specified procedures, about the unaudited financial statements and other financial information. Comfort letters are not required by the Securities Act of 1933 and are not filed with the SEC.

COMMENT LETTER.   A letter issued by the SEC describing the ways in which a registration statement does not comply with its requirements or questioning whether additional information should be included or whether disclosures should be changed. The states in which the securities are to be sold may also issue comment letters. Comment letters generally are received 30 to 60 days after the initial filing of the registration statement.

DUE DILIGENCE.   A "reasonable investigation" performed by the underwriters, the directors, the officers who signed the registration statement, and the experts (e.g., independent accountants, attorneys, or engineers) who participated in the securities offering. The purpose of the investigation is to provide the participants with a "reasonable ground for belief" that, as of the effective date, the statements contained in the registration statement are true and not misleading, and that no material information has been omitted.

EFFECTIVE DATE.   The date on which the registration statement becomes effective and the securities may be sold to the public.

EXEMPT OFFERING.   A securities transaction for which a registration statement need not be filed due to an exemption available under the Securities Act of 1933. Common exempt offerings are intrastate offerings and Regulation A and Regulation D offerings. See Chapter 3, "Private Placements."

FIRM-COMMITMENT UNDERWRITING.   An underwriting arrangement in which the underwriters commit to purchase all the securities being offered, regardless of whether they can resell all of them to the public.

FOREIGN CORRUPT PRACTICES ACT (FCPA).   An amendment of the Securities Exchange Act of 1934 that requires reporting companies to maintain adequate accounting records and systems of internal accounting control.

GOING PUBLIC.   The process by which a private company and/or its shareholders sell securities of the company to the public for the first time in a transaction requiring a registration statement prepared in accordance with the Securities Act of 1933.

GREEN-SHOE OPTION.   An option often included in a firm-commitment underwriting that allows the underwriters to purchase additional shares from the company or the selling shareholders to cover over-allotments.

INITIAL PUBLIC OFFERING (IPO). The sale of its securities to the public for the first time by a private company (and/or its shareholders).

LETTER OF INTENT. A nonbinding letter from the underwriter to the company confirming the underwriter's intent to proceed with the offering and describing the probable terms of the offering. A typical letter covers the number and type of shares to be sold, the type of underwriting, the anticipated sales price, and the arrangements for compensating the underwriters.

NATIONAL ASSOCIATION OF SECURITIES DEALERS (NASD). The role of the NASD in the registration process is to review the offering materials to determine whether the underwriter's compensation is excessive considering the size and type of offering, the nature of the underwriting commitment, and other relevant factors.

PRO FORMA. A financial presentation designed to provide investors with information about certain effects of a particular transaction. Historical financial information is adjusted to reflect the effects the transaction might have had if it had been consummated at an earlier date. In registration statements, pro forma combined financial statements are required for significant business combinations, including those that will probably occur.

PUBLIC FLOAT. The aggregate market value of the small-business issuers' voting stock held by nonaffiliates.

QUIET PERIOD. The period between the commencement of the public offering process (which begins when the company reaches a preliminary understanding with the managing underwriter) and 90 days after the registration statement becomes effective. The period is referred to as the "quiet period" because of the SEC's restrictions on publicity about the company or the offering.

RED HERRING. The preliminary prospectus circulated to prospective investors before the registration statement becomes effective. The preliminary prospectus is called the "red herring" because the following legend must be printed on its cover in red ink:

> A registration statement relating to these securities has been filed with the Securities and Exchange Commission but has not become effective. Information contained herein is subject to completion or amendment. These securities may not be sold nor may offers to buy be accepted prior to the time the registration statement becomes effective. This prospectus shall not constitute an offer to sell or the solicitation of an offer to buy nor shall there be any sale of these securities in any State in which such offer, solicitation or sale would be unlawful prior to registration or qualification under the securities laws of any such State.

REGISTRATION STATEMENT.   The document filed with the SEC to register securities for sale to the public. The most common registration statement used for initial public offerings is Form S-1.

REGULATION S-B.   Regulation S-B contains the rules governing financial- and nonfinancial-statement related disclosures in both registration statements and periodic reports filed by small-business issuers.

REGULATION S-K.   Regulation S-K contains the disclosure requirements for the nonfinancial statement portion of filings with the SEC.

REGULATION S-X.   Regulation S-X specifies the financial statements to be included in filings with the SEC and provides rules and guidance regarding their form and content.

SECONDARY OFFERING.   An offering by the company's shareholders to sell some or all of their stock to the public.

SECURITIES ACT OF 1933 (1933 ACT).   Under the 1933 Act, a registration statement containing required disclosures must be filed with the SEC before securities can be offered for sale in interstate commerce or through the mail. The 1933 Act also contains antifraud provisions that apply to securities offerings.

SECURITIES AND EXCHANGE COMMISSION (SEC).   The federal agency responsible for regulating sales and trading of securities by administering the federal securities laws, including the 1933 and 1934 Acts.

SECURITIES EXCHANGE ACT OF 1934 (1934 ACT).   The 1934 Act requires companies registered under the Act to file annual and periodic reports with the SEC and to disclose certain information to shareholders. Companies with 500 or more shareholders of a class of equity securities and total assets of more than $3 million, and companies that elect to be listed on a national stock exchange must file a Form 10 or Form 8-A registration statement to register under the Act.

SHORT-SWING PROFIT RECAPTURE.   The 1934 Act requires officers, directors, and persons holding 10 percent or more of a class of a company's stock to turn over to the company any profits they realize on the sale of shares of the company's stock that they hold for less than six months.

SMALL-BUSINESS ISSUER.   A company incorporated in the United States or Canada that has less than $25 million of revenue and public float (as defined) in the two most recent fiscal years.

STUB-PERIOD FINANCIAL INFORMATION.   Financial information or financial statements for interim periods. Under Forms S-1 and S-18, the most recent financial information included in the registration statement must be as of a date within 134 days of the effective date of the statement. This requirement is usually met by providing unaudited condensed financial statements for periods of one or more months subsequent to the latest audited financial statements.

UNDERWRITER.   An investment banker or broker-dealer who acts as the middle party between the selling company and the investing public in an offering of securities. (See FIRM-COMMITMENT UNDERWRITING and BEST-EFFORTS UNDERWRITING.)

UNDERWRITING AGREEMENT.   An agreement between the company and the underwriters that states the terms of the offering, including the nature of the underwriting (i.e., best efforts or firm commitment), the number of shares to be offered, the price per share, and the underwriters' compensation. Usually it is not signed until just prior to the anticipated effective date of the registration statement.

APPENDIX C

SAMPLE TIMETABLE FOR GOING PUBLIC

The following sample timetable presents a fairly typical registration schedule. Additional time may be required if significant corporate housekeeping is necessary or if the required financial statements for prior years were not previously audited by independent accountants. The waiting time for SEC comments can range from 30 days to 60 days or more, depending on the complexity of the registration statement and the SEC's backlog of filings in process.

Day	Tasks	Responsible Party
1	Hold an initial meeting of the registration team to discuss the preparation and filing of the registration statement, the assignment of responsibilities, and the proposed timetable; begin preparation of the letter of intent describing the structure of the proposed offering and the underwriting arrangement	All parties
2	Begin the preparation of the registration statement:	
	• Textual information, including the description of the business	Company, company counsel
	• Financial statements, schedules, and pro forma information	Company, independent accountants
	Begin the preparation of the underwriting documents:	Underwriters' counsel
	• Agreement among underwriters	
	• Underwriting agreement between the company and the underwriters	
	• Blue sky state security laws survey	Company, company counsel

(continued)

Day	Tasks	Responsible Party
	Complete corporate cleanup, as necessary	Company counsel
	Commence due diligence procedures	Underwriters' counsel
10	Distribute to directors and officers a questionnaire requesting information that may have to be disclosed in the registration statement (e.g., stock ownership, transactions with the company, remuneration, stock options)	Company
45	Circulate the initial draft registration statement, including the financial statements	Company, company counsel
50	Meet to review the comments on the initial draft	All parties
	Discuss the financial statements and the proposed comfort-letter procedures	Company, underwriter, underwriters' counsel, and independent accountants
52	Send the corrected draft to the printer for the first proof of the registration	Company or company counsel
53	Circulate the printed proof for review	Company or company counsel
55	Meet to review the comments on the first proof of the registration statement	All parties
56	Send the revised proof of the registration statement to the printer	Company or company counsel
58	Hold a meeting of the board of directors to approve the registration statement	Company
59	Distribute printed proofs of the various underwriting documents	Underwriters' counsel
	Meet at the printer to review the final proof of the registration statement	All parties
60	File the registration statement with the SEC, the states, and the NASD	Company counsel
61	Distribute the preliminary red herring prospectus to the proposed underwriters' syndicate	Underwriter
90	Receive comment letters from the SEC, the NASD, and the states	Company
92	Meet to discuss the comments and to prepare Amendment No. 1 to the registration statement. (The amendment should respond to all the comments, include material developments since the previous filing, and include updated financial statements if necessary.)	All parties
94	Meet at the printer to review Amendment No. 1 to the registration statement	All parties
95	File Amendment No. 1 to the registration statement with the SEC, the states and the NASD	Company counsel

(continued)

Day	Tasks	Responsible Party
	Inform the SEC of the date on which the final pricing amendment will be filed	Company counsel
100	Hold a due diligence meeting for the members of the proposed underwriting syndicate	All parties
110	Finalize the offering price	Company, underwriters
	File the pricing amendment and request acceleration of effectiveness	Company counsel
	Sign the underwriting agreement and the agreement among the underwriters	Company, underwriters
115	Deliver the first comfort letter to the underwriters	Independent accountants
	Receive notification from the SEC that the registration statement is effective	Company
	Issue a press release	Company
	Begin the public offering	Underwriters
120	Deliver the final comfort letter to the underwriters	Independent accountants
	Close, receive the proceeds from the underwriters, and issue the stock	Company, underwriters

APPENDIX D

COMPARISON OF REGISTRATION FORMS S-1 AND SB-2 AND ANNUAL REPORT 10-K INFORMATION REQUIREMENTS

APPENDIX D. Comparison of Registration Forms S-1 and SB-2 and Annual Report 10-K Information Requirements

	Form S-1	Form SB-2	Form 10-K
Purpose	Registration of securities with the SEC under the 1933 Act	Registration of securities with the SEC under the 1993 Act	Annual report under the 1934 Act
Dollar			
• Registrant	No limit	No limit	Not applicable
• Secondary offering	No limit	No limit	Not applicable
Eligibility for use	No restrictions	Companies must meet the definition of a small-business issuer as defined in **Regulation S-B**	No restrictions
Significant required disclosures	Summary information, risk factors, and ratio of earnings to fixed charges (S-K Item 503)	Same as S-1, except the ratio of earnings to fixed charges need not be presented (S-B Item 503)	Not applicable
	Use of proceeds; determination of offering price; dilution; selling security holders; plan of distribution; description of securities to be registered; interests of named experts and counsel (S-K Items 504-509 and Item 202)	Same as S-1 (S-B Items 504-509 and Item 202)	Not applicable
	Description of the business (S-K Item 101)	Less extensive than S-1 (S-B Item 101)	Less extensive than S-1
	Description of property (S-K Item 102)	Less extensive than S-1 (S-B Item 102)	Same as S-1
	Legal proceedings (S-K Item 103)	Same as S-1 (S-B Item 103)	Same as S-1
	Market and dividend data (S-K Item 201)	Less extensive than S-1 (S-B Item 201)	Same as S-1

(continued)

APPENDIX D. Continued

Form S-1	Form SB-2	Form 10-K
Financial statements must comply with Regulation S-X; additional financial statements are required for investees[a] and for significant acquired or to-be-acquired companies[b]	Financial statements prepared in accordance with generally accepted accounting principles; additional financial statements are required for significant acquired or to-be-acquired companies [c]	Financial statements must comply with Regulation S-X; additional financial statements are required for significant equity investees[a]
• Two years' audited balance sheets, updated by a condensed interim balance sheet as required	One year's audited balance sheet, updated by a condensed interim balance sheet as required	Two years' audited balance sheets[c]
• Three years' audited statements of income and cash flows, and reconciliations of other shareholders' equity accounts, updated by comparative condensed interim statements as required	Two years' audited statements of income and cash flows, and reconciliations of other shareholders' equity accounts, updated by comparative condensed interim statements as required	Three years' audited statements of income and cash flows, and reconciliations of other shareholders' equity accounts[c]
• Financial statements and schedules required by S-X	No schedules	Same as S-1
Selected financial data; supplementary financial information; management's discussion and analysis of financial condition and results of operations; and disagreements with auditors on financial and disclosure matters (S-K Items 301-304)	Selected financial data and supplemental financial information not required; management's discussion and analysis of financial condition and results of operations less extensive than S-1; and disagreements with auditors on financial and disclosure matters same as S-1 (S-B Items 303 and 304)	Same as S-1

Significant required disclosures (continued)		
Executive compensation and transactions with management (S-K Items 402 and 404)	Same as S-1 (S-B Item 401)	Same as S-1
Information about directors and executive officers (S-K Item 401)		
Less extensive than S-1 (S-B Items 402 and 404)	Same as S-1	
Ownership of securities by certain beneficial owners and management (S-K Item 403)	Same as S-1 (S-B Item 403)	Same as S-1

[a]Financial statements need not be audited for those years in which the significance test in rule 3-09 of Regulation S-X is not met; interim financial statements are required in a Form S-1.

[b]The number of years for which financial statements are required is determined by the significance tests in rule 3-05 of Regulation S-X; interim financial statements are required.

[c]The number of years for which financial statements are required is determined by the significance tests in Item 310(3)(c) of Regulation S-B; interim financial statements are required.

APPENDIX E

STRATEGIC ALLIANCE CHECKLIST

1. **Background**
   a. Basic information
   b. Preliminary due diligence

2. **Facilities**
   a. Land and building
   b. Equipment and tooling
   c. Services and utilities
   d. Adequacy and future needs
   e. General evaluation

3. **Purchasing and Traffic**

4. **Public Relations**

5. **Financial**
   a. General
   b. Financial status
   c. Financial operations

6. **Tax**
   a. Legal form of venture
   b. Issues affecting characterization of entity for U.S. tax purposes
   c. Selection or creation of participating parent entities
   d. Capitalization
   e. Foreign income

7. **Environmental**
   a. General occupancy
   b. Present occupancy
   c. Previous occupancies
   d. Facilities and land
   e. Regulatory/enforcement actions

8. **Legal**

9. **Markets and Marketing**

10. **Products and Services**
    a. General information
    b. Competitive factors
    c. Technical aspects

11. **Competition**
    a. Competitors
    b. Competitive products
    c. Outlook

12. **Management and Personnel**
    a. Organization and management
    b. Compensation
    c. Labor
    d. Employment

13. **Engineering and Research and Development**
    a. Projects

f. Constraints on
   transactions between
   parents and ventures
g. Tax aspects of
   termination

b. Activities

14. Manufacturing Operations
    a. Production
    b. General evaluation

════ APPENDIX F ════

OUTLINE OF A JOINT VENTURE AGREEMENT

1. General Information
   a. Date
   b. Names of partners
   c. Business description and location, or headquarters for partners
   d. Business purpose
2. Definitions of Terms
   a. Definitions of major terms for accurate and clear understanding by the joint venture parties (e.g., affiliate, board of directors, deadlock notice, GAAP, transfer price, investment costs), are detailed in appendix.
3. Organization of Joint Venture Company
   a. Form of organization and state of jurisdiction. Include the articles of incorporation (if appropriate) and the by-laws in the appendix.
   b. Name of joint venture company, principal place of business (e.g., local executive offices), and purpose (e.g., description of size and type of product and plant facilities).
   c. Names, locations, and business description of partners in joint venture as well as each partner's percent interest in joint venture.
4. Capitalization of Joint Venture
   a. Initial capital contributed by the joint venture partners (equity vs. loans with agreed-upon interest rates)
   b. Additional equity or capital contributions made by partners (e.g., required for continuation of joint venture and other types of contributions)
   c. Indebtedness (e.g., loans from sources other than joint venture partners such as banks)
   d. Loans and/or guarantees from partners with agreed-upon interest rate
   e. Transfer of patents and technology, licensing of technology, etc.
   f. Transferability of common stock
   g. Nondissolution of joint venture
   h. Financing of the new company (e.g., start-up and ongoing operations)
5. Review and Term of Joint Venture
   a. Term or length of time for operating joint venture
   b. Extension of term

    c.   Periodic review and review procedure
    d.   Termination of joint venture

6. Joint Venture Partners' Interests
    a.   Division of interests between joint venture partners
    b.   Capital contributions of joint venture partners
    c.   Failure to contribute clause

7. Management
    a.   Powers, responsibilities, and procedures of stockholders, board of directors, and operating management, officers, managers, etc.
    b.   Stockholders' meetings (both annual and special)—issues
    c.   Board of directors—composition, number of members, constitution, responsibilities, frequency of meetings, action without meetings, telephone conference, voting, quorum, deadlock by board, actions requiring unanimous vote
    d.   Operating management—composition, number of operating management members, responsibilities and authority, assignment of personnel, handling of unresolved issues (deadlock), names and titles of key executives
    e.   Employment of personnel at joint venture

8. Relationship of Parties
    a.   Parts, services, materials, installations provided by parents
    b.   Products provided by parents
    c.   Initial facilities
    d.   Products description
    e.   Engineering
    f.   Manufacturing of product(s)
    g.   Policies and procedures
        —Warranties
        —R&D cost absorption
        —Initial facilities
        —Change orders
        —Quality assurance
        —Procurement specifications
        —Proprietary information
    h.   Patents and technology
    i.   Confidentiality
    j.   Rights and third parties
    k.   Liabilities of company, indemnification
    l.   Performance bonds
    m.   Owner's right to review proprietary technology use
    n.   License of technology

9. Books and Records
    a.   Fiscal year determination
    b.   Maintenance, location, and inspection of books, records, and bank accounts
    c.   Reserves
    d.   Budget
    e.   Annual financial reports
    f.   Selection of auditors
    g.   Tax returns
    h.   Annual certification

10. Profits and Losses

      a.   Distributable amount
      b.   Distribution of cash flow
      c.   Repayment of contribution loans
      d.   Allocation
11. Allocation and Related Tax Provisions
      a.   Contribution of property
      b.   Recapture income
      c.   Miscellaneous tax allocations
      d.   Tax returns, tax credit, tax decisions not otherwise provided for
      e.   Notice of tax audit
      f.   Cost recovery
      g.   Separate reporting
      h.   Withholding
      i.   Penalties
12. Blocking Rights and Deadlock
      a.   Fundamental issues
           —Additional capital for joint venture
           —Authorization of issuance of stock
           —Declaration or payment of dividends
           —Reinvestment of earnings in joint venture
           —Indebtedness
           —Corporate officers
           —Litigation
           —Guarantee, indemnity
           —Unusual contracts or commitments
           —License agreement
           —Agreement/material transaction with one of its joint owners
           —Policy change of any kind (e.g., manufacturing, sale of products)
           —Financial policy
           —Basic change in nature of business or product specification
           —Other material transactions
           —Amendments to joint venture agreement or certificate
           —Sale and/or transfer of all or part of joint venture partners' interests
           —Admittance of new member in joint venture
           —Increase in capacity; closure or reduction of premises
           —Disposition of know-how, technology, or proprietary rights
           —Liquidation or merger of joint venture company
           —Confession of judgment against joint venture and/or its partners
           —Claim/liabilities of joint venture partners to arbitration
           —Act that makes it possible to do "business as usual"
           —Budgets for joint venture (e.g., including capital expenditures)
      b.   Procedure in event of deadlock
13. Adjustment of Joint Venture Partners' Interests
      a.   Adjustment by agreement
      b.   Adjustment upon departure, merger, or increase in capacity
14. Restrictions on Disposal of Stock
      a.   Restrictions
      b.   Transfers
      c.   Assignees and new partners
      d.   Right of first refusal
      e.   Option to put or call

f. Fair market value; terms of purchases or sales
g. Effect on distributions and allocations

15. Termination of Joint Venture
   a. Date, if any determined
   b. Events causing termination
      —End of term of joint venture and extensions
      —Written agreement by joint venture partners
      —Written notice by joint venture partner (against partner who has defaulted)
      —Change in control of a joint venture partner
      —Bankruptcy or receivership placement of a joint venture partner
      —Nonrenewal of technology exchange/license agreement
      —Court decree
   c. Rights and obligations
      —Terms for owner buyout
      —Assignment of interest (corporate)
      —Right of first refusal
      —Sale of joint venture
      —Liquidation (and liquidator)
      —Survival rights of technology
      —Implementation of grants, transfers, and conveyance
      —Release, discharge, and indemnification
      —Continuing obligations

16. Product Liability
   a. Insurance, additional insureds
   b. Claims administration for design and manufacturing, marketing, and combined claims
   c. Primary and excess coverage premium costs

17. Force Majeure

18. Confidentiality

19. Closing
   a. Terms of closing (date, place, transferred material, etc.)
   b. Conditions to the obligations of each partner
   c. Certificate from each parent, consents
   d. Attorney's opinion from each parent
   e. Approvals of information transfer (e.g., government)
   f. Delay of closing date, termination

20. Representations and Warranties (for all parents of the new joint venture company)
   a. Organization and standing
   b. Authority
   c. Absence of conflict
   d. Absence of required consents and contractual restrictions
   e. Acting on its own
   f. Property transfers to joint venture
   g. Disclosure
   h. Survival of representations and warranties

21. Miscellaneous Provisions
   a. Public announcements
   b. Governing law, consent to jurisdiction
   c. Arbitration/conflict resolution
   d. Section headings

e.   Partner covenant interests
f.   Counterparts
g.   Further assurances
h.   Currency
i.   Governing language
j.   Assignments
k.   Entire agreement, amendments
l.   Severability
m.   Legal action and fees
n.   Expenses
o.   No waiver of rights
p.   References and inclusions
q.   Investment representation
r.   Estopped certificates
s.   Secrecy obligation
t.   Waiver of partition
u.   Exhibits

Exhibits

   I.   Definitions
  II.   Articles of Incorporation (if any)
 III.   By-Laws of Joint Venture
  IV.   Business
   V.   Initial Members of the Board of Directors or Managing Committee
  VI.   Initial Management Team of the Joint Venture Company (Organization Chart)
 VII.   Technology/License Agreement
VIII.   Products
  IX.   Opinion of Counsel, Certificate of Performance, Certificate Attesting to Authority

INDEX

Acceleration request, 336
Acceptance letter of credit, 301
Account analysis, 219
Accounting methods, 277
  accrual, 278–79
  cash, 278
  changing of, 279–80
  deferring taxes, 279
Accounts payable and working capital, 214
Accounts receivable
  financing, 78–80
  financing with factoring, 79–80, 107
  pledging, 85
  as security, 10
  and working capital, 212–14
Alternative minimum tax, 270–71
Annual report 10-k requirements, 344–47
Asset-based bank loans, 8, 106–7, 331

Back-to-back letters of credit, 301–2
Bank
  development, 304
  evaluation of customer, 91, 102
    ability to pay, 91–92
    business' future plans, 97–98
    financial ratios, 93–96
    financial statements, 92–93
    signs of trouble, 99–101
  export financing, 299
    acceptance letter of credit, 301
    back-to-back letters of credit, 301–2
    confirmed irrevocable letter of credit,
      299–300
    confirmed letters of credit, 300–301
    documentary collection, 302–3
  See also Lender
Bankers' acceptances, 85
Bankruptcy laws, 9–10
Best-efforts underwriting, 336
Blue sky laws, 51–52, 192, 336
Bureau of Export Administration, 319
Business combinations, 158
  asset acquisition, 159
  consolidation, 158
  the deal, 163–65

due diligence, 163–64
implementation, 164–65
and intangible assets, 161
joint venture, 159
the process, 159–63
and self-assessment, 159–60
statutory merger, 158
target companies, 160–63
Business plan, 67
  major points, 68–69
  overall, 97–98
  venture capitalists' expectations, 67–68

Capital
  techniques for raising, 1
  venture, 1, 4–5, 55–70, 333
Caps, 11
Cash collateral, use of, 108–9
Cash-flow cycle, 206
  affected by fluctuation in sales, 209
  controlling, 207–9
  example of, 206–7
  minimizing the effect of income taxes on,
    257–60
Cash management, 5–6, 205–6
  bank services, 214–19
  controlling working capital, 209–14
  cost of capital, 223
  phases of development, 223–25
  sales versus availability, 223
  timing improvements, 223–25
  See also Cash-flow cycle
Cash-position management
  cash forecasting, 219–21
  daily cash positioning, 219–21
  electronic funds transfers, 221–22
  short-term investments, 222–23
C corporation. See Corporation, regular;
  S corporation
Certified development corporation, 150, 151
Chapter 11 and obtaining financing, 106–10
Check clearances, 90, 217–18
Collars, 10–11
Comfort letter, 336–37
Comment letter, 337

Commercial banks and debt financing, 85
Commitment fee, 91
Commodity Credit Corporation, 317–18
Community Development block grant, 136
Community Reinvestment Act, 141
Compensating balance requirements, 90
Confirmed irrevocable letter of credit, 299–300
Confirmed letters of credit, 300–301
Consolidation. *See* Business combinations
Cooperative research and development agreements, 152–53
Corporate capital, 59
Corporation, regular, 261–68
  after growth phase, 275–77
  and alternative minimum tax, 270–71
  growth phase, 274–75
  and specialized small-business investment company, 272
  start-up phase, 273–74
  See also S corporation
Credits, 6
  for increasing research activities, 283
  rehabilitation investment, 284
  targeted jobs, 284

Debt, level of, 12–13
Debt, long-term, 84
  comparison of instruments for with short-term instruments, 84
  for fixed-asset acquisition, 75–76
  and leasing, 77
  and term loans, 76, 330
Debt, short-term, 77–78
  accounts receivable financing, 78–80
  accounts receivable pledging, 85
  bankers' acceptance, 85
  comparison of instruments for with long-term instruments, 84
  current developments, 83, 85
  inventory financing, 80–82
  revolving line of credit, 82–83, 328
  working capital loans, 78
Debt, sources of
  asset-based lender, 73–74, 331
  cash-flow lender, 72–73
  finance companies, 74
  hybrid lender, 74–75
  mezzanine, 75
  secured lender, 73
Debt financing, 71–87
  advantages, 71, 86
  disadvantages, 86–87
  sources of debt capital for growing businesses, 72–75
  versus equity, 86–87
  See also Debt, long-term; Debt, short-term
Debtor-in-possession financing, 108
Department of Agriculture, Foreign Agriculture, 307, 316–18
Department of Commerce, 318–19
Department of Housing and Urban Development, 134, 136, 141
Deposit-reporting systems, 219
Depreciation, 6

modified accelerated cost recovery system (MACRS), 284, 288–89
DIP (Debtor-in-possession financing), 108
Discounted interest, 90
Diversification by initial public offerings, 19–20
Divestitures, 165
Documentary collection, 302–3
Due diligence, 34–35, 337

Economic Development Administration, 143, 156
Effective date, 337
Electronic data interchange (EDI), 216–17
Electronic funds transfers (EFTs), 221–22
EMC (Export management companies), 308
Employee Retirement Income Security Act of 1974, 248
Employee stock ownership plans (ESOPs), 12, 16, 26, 236–50
  as an employee-benefit plan, 240–41
  leveraged, 237–40
    accounting for, 239–40
    buyout, 246–47
    financing alternative, 243–44
    financing size of, 247–48
    market for shares, 244–46
    to raise capital, 241–43
    tax benefits, 237–38
    tax legislation, 248–50
  unleveraged, 236–37
Environmental issues, 10
Equity funds, 8
ERLC (Export revolving line of credit), 308–9
ESOPs. *See* Employee stock ownership plans
Estate planning and initial public offerings, 19–20, 21
ETC (Export trading companies), 308
Exempt offering, 337
Expensing, 6
Export-Import Bank, 310
  export credit insurance policies, 312–13
  guarantees, 311–12
  loans, 311
  working capital guarantees, 312
Export management companies, 308
Export revolving line of credit, 308–9
Export trading companies, 308

Factoring. *See* Accounts receivable
Farmers Home Administration, 142, 153
  agricultural loan programs, 153–54
  business and industry loans, 154–55
  defining rural areas, 153
  types of loans, 153
FIFO (first-in, first-out), 281–82
Financial ratios
  analyzing for obtaining a loan, 93–96
  current ratio, 94
  debt-to-equity ratio, 95, 100
  debt to tangible effective net worth, 95–96
  interest coverage ratio, 96
  inventory turnover, 94
  inventory turnover in days, 94
  payable turnover in days, 94
  percentage of inventory to cover deficit in quick ratio, 95

profit margins, 96
quick ratio, 94–95
receivable collection days, 93
receivable turnover, 93, 100
Financial statements
evaluating for obtaining a loan, 92–93
business hesitation in providing of, 99
Financing alternatives, 327
asset-based lending, 331
bank lines of credit, 328
corporate bonds, 332
debentures, 332
franchising, 333
government financing, 335
leases, 332
limited partnerships, 335
mortgage note, 330
public stock offerings, 334
revolver/term, 329
revolving credit, 328
short-term notes, 328
subordinate debt, 331
term loan, 330
venture capital, 333
Firm-commitment underwriting, 337
Fixed assets and government loans, 146–47
Float days, 91
Food, Agriculture, Conservation, and Trade Act of 1990, 317
Forfaiting, 304
Foreign Corrupt Practices Act, 18, 337
Foreign entities, 292–93
foreign holding companies, 297
foreign sales corporations, 293–96
tax havens, 297
Foreign government investment incentive programs
capital investment, 321
corporate tax rate, 320
employment promotion, 322
examples of, 322–25
export promotion, 322
local property taxes, 321–22
plant and equipment, 321
research and development, 321
selected industries, 321
selected regions, 321
tax holidays, 322
Foreign investment with venture capitalists, 5
Foreign sales corporation (FSC)
qualification requirements, 293–94
shareholder taxation, 296
small exporters, 296
taxation of, 296
tax exemption rules, 294–95
Form 8-K, 38–39
Form 10-K, 37–38
Form 10-Q, 38
Franchising, 11–12, 251, 333
advantages of, 254–55
defined, 252
disadvantages of, 255
fees, 255–56
legal components, 256
methods, 252–53

when to consider, 253–54
Funds concentration, 218

Going public, 337, 341–43
Going Public: The IPO Reporter, 24
Government financing, 7, 133–57, 335
Bureau of Export Administration, 319
Department of Agriculture-Foreign Agriculture Service, 316–18
Department of Commerce, 318–19
Department of Housing and Urban Development, 134, 136, 141
direct loans, 138–39, 142–43
direct payments, 140, 142–43
enterprise zones, 141
equity participation, 140–41
Export-Import Bank, 7, 310–13
export programs, 305–20
federal, 137, 305
guaranteed/insured loans, 139–40, 142–43
insurance, 140, 142
International Trade Administration, 318–19
lender expectations, 137–38
local, 7, 61, 135
Overseas Private Investment Corporation, 313–16
programs, 141–57
project grants, 140, 142–43, 156
Small Business Administration, 7, 134, 138, 305–10
state, 7, 61, 135–36
state export assistance, 320
Urban Development Action Grant, 134
U.S. Trade and Development Agency, 319–20
Green-Shoe option, 337

Harrigan, Katherine Rudie, 112
Hybrid lenders, 8

Individual investors as venture capitalists, 60–61
Initial public offerings (IPOs), 1, 14–39, 176, 334
advantages to company, 16–17
advantages to owners, 19–20
cost, 18
defined, 338
disadvantages to company, 17–18
disadvantages to owners, 20–21
obtaining marketability, 18
prevention of, 40
registration, 23–33
risk, 23
Securities and Exchange Commission involvement with, 17, 20
stock market, 22–23
stock price, 19
suggestions, 35–37
timing of, 21–23
Intangible assets, 161
Interest-rate protection, 10–11
International expansion, 298–99
bank export financing, 299–303
export programs, 303–4
foreign government investment incentive programs, 320–25
government export-finance programs, 305–20

International private insurance, 303–4
International Trade Administration, 318–19
International trade loan program, 309
Inventory
  determining, 281–82
  cost flow of, 281–82
  FIFO (first-in, first-out), 281–82
  high levels of, 99
  LIFO (last-in, first-out), 281–82
  tax accounting for, 280–82
  valuation of, 280–81
  and working capital, 211–12
Inventory financing, 80
  blanket inventory advance, 81
  floor planning, 81
  warehouse financing, 81–82
  See also Debt, short-term
Investment banking firms and venture capital
      funds, 59–60, 333
Investors in private placements, 42–43
IPO. See Initial public offerings

Joint ventures, 2, 4, 111–20
  agreement outline, 350–54
  when to create, 113–14
  defined, 113
  See also Strategic alliances
Joint Venture Success, Managing for, 112

Laws
  bankruptcy, 9–10
  consumer, 9–10
  retail, 9–10
Leasing, 3–4, 77, 121, 332
  advantages of-capital, 124
  advantages of-operating, 122–23
  capital, 123–25
  financial statement reporting for, 125–29
  leveraged, 131–32
  master real estate, 125
  modified, 123–25, 126
  operating, 122–23
  personal, 130
  pricing, 130–31
  sales and leasebacks, 132
  tax advantages, 131
  tax reporting for, 129–30, 289
  traditional, 122–23
  venture, 125
Lender
  asset-based, 73–74, 331
  cash-flow, 72–73
  characteristics, 89–90
  defined, 72
  evaluation of, 89–91
  evaluation of customer, 91–101
  finance company, 74
  hybrid, 74–75
  priming of existing, 109
  secured, 73
Lender, negotiating with
  collateral agreements, 103–4
  future borrowing constraints, 104
  general guidelines, 105–6
  interest rates, 103

  the loan package, 101–3
  payment terms, 104
  personal guarantee of indebtedness, 104
  ratio requirements, 105
  use of capital, 104
Letter of intent, 338
Leverage buyouts (LBOs), 2, 3, 6
  employee stock ownership plans in, 12
  and management buyouts, 227
Liability
  lender, 9–10
  registration, 34–35
LIBOR (London Inter-Bank Offering Rate), 9
LIFO (last-in, first-out), 281–82
Limited partnerships, 4, 335
  and equity R&D arrangements, 186–88
  pooled R&D arrangements, 188–89
  and private placements, 49–50
  and research and development, 180–89
    additional types of arrangements, 186
    basic technology, 182–83
    the contract, 183
    after the completed project, 184
    compensating partners, 184–85
    trade-offs, 185–86
Loan production offices (LPOs), 83
Loans, obtaining, 88
  ability to repay, 91–97
  business' future plans, 97–98
  company age, 96
  cost considerations, 90–91
  credit reports, 96–97
  factors that increase available capital, 91
  factors that reduce available capital, 90
  financially troubled companies, 106–10
  signs of trouble, 99–101
  term of present management, 96
  trade reports, 96–97
  years of continuing increases in profits, 96
  Z-score, 97
Loans, short-term, 8, 328
  asset-based bank loans, 8, 331
Loans, term, 76, 330
Local development company, 148–49
London Inter-Bank Offering Rate, 9
LPOs (Loan production offices), 83

Management buyouts (MBOs), 2–3, 226
  accounting issues, 230–31
  the acquisition, 228–29
  advisory services, 232
  cash flow, 229
  defined, 227
  financing requirements, 231
  managements stake in, 233–34
  operations after, 234
  ownership expectations by management, 230
  parent company's strategic and financial
      position, 227
  price of, 232
  raising debt and equity, 232–33
  is risk worth it, 234–35
  structuring, 229
  subsidiary's strategic and financial position, 227
  tax issues, 230

transaction fees, 232
valuation of subsidiary, 227–28
Managing for Joint Venture Success, 112
Matched funding, 9
MBOs. *See* Management buyouts
Merger. *See* Business combinations
Mezzanine debt, 8, 75 172. *See also* Debt,
   sources of

National Association of Securities Dealers
   (NASD), 30–32, 338
National Technical Information Service, 157
National Venture Capitalists Association, 66
Niche and venture capitalists, 4

Overdrafts, 99
Overseas Private Investment Corporation, 313
   finance program, 314–15
   political-risk insurance, 315–16
Ownership of company and venture capitalists,
   69–70

Partnerships, 4, 261–68, 269–70
   after growth phase, 275–77
   growth phase, 274–75
   limited, 269–70, 335
   private, 57–58
   start-up phase, 273–74
Points, 91
Pratt's Guide to Venture Capital Sources, 66
Preferred stock, designer, 173–74
Prepayment penalties, 91
Pricing options, 9
Private placements, 6–7
   defined, 40, 41
   exempt offerings, 43–51
     $5 million, 45–48
     intrastate, 50
     Regulation A, 51
     Regulation D, 44–45
     small business, 45
     unlimited, 48–50
   memorandum, 54, 192–94
   problems with, 52–54
   state securities regulation of, 51–52
   types of investors, 42–43
Pro forma, 338
Proprietary rights, 194–95
Prospectus, 28, 29, 192–94. *See also* Registration
Proxy rules, 39
Public float, 338
Public funds, 58–59
Public offerings, 172. *See also* Initial public
   offerings

Quiet period, 338

Real estate
   government loans for, 146–47
   lending, 10
Real property, equity in 109
Red herring, 28, 338
Registration
   amending, 32–33
   assembling a team, 23–24

closing, 33
due diligence, 34–35
filing, 30–32
financial statement requirements, 29–30, 31
Form S-1, 27, 344–47
Form SB-2, 344–47
information requirements, 26–27, 28–29
in-house questions to ask, 25–26
initial meeting, 27–28
initial regulatory review, 30–32
initial statement, 28–29
liability, 34–35
planning, 25–27
publicity restrictions, 33–34
Regulation S-B, 27
sample timetable, 341–43
significant steps, 25–33
statement, 339
underwriting, 23–24
Regulation, securities
   state, 51–52
Regulation S-B, 339
Regulation S-K, 339
Regulation S-X, 339
Reporting requirements, public
   Form 8-K, 38–39
   Form 10-K, 37–38
   Form 10-Q, 38
   insider trading, 39
   proxy rules, 39
   tender offers, 39
Research and development (R&D), 166
   accounting treatment of, 189–91
   arrangements, 167–68
     acquiring technology, 171–72
     carve-outs, 175–76
     corporations, 177–78
     foreign, 4, 179–80
     government, 4, 174–75
     joint ventures, 4, 176–77
     and limited partnerships, 4, 180–89, 335
     mezzanine financing, 172
     partnerships, 4
     preferred stock, designer, 173–74
     public offerings, 172
     seed-capital rounds, 172
     selling technology, 171–72
     spin-offs, 175–76
     strategic alliances, 167, 168–71, 348–49
     tax concerns for corporations, 203–4
     tax goals for investors, 196–203
     venture capital, 172
   and business considerations, 167
   and foreign investment, 321
   initial steps before, 167
   and legal aspects, 191–95
     blue sky laws, 192
     federal securities law, 191–92
     proprietary rights, 194–95
     prospectus and private placement memoran-
       dum, 192–94
   and tax aspects, 195–204, 282–83
Revolving line of credit, 82–83, 328
Risk
   and debt financing, 72, 73, 74

initial public offering, 23, 334
joint ventures, 2
limiting interest-rate, 10–11
strategic alliances, 2
and term loans, 76, 330
and venture capitalists, 4, 55–56, 62, 63

Savings and Loan (S&L), 10
SBA. *See* Small Business Administration
S corporation, 261–68, 272–77
    after growth phase, 275–77
    eligibility requirements, 272
    growth phase, 274–75
    start-up phase, 273–74
Secondary offering, 339
Securities Act of 1933, 24–25, 37, 339
    and private placement, 40–41
Securities and Exchange Act of 1933, 191–92
Securities and Exchange Commission (SEC), 17,
    20, 27, 339
Securities Exchange Act of 1934, 18, 37, 339
Service Corps of Retired Executives, 309
Short-swing profit recapture, 339
Small business
    and private placement exemption, 45
Small Business Administration (SBA), 7, 60, 134,
    138, 142, 144–53, 272, 305–310
    7(a) program, 146–48
    502 program, 148–49
    504 program, 149–51
    definition of small business, 144
    rules for loans and loan guarantees, 144–46
    special programs, 151
Small Business Development Centers, 310
Small Business Initiatives, 1992 SEC, 45, 51
Small Business Innovation Research program,
    141, 143, 151–52, 156–57
Small Business Investment Companies (SBICs),
    60, 309
Small Business Investment Incentive Act of 1980,
    41
Small Business Issuer, 339
Sole proprietorship, 260–69
Specialized Small Business Investment Companies
    (SSBICs), 60, 272
Stock
    advantages to selling, 16–17, 18–20
    used for acquisitions, 16
    deciding to go public, 14–39
    disadvantages to selling, 17–18, 20–21
    as employee incentive, 16, 26
    enhancing company prestige, 16–17
    market, 22–23
    phantom plan, 287
    restricted, 285–86
    See also Initial public offerings
Stock appreciation rights, 16, 287
Stock options, 16, 26
    incentive, 286–87
    nonqualified, 286
Strategic alliances, 2, 111–12, 348–49
    approach for considering, 116–20
    arbitration, 119–20
    in automotive industry, 2

between companies to complement tech-
    nologies, 169
between technology-rich companies and larger
    corporations, 169
and blocking rights, 118–19
checklist, 348–49
in computer industry, 2
coordinating committee, 119
enhanced credibility through, 170–71
finding a partner, 117
initial contributions, 118
joint ventures, 113–14
licensing, 115–16
for manufacturing purposes, 169–70
for marketing and distribution rights, 170
minority equity investment, 114–15
negotiating the agreement, 117–20
and research and development, 168–71
Stub-period financial information, 339–40
Subordinated debt, 8, 75, 331
Subsidiary, sale of, 109–10
Syndications loans, 8–9

Taxes, income
    minimizing effect on cash flow, 257–60
Tax incentives and employee stock ownership
    plans, 12, 16
Tax liabilities, minimizing, 282
    debt versus equity, 288
    deferred compensation plans, 287–88
    depreciation, 288–89
    local taxes, 290–91, 321–22
    organizational expenditures, 289–90
    qualified retirement plans, 287–88
    research and development, 282–83
    start-up expenditures, 289–90
    state taxes, 290–91
    stock compensation techniques, 284–88
    tax credits, 283–84
Tax payments, minimizing
    estimated tax requirements, 291–92
    with foreign investment, 321–22
    quick refund, 292
    refund claims, 292
Tax planning
    accounting method selection, 277–80
    alternative minimum tax, 270–71
    comparison table of legal business form,
        261–68
    C Corporation, 261–68, 270–72
    using foreign entities, 292–97
    for inventories, 280–82
    legal business form, 260–77
    local taxes, 259
    minimizing the effect of income taxes on cash
        flow, 257–60
    minimizing estimated tax payments, 291–92
    minimizing tax liabilities, 282–91
    partnership, 261–68, 269–70
    S Corporation, 261–68, 272–77
    sole proprietorship, 260–69
    state taxes, 259
    See also Taxes, income; Tax liabilities, mini-
        mizing; Tax payments, minimizing; Tax
        strategies

Tax Reform Act of 1986, 248
Tax strategies, 5–6, 258–59
  capital structure, 6
  credits, 6
  estate planning, 19–20, 21
  expensing, 6
  income deferral, 6
  for management buyouts, 230
  for R&D, 195–204
Tender offers, 39

Underwriter, 340
  letter to, 336–37
Underwriting
  agreement, 340
  best-efforts, 336
  commissions, 18, 32
  firm-commitment, 337
  and initial public offering, 20, 22–23, 27
  loans, 8–9
  and registration, 23–24, 27–28, 32
Uniform Customs and Practices, 300–301
United States Agency for International Development, 307
United States Trade and Development Agency, 319–20

Venture capital, 333
  and the business plan, 67–69
  corporate, 59
  defined, 55
  finding, 66–67

funding process, 64
individual, 60–61
investment banking firms' funds, 59–60
investor expectations of business plan, 67–68
and ownership in company, 69–70
points of business plan, 68–69
private partnerships, 57–58
public funds, 58–59
and research and development, 172
Small Business Investment Companies, 60
Specialized Small Business Investment
  Companies, 60
sources of, 57–61
and state government funds, 61
withdrawal of, 65
Venture capital firms, 61
  acquisition financing, 65
  buyout financing, 65
  early-stage financing, 62–63
  finding, 66–67
  second-stage financing, 63–64
Venture Capital Sources, Pratt's Guide to, 66

Wire transfers, 219
Working capital
  controlling, 209–10
    using accounts payable, 214
    using accounts receivable, 212–14
    using inventory, 211–12
  government loans for, 146–47
  loans, 78

Zero-balance accounts, 219

EY/FastPlan^{SM}, Ernst & Young's affordable, easy-to-use financial forecasting software program, can help you generate financial forecasts, allocate resources, and identify your company's growing capital and financial needs.

Using an IBM-compatible or Macintosh microcomputer plus Microsoft Excel, this user-friendly, financial projection and reporting model can help you identify financial needs, analyze the impact of various alternative operating plans, and better allocate company resources. Five-year annual and quarterly business projections, essential to making better business decisions, are easily generated.

The *EY/FastPlan* program is specially priced at $99 and can be charged on your American Express, VISA or MasterCard.

To receive a copy of *EY/FastPlan,* please complete the coupon below and mail or FAX to:

Ernst & Young
Entrepreneurial Services
National Office
2001 Ross Avenue, Suite 2800
Dallas, Texas 75201
FAX: (214) 979-2333

☐ Enclosed is my check made payable to Ernst & Young, or

☐ Please charge my American Express, VISA, or MasterCard
(circle type of card used—signature required)

Card Number _____ Expiration Date_____

Signature _____

Print Name _____ Title _____

Company _____

Shipping Address _____

City _____ State _____ Zip _____

Business Phone ( ) _____

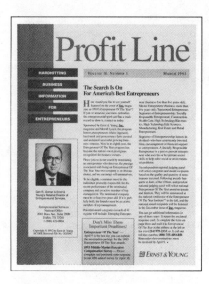

Profit Line is the newsletter of the Entrepreneurial Services Group of Ernst & Young. Distributed nationally on a quarterly basis to over 100,000 companies, the newsletter contains articles on topics ranging from financing assistance and business management to employee benefit programs and tax-related topics.

To receive your **free year** of *Profit Line,* complete the coupon below and mail to or fax:

Ernst & Young
Entrepreneurial Services
National Office
2001 Ross Avenue, Suite 2800
Dallas, Texas 75201
Fax (214) 979-2333

Print Name _____ Date _____

Address _____

Company _____

City _____ State _____ Zip _____